Happy Christmas, Peter
from Dave, Catherine
and James.
25-12-77

Follow On

FOLLOW ON

E. W. Swanton

with Foreword by
TIM RICE

COLLINS
St James's Place, London
1977

William Collins Sons & Co. Ltd
London · Glasgow · Sydney · Auckland
Toronto · Johannesburg

First published 1977
ISBN 0 00 216239 3
Set in Intertype Baskerville

Made and printed in Great Britain by
William Collins Sons & Co. Ltd, Glasgow

Contents

Acknowledgements

I am indebted to several people for their contributions to this book: to Tim Rice, author of *Jesus Christ Super-Star* and other musical works, for his warm and amusing Foreword; to J. D. Coldham, editor of the *Cricket Society Journal*, for undertaking with his usual meticulous care the compilation of the index; to the Earl of Gowrie, Viscount Montgomery of Alamein and Mr R. V. C. Robins for permission to publish letters written by their respective fathers; to Alan Gibson for allowing me to quote from his address at the Memorial Service to Sir Neville Cardus; to Mr Gilbert Mant, formerly of Reuters, who has allowed me to print a letter from him throwing new light on the Bodyline Tour, and to Mr Leonard Crawley for leave to publish a letter to the editor of *The Times* on the same subject; to Mr Gilbert Ashton whose first-hand account of the defeat of the Australians by A. C. Maclaren's XI in the classic match at Eastbourne I have lifted from the *Cricketer*; to Mr George Cox, whose tribute to the late H. S. Altham I have been able to reproduce from *The Heart of Cricket*; to others for shorter quotations; and not least to Ann, my wife, who has suffered patiently the household dislocations of authorship.

Finally, because of a production slip, I must amend here the picture captions in two particulars. In No. 2 Martha Woolley, Frank's wife is lunching with us in the garden. In No. 5 Charles Ambrose is sitting beside R. H. de Montmorency on the other side to Percy Chapman. The two figures standing are unidentified.

Illustration Credits
J. M. Flint – 1; Ann Swanton – 2; MCC – 3, 4, 10; Sport & General – 5, 14; Worcester College, Oxford – 6; Author – 7, 8; F. J. Pitts – 9; Hollis & Carter Ltd – 11; Anon – 12; Patrick Eagar – 13, 17, 18; BBC – 15; TVW Channel 7, Perth – 16.

Foreword

The men who wrote introductory essays to E. W. Swanton's last book, *Swanton In Australia*, were Sir Robert Menzies and Sir Donald Bradman. That two gentlemen of such great distinction contributed to Jim Swanton's book is itself an indication of his stature as a cricket writer; and of course the actual text of Sir Robert's Foreword and of Sir Donald's Introduction further emphasized the pre-eminence of E.W.S. in his world.

It is possible (but only just) that there are a few cricketers or cricket-lovers who do not know about E. W. Swanton. If they exist these unfortunates are unlikely to be instantly converted to appreciation of E.W.S. simply by the words 'Foreword by Tim Rice' – though, who knows? Maybe my Foreword will help *Follow On* to find its way to the dressing-rooms or recording studios of one or two musical or theatrical institutions which might otherwise have been Swanton-less? Anyway, I hope that those kind enough actually to read beyond that title will soon become aware of the pleasure Jim's writing has given me for two-thirds of my life, and will detect in this article the same enthusiasm for my subject as that displayed by my two immediate predecessors.

Despite having had the honour of being asked to contribute to an important cricket book, I am such an untalented cricketer that details of my feats in flannels have not been made over-available to the general public. I must therefore briefly reveal the actual connections with cricket that I have. (This is something the Don did not have to do when writing about *Swanton In Australia*, but I hope that the great man, if ever asked to write a sleeve note for a long-playing record, will let his readers know that in 1930 he released a single 78 r.p.m. record on Columbia DB 270. One side, 'Old Fashioned Locket' and 'Bungalow of Dreams', featured some fairly natty piano playing, while the other, a 'friendly chat' entitled 'How It's Done', informed listeners how they, too, could score over 300 at Leeds in a Test Match. A rather worn copy of this platter is a highly valued item in my record collection, even though it does not seem to have made the charts.)

I realized, in late 1972, ten years after my last game of cricket at school, that the only way a player of my ability could guarantee his regular selection for an XI was to form his own team, and to become his own captain and selector. Thus Heartaches CC was born. It has been a startling success, and as my team gets ready for its fifth season of fixtures I can honestly say that of all the amazing things I have been lucky enough to experience since Andrew Lloyd Webber and I first found our feet as songwriters the enjoyment I have got from my cricket team (the lads in red, pink and green) is the equal of them all. The club now has caps and colours, almanacks and annual dinners – and a magic for me that gold discs somehow lack. Despite advice from non-cricket-loving accountants I have not emigrated to escape the clutches of the Inland Revenue, as I cannot face the prospect of a summer in which I shall not patrol the covers or order the heavy roller, plan the batting order or change the bowling.

So therefore I now play nearly every summer week-end. Heartaches CC have about a dozen fixtures each year, and charity matches organized by such bodies as the Lord's Taverners and Christopher Martin-Jenkins keep me busy on many of the remaining Saturdays and Sundays of the season. At some of these games I have been able to meet and to play with the owners of some of the most famous names in cricket. Colin Cowdrey, for instance, once lent me a magnificent bat just after he had scored a century with it; I can now reveal that the genius of that innings lay with the batsman, not the bat – I made a less than memorable two. On another occasion I dropped a catch off the bowling of John Snow. I am indeed fortunate that a few songs have brought me cricketing privileges that my skills with bat or ball never could.

One of my cricketing friendships I value most is that with Jim Swanton – and yet it did not come about as a result of this heady mixture of cricketing and musical society. Far from it. After reading Jim's *Sort of a Cricket Person* I wrote him a fan letter which to my delight resulted in his suggestion that we should meet at Lord's. I had been wanting to write a letter of admiration to E.W.S. for almost 20 years, and after reading his autobiography I could restrain myself no longer.

I remember having an earnest conversation with my mother when I was still a long way from long trousers about the advisability of writing to a popular TV programme of the day called 'Ask Pickles' in which Mr Wilfred Pickles attempted to satisfy the hitherto impossible wishes of half a dozen viewers each week. My unreachable dream was to meet E. W. Swanton, but my courage failed me and I never did ask Pickles. Two decades later I was braver, and did not even consider using Wilfred as a middle man in my quest to thank Jim for encouraging my love for and appreciation of cricket.

I first came across Swanton in print in 1956 – the report of the First Test against Australia of that year in the *Daily Telegraph*. But I had been a Swanton man (or rather, boy) well before that, having been mightily impressed by his words and by his voice on the radio and television since the 1953 series, of which the Ashes-winning Oval match was the game that actually sparked off my fanatical interest in cricket. Not until my parents wisely switched newspapers just in time for me to read about the whole of the astonishing 1956 series through the eyes of E. W. Swanton did I realize that my hero of the commentary box was a giant of cricket journalism too.

Of course it is ludicrous to dismiss E.W.S. as simply a journalist when he sets pen to paper. When one reads a collection of his match reports together assembled they have a continuity and style that elevates them beyond journalism. The only good thing to have resulted from Jim's departure from regular cricket reporting in the *Daily Telegraph* has been an increase in his output of longer pieces of writing in book form – rarely can one writer have produced in just five years three works of cricket literature to match *Sort of a Cricket Person, Swanton In Australia* and now *Follow On*.

I could wax eloquent for some time about the particular merits of Jim's work, but I would be covering ground many have covered before. However, I would like to echo the sentiments of others as far as one or two of the outstanding qualities of his writing are concerned, and I would then like to dwell a while upon the subject of Swanton the broadcaster. Finally I can turn my attention to this volume in particular, where I do have the edge over other Swanton-philes in that I am getting first crack of the whip.

First, the echoes of the verdict of those who have read much Swanton : Jim's writing does great service to cricket. A man who knew nothing whatsoever about the game, who had never heard of any of its myriad of technical and poetical terms, would realize when reading an article by E. W. Swanton that the game was more important than the winning or the losing, that this thing 'cricket' was not just another device whereby men of different nationalities or different sponsorship can grind each other into the dust by fair means or foul. He has never rushed headlong into instant sensation. He will consider the point of view of all sides in every clash, on or off the field, within or without the laws of cricket, and come down every time on the side of cricket. He has humour, often through understatement ('There has been no official complaint from the Australians, but since they are not deaf mutes they have conveyed what they feel' – Swanton writing about the Australians' thoughts about the pitch on which they were destroyed by Laker at Old Trafford in '56); and he has total command of English. Perhaps his only fault is that, like one of the cricketers he most admires, Colin Cowdrey, he is too modest, which sometimes means we learn a little less than we would like about the writer who entertains us so well; however, I believe readers of *Follow On* will discover that in this new book he has seen the error of his ways in this regard.

Second, Swanton the broadcaster: obviously, all the comments I have just made about Jim's writing apply to the words he chooses when he talks on radio or television, but I can never listen to Jim on the air, even today, without remembering that what first interested me in E. W. Swanton was the way he spoke, not what he actually said. I have never quite understood why John Arlott has such a stranglehold on the 'voice of cricket' title. I am second to no man in my admiration for Mr Arlott's magic vocal delivery, but I have always believed that in cricket there is many another larynx deserving of the awed respect accorded to the Arlott vocal chords. Jim Swanton's is one, and as more and more of the voices of sport become totally indistinguishable from one another, hysterical and nasal, lacking class and region, a voice such as Jim's becomes even purer gold.

Finally, Jim's latest work, this book, *Follow On*. I must confess that while I had no hesitation whatsoever in agreeing to write this Foreword I was a little worried when the manuscript of *Follow On* arrived on my desk that it might not reach the standards of its predecessors. I need not have worried – it is in many ways the best of the three, though probably to be most enjoyed by those who have already read *Sort of a Cricket Person*, which it complements perfectly.

Free from the confines of chronology which inevitably governed much of the pattern of *Sort of a Cricket Person*, Jim has been able to strike out in a variety of different directions. The only serious criticism encountered by *SOCP* (as Jim himself refers to his earlier book in *Follow On*) concerned what he left out of his memoirs. How much better to receive that kind of complaint than the charge of long-windedness! To leave the customers crying for more at the end of the show is the aim of every theatrical producer in my profession, and can only be a good thing for an author to achieve too. *Follow On* should satisfy all those who wanted more of Swanton on Swanton, but not in the way they might have expected. We learn more about Jim through his perceptive and colourful essays on topics that range from Bodyline to the Church, Montgomery to the *Cricketer* magazine. His chapter 'Aspects of Oxford' in particular leads him into fields some distance from the bat and ball – or does it? For Jim Swanton, the spirit of the interpretation of the rules is what matters, and not just on the pitch, or during the game. One can see in chapters such as this that the description of E. W. Swanton as a great cricket writer does not do him justice – he is a great writer whatever his subject.

TIM RICE

Great Milton, March 1977

Author's Note

This book was completed in the spring of 1977 when the only sporting connotation attaching to the name of Packer, so far as I know, concerned the challenges made by the late Sir Frank Packer for the America's Cup with his yacht, *Gretel*. He was the owner of a chain of Australian newspapers and magazines, with a controlling interest also in Australian commercial television. On the death of Sir Frank the press and TV empire he had created passed to his son, Kerry, who, as we go to press, has shocked the cricket world by announcing that, completely unknown to the authorities either in Australia or elsewhere, he has contracted some 35 leading players, half Australian and half drawn from England, the West Indies, South Africa and Pakistan, to play a series of matches over the next three years. The first such series would be held in Australia this coming winter between his Australian mercenaries and the remainder. This would coincide with two Test series, between Australia and India in Australia, and the West Indies and Australia in the West Indies. The fact that it would clash, too, with two English series in Pakistan and New Zealand, is by comparison almost – though not quite – co-incidental.

So far as English cricket is concerned, the immediate effect was to cause the Cricket Council to eliminate Tony Greig from consideration as captain of England for the summer's rubber against Australia, because by helping to recruit other current England players (Knott and Underwood) to what was promptly dubbed 'Packer's Circus' he had 'inevitably impaired the trust which existed between the cricket authorities and the captain of the England side.'

At the moment of writing the special meeting of the International Cricket Conference called to consider the grave threat which this enterprise poses to Test cricket has yet to take place. In any case it is scarcely possible to envisage a quick or an easy solution. On the face of it Packer's manoeuvres constitute nothing less than an act of sporting piracy. The leading players concerned have been brought to the top at considerable cost by the established system. The game in all the countries concerned is nourished largely by the gates and other emoluments from Test Matches. What is being attempted is simply to filch these men from the allegiances to which they owe their name and fame, in so doing putting the financial structure of cricket at risk, in order to swell the profits of a television company.

One can understand, up to a point, the dilemma of the cricketers themselves, before whom the bait of very large three-year contracts has been dangled – especially the Australians whose own system offers no substantial security, and the South Africans, who cannot now augment their earnings by the various rewards, direct and indirect, that stem from Test Matches.

In the short term the country chiefly under duress is Australia. However, the prosperity of cricket among the Test-playing countries is indivisible. The next England-Australia series is due in Australia in 1978, and it is this most ancient of rivalries that underpins the whole fabric of Test cricket – upon which, as I say, the first-class game depends.

England can no doubt absorb the loss of three of the foremost players – even though at the moment there is no abundance of talent. But can Australia in a few months build a fresh team, starting from scratch? Quickly though their sportsmen mature this is a tall order. Altogether it is a black and ugly cloud which has suddenly overshadowed the face of cricket, ironically enough when in the after-glow of the Melbourne Centenary Test all seemed set fair. (It is a bitter thought that so many of those engaged had already and in secret sold their future services.)

There is no alternative surely for the ICC members than to ride out the storm, confident that though exhibition matches with the personalities involved may have an initial appeal in Australia they can be no substitute in the long run, so far as the public is concerned, for the real thing.

In the light of the Packer business my chapter on 'The Post-War Breed' and my final 'Reflections' – neither of which I have altered in proof – may bring a wry smile to my readers. Some may think that the sentiments I express there have a more acute relevance than when they were written. One point I made at the end – that the top players nowadays do pretty well out of the game, and are likely to do better – is worth underlining. This is true of no one so much as Greig, whose income since he was elevated to the England captaincy is estimated as at least £50,000 a year, with every prospect of a long-term security. Questions of loyalty aside, his decision reflects a temperamental instability of judgement which has always had to be measured against his undoubted qualities. How sad that his priorities have shifted such a long way since he stated a year ago, in answer to questions as to his future:

'I have always said that any man worth his salt will, if picked, play for England whether at home or abroad. To play for England is the ultimate for any sportsman. That is something I passionately believe. First and foremost – as I did before I went to Australia last winter – I have put everything before the authorities at Lord's and nothing will be undertaken without their full approval.'

When the news of Packer's take-over bid broke I recalled an exchange I had had with Kerry Packer's father over the dinner-table at Sydney during the 1965-6 MCC tour of Australia. Cricket, said Frank Packer, with all the certainty of a man unaccustomed to being contradicted, was a dying game. In Australia, he added, baseball was the coming thing. I said I was sorry his sporting staffs did not keep him better informed. Would he accept my word that more people were playing the game in Australia than ever before, that half a million Australians out of a total population of fewer than ten million had rung to know the Test score in the preceding series, *et cetera*? No, he replied, he wouldn't. Knowing he gambled on everything – to the extent of losing large sums regularly on the golf course, despite receiving two strokes at the par fours and fives and one stroke at the short holes! – I suggested that he put his money where his mouth was. I see from my diary that the date was 7 January 1966, and the stake was £10. I sent Packer an affirmation from Alan Barnes, secretary of the Australian Board of Control, of the facts I had quoted, and duly pocketed the cheque he sent in reply.

I firmly believe that in his estimation of the strength and taste of the Australian cricket public the son will prove as wide of the mark as his father.

Sandwich
June 1977.

I

Come Dancing

E. W. Swanton is to cricket what Peter West is to 'Come Dancing' : one feels it could not continue without him.

Looking over a profusion of old papers, wondering whether or not a fresh selection of memories might be acceptable to the great cricket public (and even, with luck, to a few beyond its boundaries), I came across this crisp review – that's all there was of it – of my last book but two, *Cricket From All Angles*. It appeared in the *Times Saturday Review* of 14 December 1968.

Anonymous reviews, of whatever length, are apt to leave the author asking himself unanswerable questions. In this case, for instance, was the reviewer aiming to pay the most telling compliment possible within his prescribed length of twenty words? After all, my friend and erstwhile fellow-commentator, Peter West, with his black tie and bonhomie, was for a long time the indispensable TV guide to the world of ballroom dancing. Whether or not those well-groomed couples could have gone twirling on, Friday after Friday, without him, they never did until after what he described as 'fifteen years hard'. He then called it a day in favour of more time for cricket and rugger.

Or was this aphoristic gem the work of some sharp young man at Printing House Square, to whom cricket and dancing were alike anathema, the sort who might pray in the words of Arthur Marshall: 'Oh, God, if there be cricket in Heaven, let there be rain as well'? One can only guess.

Continuing my rummaging-about – and it is one of the consolations of advancing years to have the leisure to potter among old records – I happened across a lengthier estimate of my place in cricket literature emanating from the same stable – it appeared in the *Times Educational Supplement* – and at about the same time :

First, Mr Swanton's style : it is pawky, dull, at times embarrassingly pompous. He has always liked to speak with authority, but, read retrospectively, many of his pieces are clichéd and repetitive, faintly nineteenth-century and ponderous.

Cricket writing (*vide* Alan Ross and John Arlott) needs a dash, but not an overdose, of poetry. Mr Swanton is very prosaic.

It was a schoolmaster, surely, who made this flattering judgement – beta minus at best, more probably a plain gamma. If the cutting hadn't remained forgotten in obscurity I might never have had the nerve to embark on *Sort of a Cricket Person*, to say nothing of *Swanton in Australia*, both of which, it is perhaps fair to all to say, were very kindly noticed in *The Times* proper, and even sold out – pompous, pawky, prosaic or not – several editions apiece. So far at least the decline from anonymity in that quarter seems to have worked to my advantage.

But is one wise to risk another book of memoirs? To perpetrate one volume of autobiography is said to be an unmistakable mark of vanity. How can a successor to *Sort of a Cricket Person* (which for convenience's sake I shall henceforth shorten to *SOCP*) be excused? Well, I'm afraid I don't intend to make the attempt. My intention is to retrace much of the same journey again, but keeping, as it were, more to the side-roads, and so encountering people and places either missed or only briefly saluted the first time. I shall follow a long-held belief that what gives pleasure to write about may be interesting to read.

As to any charge of vanity I find that as one gets old one becomes less sensitive to criticism of this kind. Perhaps I may even fortify myself by the remark of H. S. Altham, who first fired my ambitions towards authorship, in alliance with journalism, when he asked me, when I was 30, to collaborate with him in the second edition of *A History of Cricket*. After his retirement as a schoolmaster at Winchester Harry was in constant demand as a speaker at every sort and condition of cricket occasion and such was his good nature and love of the game he rarely declined. Someone asked him whether he worried about telling the same stories, or uttering the same sentiments twice. 'Not in the slightest,' he replied; 'if they've heard it before, they've probably forgotten it. And if they haven't forgotten it they're damned lucky to get it again.'

As will be imagined, Harry Altham had a special claim on my

affection, as he had with many of all ages, and though some will have read *The Heart of Cricket*, the book about him, with contributions on various aspects of his life, which Hubert Doggart edited for the *Cricketer*, I have attempted a further picture of him since he epitomized perfectly the concept of *mens sana*, now, to our detriment, somewhat in decline.

There are others of the generations senior to mine who personified the amateur ideal and whom I know or knew well enough to say something about: Sir John Masterman, for instance, that pillar of Oxford for more than half a century; Gubby Allen, who has meant so much to MCC, and MCC to him; Raymond Robertson-Glasgow, scholar-player-writer-friend; Leonard Crawley, my idiosyncratic, dyspeptic, endearing *Daily Telegraph* colleague for so long; and many more. With some trepidation I shall also attempt as an act of filial-in-law piety a short tribute to someone well known to all of these but not unfortunately to me, my wife Ann's father, R. H. de Montmorency, known widely in the sporting world as 'Monty'.

It is a temptation to linger in the past, but there are also places and people, some recently encountered, of a strange assortment of backgrounds, with which and with whom I want to familiarize the reader: Lord's and the men who've made it; the inter-war figures; the heroes of the post-war breed; familiar haunts, and home pastures, not excluding our Cinque Port of Sandwich, which by the mercy of Providence is being saved from destruction in the nick of time by the long-overdue building of a by-pass. It is a privilege to be associated with traditional places, to have Canterbury itself only twelve miles down the road; also, of course, to be seeing MCC from the inside as a member of the Committee.

Lord's is a word that conjures up a wide variety of emotions, ranging from blind, uncritical veneration to – among some – distaste and disrespect as representing in their minds the darkest forces of reaction. Over more than forty years of membership I have seen the Club treble in size from its 6000 of the mid-'30s, and its staff and ramifications multiply. Ten sub-committees now deal with different branches of MCC administration, and, though there is some overlapping of function, to be in the middle of the web is to realize that this could perhaps only be avoided if executive powers were to be vested in an enlarged secretariat or a salaried board of management. Of the present 18,000 members about a hundred serve the club on committees, and they form a democratic cross-section which would pass the scrutiny of most fair-minded men. 'Declaring an interest' naturally, I believe that Marylebone Cricket Club would come out at least as favourably from a Commission of Enquiry as most national institutions, sporting or otherwise.

Though MCC has been itself instrumental in delegating some of its former powers its influence scarcely grows less, and I expect it will adapt its ways to changing patterns, and continue to stand for what is best in the game in the future as it has done since its inception getting on for two hundred years ago, even though at first-class level the independent cricketer, from which type MCC used largely to recruit its committees, has disappeared.

I speak of the independent cricketer rather than the amateur since it is the independence rather than the distinction in status which was surely the chief loss. On the social side it has always been one of the charms of cricket from earliest days that it brought together all classes from the duke to the dustman – sorry, refuse collector. It was from this uniquely wide cross-section that there evolved an unwritten code of sportsmanship which from the earliest days has bound cricketers of all sorts in a common fellowship.

The higher the level at which the game is played the more hangs upon winning – in material terms. For the generality of cricketers the game is at its best and most enjoyable surely when what matters deeply while the players are at it recedes swiftly in importance once it is finished. I am not against cups and leagues, points and prizes in themselves; there is, however, a clear threat to the character of cricket if as a general thing the result begins to mean too much to too many.

But these are solemn sentiments which I promise to restrict, in what follows, to the smallest and most infrequent doses. I am led to them by a review of *Swanton in Australia* by Nicholas Richardson in *New Society* in which he pictures me as something of a bereft, disconsolate defender of the spirit of times past:

His autobiography contained a chapter on 'Cricket in distress'; and from the evidence of this book his melancholy remains unpurged. Few of the phenomena he laments – throwing, the excessive use of the bumper, deliberate time-wasting, histrionic behaviour, even rioting – are new. After all, the first English tour abroad was stopped not by riot but revolution : that was to Paris in 1789. But behind the changes he details, Swanton sees a new spirit, an abrasive bloody-mindedness that is in part a reaction against the amateur ethic. But the Greeks would have understood. Their word for amateur had a wide range of meanings – from the untrained to the ignoramus. And so should Swanton, whose writing has a curious elegiac quality reminiscent, if not of a chorus-ending from Euripides, at least of the last episode of *Upstairs, Downstairs*. For by a supreme irony he was decorated the same year as the Beatles : and if the amateur is dead, then the future may well belong to the Fools on the Sydney Hill.

After the last Sydney Test I saw (Australia *v* England in January 1975), I confess I can scarcely think of the Hillites without a shudder. Mr Richardson has got me on the raw there, even though I'm sure the grossly insanitary discomforts of the Hill when full of people – and the people full of beer – make its inhabitants the fools they seem to be. The latest news is said to be that the Hill is to be replaced by a stand : so much the better. Like most cricket-writers apparently I have 'small use for social observations', so I should perhaps beware of contradicting a reviewer who sees me as

in appearance and *auctoritas* a little like some late Roman Emperor, in style a not unbecoming blend of Charles Pooter and Major Pendennis.

Hark at that ! It remains only to lighten the ignorance of less lettered readers by revealing that Pooter, an assistant in a mercantile business, was the subject of George and Weedon Grossmith's amusing late-Victorian *Diary of a Nobody*. The Major is uncle to Thackeray's *Pendennis*, a more worldly not to say conspiring fellow than the simple Pooter, though equally well-meaning. H'm ! On the whole I think I prefer the Emperor bit.

Talking of book reviews, there's no denying the satisfaction derived by the author from anything reasonably favourable, and if there are sufficient of such the odd sour notice seems not to matter very much. I was lucky with *SOCP* in that it touched agreeably nostalgic chords in several reviewers, who were kind enough to recommend it as a Christmas present. Tommy Joy, the presiding genius of Hatchard's, the Piccadilly book-shop, seemed to be con-

firming that the reviewers' advice was being taken when he said:
'It's what I call our Uncle Fred book.' On being asked to explain,
he added, 'Oh, you know, what the devil can we give Uncle Fred?'
It was agreeable to hear from some of these venerable contemporaries that they had enjoyed it even if some may not have had
their full money's worth. I heard of two friends who died with the
book at their bedside, though one certainly had nearly finished it.
Whether life was shortened or prolonged one will never know. The
other was that magnificent all-round sportsman and charming fellow
who is chiefly remembered as one of the greatest of all scrum-halves,
C. A. Kershaw. At a British Sportsman's Club luncheon 'Kay'
brought the book for me to sign. He looked as fit as ever but said:
'This hip is giving me gyp. I'm going in to have it fixed tomorrow,
and taking your book for company.' He suffered a relapse after the
operation and within a week or so was dead.

Others were luckier, including the stranger who wrote from Stock-
port that he was 90 and just recovering from double pneumonia,
'but sheer gratitude constrains me to tell you how much I enjoyed
your book . . . It is logical, I think, to assume that the pleasure its
reading has given me has helped in my convalescence.' I liked that
'logical'.

It is pleasant, as I say, to think that one is giving comfort to the
elderly but even more satisfactory when one's correspondent is a
young man – such, for instance, as he who dated his first cricket
reading precisely as the *Daily Telegraph* report of the First Test
against Australia at Trent Bridge in 1956. He was then eleven and
wrote that he had not missed one since.

Finally, I cannot resist quoting the views of Benny Green, who
greeted the paperback edition of *SOCP* thus in the *Spectator*:

E. W. Swanton's memoirs possess a kind of rubicund flush which
used to be par for the course in the Fleet Street reminiscences of
press-box sportsmen, but which has almost disappeared in these
utilitarian times. Swanton has never been a very elegant writer,
but he is honest and accurate. What is surprising is the added
bouquet of charm which insinuates itself in the mind of the
reader. Charm is hardly the word I would have thought of to
describe Swanton's prose, but the narrative is disarming . . .

Well, it's something to have disarmed so sharp a critic as

Mr Green. But I have a feeling this introspection has gone on long enough, and that, with all the virtues I can command, I'd best be getting down to my muttons.

I propose first, however, perhaps as something of a personal quirk, and possibly to inject an occasional fresh note in the story, from time to time to introduce an imaginary companion on my journey.

When I was a prisoner-of-war – 'in the bag' as we old lags are still inclined to say – I used sometimes to while away the night hours by making imaginary journeys from my house in the Temple, pausing at each ground I'd played on and recalling some of the games and my own contributions to them. In this way before falling off to sleep I contrived to tot up a lot of runs; but I dare say under-nourishment may have softened the brain and blurred my arith-metical processes. In any case, the point is immaterial – or as Maurice Tate and/or Frank Chester would have said, 'immemorial' – and merely serves as a way of informing readers of this book who are not acquainted with *SOCP* that I used in my day to fancy myself rather as a batsman.

On this tack I used to be accused by a brash young Australian when he was playing Arab cricket that I would transport him miles out of the way to show him grounds whereon I'd made hundreds. This slander probably derived from my having driven to Oxford, long before the days of the M40, by the longer but far more pleasant Thames Valley route, so passing that charming little ground tucked into the side of the hill as one descends to Henley Bridge. Henry Longhurst and I with other companions once enjoyed a river holiday by motor-launch. One day I hopped off at the Phyllis Court landing-stage and managed to get a hundred there for MCC.

Well, remembering my nostalgic nights on the bamboo-slats of Kinsayok and Kanburi gives me the notion that to make certain English pilgrimages in the mind's eye might be as acceptable a way as any of stimulating half-forgotten memories of places and people. *Wisden* will be, as ever, at my side, to say nothing of a collection of Badminton diaries and a long shelf of cuttings-books: but I shall hope to need only occasional recourse to the records. And it will be a good idea perhaps to provide myself with a hypothetical companion with a feeling for cricket and character. Who better than that self-same Aussie now tending his sheep-stations somewhere in the South Australian out-back?

2

In the Beginning

Can I as a start, I wonder, do anything to satisfy those reviewers
of *SOCP* who remarked they would have liked to know more of
my early years, normal, happy and uneventful though I had said
they were? I stick to my contention that in most cases the interval
between the cradle and adolescence is best taken as read unless it
has been in any important respect extraordinary. In such a category,
for instance, one might include the childhood of another recent
cricket autobiographer, Colin Cowdrey, who tells us that for more
than seven years, from just under six until he was almost thirteen,
he was separated because of the war from both parents. They were
in India, he in the care of relations. I've no doubt that, when they
were at last reunited with their son, Colin's father and mother must
have rejoiced that he had been so well taken care of. Nevertheless –
to me at least – there is a side of his nature which attracts one's
sympathy in the knowledge of what he missed of security and
parental affection in those years of war. In this case the boyhood
story has significance.

Not so with me; I was always comfortably and affectionately
surrounded, and duly grew up, taught pretty rigorously to mind my
manners, work hard at my books and wash behind the ears, but
with few other limits on my behaviour. However, for the benefit of
those professing an interest in embryonic matters, let me record with
pride that I was conceived in that great and glorious year wherein
for the first time Kent won the County Championship. True, within
a few days from when this epoch-making event may be presumed
to have occurred, and only a mile or so from my birthplace at Forest
Hill, on the Private Banks ground down at Catford Bridge beside
what is now the South Circular Road, Kent in their opening match
of the season took a hammering from Yorkshire.

That was hardly a hopeful beginning, but in mid-June there
occurred the most auspicious event in the illustrious history of Kent,
the emergence of 'the colt Woolley' who, so *Wisden* tells us, had

been 'regarded for some little time as the most promising of the young professionals at the Tonbridge nursery'. Never mind my little suburban nursery (wherein I duly arrived on 11 February 1907) – here was one that really mattered!

This is an unashamedly self-indulgent book, so let us linger over my pre-natal summer of 1906 at least long enough to re-record certain important moments. In his first match, at Old Trafford in early June, Frank fielded out while J. T. Tyldesley made 295 not out, and, as is well known, dropped him early and made a duck. However, in the second innings he scored 64, and so was fairly launched. His first home game directly afterwards was on the Bat and Ball ground at Gravesend, wherein he made a major contribution to victory by taking six Somerset wickets for 39 with that steep trajectory and humming spin: and his next at home, on the Angel ground at Tonbridge, his birthplace, wherein he made 116, the first in his roll of 145 scores of three figures – to say nothing of 35 90s.

A few weeks past his 19th birthday the tall, spare figure walked in – always a bit stiff-legged – against Hampshire with the board showing 23 for three. Whereupon he 'drove so brilliantly on the off-side that he made his hundred in about an hour and a half'. Yes, the maiden hundred of this untried youth contesting for his place took an hour and a half. With eight wickets in the two innings for 57 runs Frank had quite a match. It can hardly, however, have come as a surprise since in between these games at Gravesend and Tonbridge, in the first of the two blood matches with Surrey, he had put up perhaps an even more extraordinary performance with 72 and 23 not out, and eight for 119.

'When does Tom Hayward come in?' the green young man is said to have asked after two or three wickets had fallen. 'Hayward?' he was told, 'He was the one you bowled out first.'

What else about the summer of 1906? Well, Kent went from strength to strength, scoring 568 and 479 in the Canterbury Week and crushing Sussex and Lancashire respectively by an innings and plenty. Proceeding finally to Bournemouth where they needed only to draw to finish on top, they made 610 in six hours and won, again, by an innings. Young Frank, for the first and last time, had to stand aside for the amateurs at Canterbury: the Kent batting averages were headed by five of them, C. J. Burnup, K. L. Hutchings, E. W.

Dillon, J. R. Mason and R. N. R. Blaker ('Pinkie', Kenneth or Quartus, Ted, Jack and Dick as we should say today), the first two finishing in the sixties, the rest in the forties. Frank's own figures from fourteen matches were 626 runs, average 28, and 42 wickets at 20 runs each. His feet were firmly on the ladder, and his style of play definitely established, deriving, as he has often said, from these brilliant amateurs and others in the same mould.

Hero of my youth! How could I have chosen any other?

Kent were the team of the season, yet they would have finished second to Yorkshire but for the latter's defeat by one run at Bristol in their last match. Eleven runs were needed when Billy Ringrose, afterwards Yorkshire's scorer, came in last: nine were made before G. L. Jessop brought himself on and with his third ball had Ringrose LBW. 'Captain's decision'? Plumb as plumb? A straight full-pitch perhaps? On what brief digital movement, swiftly determined, does history depend!

Thus were Yorkshire thwarted and that despite the greatest all-round performance in the history of cricket, George Hirst's immortal and unique double of 2385 runs and 208 wickets. It is a sadness that I never met George Hirst, almost the only considerable cricketer of the post-1918 period whose company I was never in. So I can only salute his great qualities as man and cricketer at second-hand. At Eton where he had a long and happy reign as coach they loved his blunt judgements as when a captain (was it Willy Hill-Wood?) sought his reasons for an unexpected defeat – either that or a failure to force victory: 'Ye bowled too long, and ye bowled too bad.'

What a study in character must have been the partnership between C. M. Wells, master-in-charge of cricket on Hirst's arrival, and the all-round ideal which I shall exemplify later on by men nearer my own time. Wells was a classical scholar, a rugger international and double blue, distinguished Middlesex cricketer, an authority on wine and fishing, stamps (of which he swapped knowledge with King George V), South African mines, and no doubt much else besides. He was said to read the *Financial Times* from cover to cover. To emphasize the boys' own responsibility for their cricket he expected an invitation each morning from the captain to run the practice: otherwise he wouldn't be there. He demanded and generally achieved high standards. In 1918 on Agar's Plough

Eton bowled out Charterhouse for 13. The comment years later of Robertson-Glasgow who was playing for Charterhouse, as I remember, being, 'And Plough was the word.' Wells's reputed verdict was, 'All right, but it should have been nine.'

Wells was Gubby Allen's housemaster, and in the years before he died at the ripe age of 92 Gubby used to give a dinner party for him at the Conservative Club on his birthday. Plum Warner would be there and Dick Twining and other of the Middlesex players of differing generations, and once or twice Gubby was kind enough to ask me. The cricket talk was of a high order, though I'm afraid the only remark of Wells's that sticks in the mind is not indicative of the mutual affection that existed between master and pupil.

'They tell me Allen – ' Wells always put an equal stress on both syllables – 'is writing a book. I never knew he read one.' In fact Allen, almost alone among the great men of cricket, never has published a book under his own name, and it's a fair bet that now he never will. But within the last year or so he has almost rewritten, and with the utmost care in every paragraph, *The MCC Coaching Book*, a labour of love if ever there was one.

The year 1907, in addition to the strictly personal event on 11 February already referred to, saw not only the further blossoming of Frank Woolley, now fairly launched in the Kent XI, but also the promotion to the ranks of the MCC touring team to Australia of the cricketer a few years senior to him destined possibly to an even wider fame, though since one was a batsman and the other an all-rounder, they are properly ranked jointly and of equal lustre.

Jack Hobbs's beginning in 1905 was about as auspicious as Frank Woolley's was to be a year later. Who can say that the affairs of cricket are not guided by one of the more romantic branches of the celestial civil service when we find that in his first match for Surrey young Hobbs, destined to be known throughout the cricket world as 'The Master', found himself on opposite sides to the bearded patriarch, whose initials, W.G., meant only one thing to every living Englishman, and who was equally familiar as 'The Champion'?

In those hardy days the Oval season began with the visit of the Gentlemen of England on Easter Monday, and 24 April was not too early for the 56-year-old who, by all report, made a few of those curiously high-pitched comments, of a complimentary kind, about the 88 scored in the second innings by the slim young opening bat from Cambridge whom Tom Hayward had brought up to try his luck with Surrey. Like almost all the truly great ones Jack 'never looked back'. He and his mentor, Tom, forthwith began to set up the first of the three opening partnerships that were to span his cricket life: 1317 runs he scored in his first season, 1913 in his second, and in the phenomenally wet summer of 1907 he made 2135.

MCC had difficulty finding their second side to Australia: two or three of the amateurs couldn't go, and four of the pros wouldn't, on a matter of terms. And so Hobbs (J. B.) was given his chance. The career of the man who was to make more runs than anyone in history, more hundreds, and in particular more runs and more hundreds than any Englishman against Australia, was fairly on its way. He had had little cricket before the First Test, and was not chosen, and I seem to recall Philip Trevor, MCC's manager on that tour, who subsequently so befriended me in my early days in the press-box, saying it took Jack a long time to get over the sea voyage – he was always a terrible sailor.

However, he was named for the Second Test in Melbourne at the New Year, went in first and made 83 and 28 (England winning the most exciting of victories by one wicket); it was the first of his 41 Tests against Australia, the beginning of the Test story that ended, nine series later, when the Australians at the Oval in 1930 surrounded him as he came in to play against them for the last time, and raised their caps and cheered in final salute.

It is not easy to find phrases to describe a man of such attainments without descending to cliché. It must be accepted that he was the nearest approach to perfection on all types of pitch and in every variety of situation: particularly of pitch for, apart from the South African mat, there was much more variation in terms of texture – the Australian 'looking-glass' to the sticky – of pace, and lift and turn in days when only the creases were ever covered. Technically his equipment was all but faultless: temperamentally one has only to study the serenity of expression in all the photographs of his going out to bat to be sure that he was not to be flustered or discomposed. Rather he seems to be saying, 'I'm going to enjoy this – and I hope you're all going to enjoy it too.'

There were two tributes to him at his death which said all that there was to say: 'Sir John Berry Hobbs', by Neville Cardus in the

1964 *Wisden,* and the Memorial Address at the service in South-
wark Cathedral by Harry Altham that is republished in *The Heart
of Cricket.* On the anniversary of his death last year I wrote a
nostalgic piece which the *Daily Telegraph* entitled 'Hobbs – The
Legend Lives On'. It was illustrated by the famous photograph
showing him moving out to drive, a study of poetry in motion that
every aspiring young batsman should know and possess. There was
nothing in my article that seemed likely to encourage people to
write, but write they did in the most charming way and in almost
embarrassing numbers.

Two points were seized on, one a matter of batting method, the
other a personal story illustrative of the high regard in which he was
held by all who knew him. The first had to do with his back-lift
which I presumed to tell the moderns they would do well to imitate
– strange indeed though they would find it. One reader told how
in the '20s his coach advised him to see all he could of the great
players such as Hobbs, Woolley and J. W. Hearne ('Young Jack').
At Lord's one day Hobbs got out after lunch, and my correspondent
was lucky enough to spot him later in the afternoon going round
to the nets where he batted for an hour in what is described as a
photographic session, probably in order to illustrate a text-book.

'Watch particularly Jack Hobbs's early and high back-lift, and
see how this gives him more time to position himself for every
stroke,' the young hopeful had been told by his coach. So he
stationed himself behind the net and, wrote my reader, 'to this day
I can recall the Master's words as he made exactly the point you
mention.' Then quoting Hobbs talking to the author of the book
(as he supposed) while batting : ' "Come *down* on the ball with the
full weight of the bat," he said, demonstrating the late-cut. "To do
that the back-lift must be high, and to gain height you may even
have to rise on your toes to get right over the ball. Never just push
at it, that's the way to get caught." '

My reader regards that enchanted hour as the one that shaped
his attitude to batting, and though he was modest about his own
play in his letter, thanks to his wonderful free lesson I believe he
gave fast bowlers who bowled short to him pretty short shrift when
in due course he became a very successful cricketer.

I mentioned, too, in my article on Jack a man who had told me
that whenever Surrey were playing at home at the week-end, though

they attended different churches, he used to take his family a longer way round on the chance of seeing the Hobbs parents and children on their Sunday morning church parade. Jack was anything but a sanctimonious person, but he was a devout Anglican all his life. His first cricket team, Cardus tells us, was the choir of St Matthew's, Cambridge, and the first innings he remembered was for the choir of Jesus College, who 'borrowed' their groundsman's promising young son. Parishioners of two churches at Clapham Common wrote with affectionate memories, and an Air-Commodore who seemed only to have met him once as a boy idolized him all his life. All in all, I felt fortified in the point I was making, which will recur in this book (though I hope not to excess) that the national fascination for cricket has always been much bound up with the men our famous players are, as well as with the way they play. It's a tradition that has taken some hard knocks from time to time, but, in the words of the headline, it 'lingers on'.

Even I actually once played with Jack Hobbs. Andy Kempton, a noted maker of pies and a patron of Surrey as well as a high-class wicket-keeper, took in the mid-'30s a richly-assorted team down to Stinchcombe for a one-day match against the Gloucestershire XI in aid of one of their benefits, and we had also P. G. H. Fender and Jack O'Connor, and a few more stars whose lustre has dimmed over forty years ago and more. Behind the Pear Tree inn was a lovely field with natural banking and what we were assured was a beautiful wicket. On Friday night I expect it was, but as we slept down came the rain, out – so we were afterwards told – went mine host of the Pear Tree, nobly dragging the tarpaulin that was to protect the sacred pitch. If ever virtue went unrewarded this was the time. In the dark his tarpaulin was hauled to the wrong spot, and there we were next day, before a splendid crowd sunning themselves on the slopes, and as the last meet of the season streamed away on the skyline, facing Tom Goddard and Charlie Parker on a sticky dog. However idly they went through the motions even the Master was reduced to mere mortality. As for the callow young journalist, one from Parker that pitched leg-stump and hit off 'were wasted' on him, but as we were changing afterwards in the little dressing-room he remembers with gratitude to this day Walter Hammond saying, 'Rather you'd had that one than me.' Come to think of it, no doubt that's what I chiefly recall about the day – that and the Master and

I strolling about together in the covers.

My last Hobbs recollection comes at second-hand, but I fear my modesty is not proof against repeating it. In his review of *SOCP* for the *Daily Telegraph* I had to forgive John Warr many of the witticisms that seem to flow so effortlessly from his pen – such as that my prose style had been likened to 'somewhere between Enid Blyton and the Ten Commandments', or that I had been tipped as the next Governor-General of Barbados – when he quoted Jack slipping away from Lord's at the tea interval of an England-Australia Test, and excusing himself by saying, 'It was getting a bit dull, I've met all my friends, and I can read Jim Swanton in the morning.' That surely was a real Oscar.

I read recently – without any sense of particular pride or personal involvement – that London in 1907 was the biggest, most powerful and most sophisticated city in the world. In fact, if British civilization could be said to have had a peak then 1907 has a strong claim to being its date. The long golden Edwardian summer had still three years more to run . . . and so on. So be it. In the world of cricket it was not only the emergence on the international scene of England's finest modern batsman but the development in England by four highly talented South Africans of a fundamental new weapon in the bowling art. This was the birth of the googly, the ball that is expected to turn from leg to off, and instead does the contrary. Its four exponents, Faulkner, Schwarz, White and Vogler, all achieved marked success, three of them mixing, out of the back of the hand, the leg-break with the googly. Schwarz apparently did not command the leg-break but did have the top-spinner, and thus armed fared as well as the others. What was extraordinary was that the new method, no doubt by its very novelty, made such an impact despite the wetness of the summer. One of the great virtues of wrist-spin is that it will turn the ball on plumb pitches which may be almost impervious to orthodox finger-spin. Nowadays, of course, in most classes of cricket the discouraged, dwindled band of wrist-spinners scarcely get given an over by their misguided captains unless the off-breakers and left-armers can't turn it an inch – or alternatively unless the attack is in almost total disarray. Aubrey Faulkner, of course, was *the* great South African criceter of that generation, and I will not presume to add here to Ian Peebles's admiring first-hand portrait of him in his recent autobiography. (The two of them are inevitably associated in my mind because I met Ian first at the Faulkner School of Cricket at Walham Green, whither in 1931 I had been sent by the editor of the *Evening Standard* to entice him to write a weekly article for us during the cricket season – which without much persuasion he consented to do. But that's jumping ahead a bit.)

It is interesting surely that the arrival of wrist-spin 70 years ago is the last basic addition to the bowler's repertoire – apart, that is, from Bodyline and the contemptible modern cult of intimidation : to be precise, let me say the last *legitimate* development. Have all possibilities now been explored? I suppose there remains Conan Doyle's Spedegue Dropper, the high parabolic full-pitch aimed to land on top of the bails. If sufficient accuracy could be perfected I can imagine this method proving disconcerting and effective. Not cricket, Sir? Maybe not – nor, even more emphatically, the under-arm grub that sneaks along the floor. If anyone seeks to save a match by descending to that we may indeed all abandon hope.

In 1909, when I was two, Kent again won the Championship, as they did also in 1910 and 1913. 1912 was the year of the Triangular Tournament, and of my first conscious recollection. That was of the slate with which I was provided on my first day at kindergarten, with my name and the date, May 1912, inscribed on the wooden frame. I also remember the hymn we sang at our first assembly, No. 4 in the *Ancient and Modern*, 'New Every Morning is the Love'. And standing next to me was a boy who didn't sing a note, one Alec Edwards who afterwards succeeded his father as my parents' family doctor. He didn't sing because he was a Roman Catholic !

One may deplore the centuries-old anti-Catholic prejudice and antipathy in Great Britain, in these more ecumenically-minded days mercifully growing less, but surely nothing could have been better designed to fan the flames thereof than to tell a little boy that he must not sing a hymn with fellow-Christians. Isn't it significant that this tiny cause of discord – repeated, no doubt, in schools everywhere – has stuck in my mind for 60 years and more? Thank God things are better now. On which hopeful note perhaps I can bring these random thoughts of early years to an end. I wonder whether I have satisfied those who regretted my having skimped them last time . . .

3

The Mecca

There is only one starting-point for anyone, and especially for an Australian, anxious to explore the mysteries of cricket, and that is its headquarters at St John's Wood called Lord's. For anyone with a fondness for cricket who has any spark of imagination the story of MCC, and of Lord's which has been its home since the time of Waterloo, must have a strong romantic appeal. Much of my own enjoyment of cricket has centred on Lord's, too, so I feel something of a personal involvement in its history.

The game was played, of course, and flourished in and around the Weald – had even reached as far north as Nottingham and Sheffield – long before Thomas Lord and the new Marylebone Cricket Club first became associated, to their mutual advantage. But from that time – and remember we are now only ten years short of the Bicentenary of the foundation of MCC – cricket had a metropolitan focal-point, and henceforward to a large extent the growth and development of the game and of MCC went hand in hand.

The interplay of chance and coincidence that are the stuff of history are fascinatingly evident if we trace the evolution of the club and of its premises. Thomas Lord's father is a prosperous yeoman farmer in the North Riding of Yorkshire and a Catholic who, with his own troop of 500 horse, goes to the aid of Prince Charlie in the '45 Rebellion, suffers in consequence the confiscation of his lands, and so migrates from Thirsk (where in the pavilion of the cricket club there is today a Lord commemorative plaque) to the quiet Norfolk market-town of Diss.

In due course the handsome Thomas moves on to seek his fortune in London, enters the wine trade, and also becomes ground bowler and general factotum to the aristocratic White Conduit Club which plays on the public fields of that name at Islington. The White Conduit decide they want the privacy of an enclosed field, and they back young Lord to procure one. First they inhabit a ground in the rural area which became Dorset-square, at which point (1787) the

31

White Conduit become Marylebone whose noble members, according to popular request, promptly undertake a revision of the first Laws of 1744.

The great days of Hambledon are over by this time, as its patrons shift their interest from Hampshire to London, and there is no disputing the authority of what from its earliest days was recognized as the leading club. The expansion of London in the first years of the new century forces Lord farther north, first (taking his precious turfs with him) to a plot that became absorbed into the Regent Canal and thirdly and lastly, turfs and all, to its present situation to the west of the newly-built St John's Wood Church, of which parish, by the way, he, now presumably Anglicanized, becomes a vestryman.

To every cricket historian this is all familiar ground : lo ! is it not written in the book of the prophet and evangelist, Altham? But it may be new to my young Australian friend, and if I am to conduct him round a sentimental English cricket pilgrimage there is only one possible place to start.

When I first knew Lord's, from the late '20s on, my generation used often to refer to it, in inverted commas, you understand, as 'The Mecca'. It has had several subsidiary titles. The Press have often used the tag 'Headquarters', which is explicit enough, while Plum Warner used to quote, with an ecclesiastical intonation and a twinkle in his eye, Sir Robert Menzies's description, 'The Cathedral of Cricket'. After the clamour of Melbourne and Sydney the holy calm of Lord's used to strike visiting Australians with particular emphasis, and Bob Menzies's appellation perhaps might still be applied over most of the season though he would have something more pungent to say about the can-banging and the slogan-chanting by the minority that now take away so much of the pleasure from Test Matches and Cup Finals.

Again, some of the old pre-war landmarks have gone, notably the Tavern and Members' Dining-room, the low stands, A and B and P and Q, flanking the pavilion on either side, cosier and more personal places, all of them, than their more commodious, efficient successors. Yet withal Lord's is still 'The Mecca', the shrine to which pilgrims come from wherever in the world cricket is played, and which has still an atmosphere quite distinct, exclusive to it.

Suppose my friend and I come in from St John's Wood Road and make a tour of the ground before entering the cathedral sanctuary.

We pass through the Grace Gates which were put up in 1923 –
suitably imposing and substantial – simply inscribed to 'William
Gilbert Grace, The Great Cricketer'. Plum records that there was
much discussion in committee about the wording of the commemorative stone, and many suggestions were received, in English,
Latin and even Greek – which would no doubt have caused the
Old Man to pluck at his beard a bit – before Stanley Jackson came
up with the phrase that says all that needs be said.

I will postpone making an assessment of W.G.'s unique place in
the game as we pass on, leaving the new Tavern, practical if unlovely, to our left. Next comes a pleasant memorial to another of the
great men of cricket (like W.G. what would now be called a *controversial* figure), the Harris Garden. It is in the shape of a lawn-
tennis court, which is exactly what is used to be.

Whereby hangs a story. The late Lord Harris was a stickler
among other things for county qualifications, and was instrumental
in preventing certain men from playing until the regulations had
been complied with. One such was Walter Hammond, born close
to the Harris country at Dover where his sergeant-major father
happened to be stationed, but schooled at Cirencester in Gloucestershire for whom he played once in 1920 as an amateur. Kent (i.e.
Harris) promptly objected, and it was two years before Hammond
could appear again. Another was Leonard Crawley whom Worcestershire, hard pressed as usual for good cricketers, recruited (as
Somerset used to do) quite irregularly.

This time his lordship was slower off the mark, and Leonard
played in the school holidays of 1922 without complaint. He did
so again next year but before Worcestershire's last match of the 1923
season a telegram arrived from Lord's (i.e. from Harris) ordering
that Crawley not be played as he was not qualified. According to
the victim, Worcestershire, who knew the game was up, decided to
cock a snook at authority, pretending that the wire had not been
delivered until the match was in progress. So he had, literally, a last
fine fling, making 112 out of 176 in a couple of hours or so. That,
it was reckoned, would make the old meddler splutter into his tea
as he read the stop-press. Incidentally, when next they met, Lord
Harris is said to have received a famous reproof in the Long Room
from his fellow-peer, Deerhurst, president of Worcestershire, who
raised his hat and observed in icy tones : 'May I congratulate you,

C   33

my Lord, on having b——d the career of another young cricketer?'

Coming belatedly then to the point, it was reportedly a school-master who, on seeing the tennis-court converted to a Harris memorial and the inscription on the far wall, banged his umbrella on the ground, and said: 'There! He stopped them playing while he was alive, and he's stopping them playing now that he's dead.' Despite all this, Lord Harris's influence on the game was almost wholly for its good.

Directly following the garden is the block comprising the Real Tennis and squash courts and also the War Memorial Gallery which replaced the old Racket Court. I played tennis – the real or royal game – just enough to be able to imagine the extraordinary fascina-tion it has for all who take it up. I only did not continue because of so many absences abroad in winter, which was the only time I would otherwise have been able to play. The court at Lord's is rarely empty, and neither for that matter are the squash courts.

The Imperial Cricket Memorial Gallery as it is today conjures in me mixed emotions – on one hand admiration and approval for its dignified and handsome appearance, and for the good taste surrounding the wide range of cricketana, pictures, bats and relics of every sort that make up the exhibits; on the other sadness that the chance was missed of erecting a more practical tribute to the fallen such as a cricket school which at long last has come, after subsequent plans had foundered, a quarter of a century later.

The original memorial plan incorporated a library as well as a gallery, and it was certainly at least as necessary to display to the best advantage MCC's unique book collection as its other valuable treasures. But soaring costs limited the scheme and so Diana Rait Kerr, daughter of the then secretary and for upwards of a quarter of a century MCC's brilliant curator, had to make do as library with a converted office in the pavilion, which was adequate possibly but far from ideal. Now the library is less accessible, having been moved across and up too many stairs for old legs to the court block.

It was the Hon. George Lyttelton, the Eton master, not the least distinguished member of the famous family, who this time produced the approved line: 'Secure from change in their high-hearted ways', below the inscription:

To the memory of cricketers of all lands who gave their lives in the cause of freedom, 1914–1918; 1939–1945.

The author is the nineteenth-century poet James Russell Lowell, he who wrote:

Once to every man and nation comes the moment to decide,
In the strife of Truth with Falsehood, for the good or evil side.

Once? Or twice? Or three times?

Many of MCC's best landscape pictures are hung in the Memorial Gallery, for they came largely from the bequest of Sir Jeremiah Colman, who asked that in so far as was possible they should be hung together. Dominating the far Gallery wall is one such, the celebrated composite by H. Barrable and R. Ponsonby Staples, showing the ground as it was in the late '80s with a great match in progress. W.G. has hit to the extra-cover boundary in the foreground, and T. W. Garrett is fielding the ball immediately in front of the old 'A' Stand which was then the focus of beauty and fashion. Those present seem to be giving only perfunctory attention either to the cricket or to the Prince and Princess of Wales who have arrived almost unnoticed. They are equally oblivious to the discomfort of the lady whose slim waist seems to be wedged between the back-rest of one seat and the lower bar of the one in rear, with nothing to sit on!

The eye as one enters the gallery takes in two objects: one is the picture just referred to, the other the marble bust of W.G., placed centrally on the first elevation as though on the quarter-deck of his ship – as maybe in a sense he is. This is the bust, then in the Long Room, about which Cardus told his ever-popular story. The last game of the summer of 1939 – Middlesex v Warwickshire – was pursuing its placid way when Cardus saw two overalled figures approach the statue and, between them, with no word spoken, bear it carefully away. Two old members also witnessed the scene, whereupon one, according to Cardus, gravely remarked to the other: 'Mark my words: this means war.'

We move on round the periphery with an admiring look at the Coronation Garden with its weeping ash and seats among other shady trees and air of peaceful refuge behind the Warner Stand. This stand is part of the newer Lord's, two-storeyed, confined to

Members and Friends, with a big bar and buffet, giving on to the field, and surmounted by the Press-box, ample and well-equipped, appropriate maybe in that Plum was among many other things in the game a cricket-writer, but ill-placed in that the view is over extra-cover and long-leg. The senior writers have a medallion which admits to all pavilions, Lord's included, yet the fact is they are at a disadvantage compared with their brethren of TV and radio.

They are better placed than I was at the Lord's Test of 1930, in a Press annexe, under the canopy of the new Grand Stand, more or less behind cover-point – but, naturally, I was pleased enough to be there, watching, as it turned out, one of the most memorable and spectacular of all games, wherein among other things Don Bradman sealed his fame with his chanceless 254, in his own view *the* innings of his life.

What can one say about the Grand Stand? It is greatly in its favour that it has dignity, and blends well with the pavilion. On the other hand, considering its size it gives a satisfactory field of view to the minimum number. Some seats are unsaleable since from them can be seen only one set of stumps! At its rear is a honeycomb of stairs and passages, and some of the dining-rooms are situated in bizarre relation to the boxes they were designed to serve.

It cost £46,000 – no flea-bite in 1926 – and on its completion MCC were reputedly none too happy with their bargain. The architect, Sir Herbert Baker, disarmed criticism, however, by affixing at its apex, and immediately above the main scoreboard, as a surprise present, the Father Time weather-vane showing the old man with the scythe affixing the second bail – at least it is to be assumed he is putting them on rather than taking them off – which is now a symbol of Lord's all over the world. And there is at least a splendid view from the Grand Stand balcony.

We come next to the North Clock Tower where are inhabited the ground-staff. Here many who became famous had their initiation to the game, from young Jack Hearne, Pat Hendren and Denis Compton to John Murray and Fred Titmus downward. On either side of the sightscreen is the two-storey stand known as the 'Free Seats', seeing that admission to the ground (with certain reservations now, I think) gives access to them. From them one gets as good a view as anywhere, plus as much sun as there is – in contrast to the pavilion seats which are in shadow from noon on. Curious how allergic the Victorians were to the sun!

Come to that, they were allergic to a good deal, including almost any sort of change – such, for instance, as the new-fangled mower, which only won grudging and belated acceptance. This north-east corner was the site of the sheep-pens, the inhabitants of which kept the turf cropped, their efforts augmented on Saturdays by four or five hundred sheep who were driven through Lord's, almost perhaps for their last square meal, on their way to Smithfield market. The coarser grass, unpalatable to the sheep, was pulled out by hand by groups of boys – much, I suppose, as rows of black women moving forward almost imperceptibly on their haunches picked out the weeds one by one on the old Wanderers' ground at Johannesburg when I first saw it nearly 40 years ago.

These early-Victorian English boys were luckier than the South African Bantu, male or female, since the public on all but match-days could hire a pitch on the outfield for a shilling, the fee including stumps and a ball and even a couple of Mr Dark's bats. The willow for these, by the way, was stacked in blocks to mature, just opposite, near Dark's workshop over beside St John's Wood Road.

The Nursery or Practice Ground, which extends behind the Free Seats right back to Wellington Road, has had any number of uses and now, most importantly, inhabits the MCC Indoor School. The nets are here, and here throughout September the Cross Arrows, drawn from past and present playing staff and also MCC members, fulfil a match programme. Although the straight boundaries are on the short side the Nursery square is ample to take a lot of cricket and there are those who would like to see MCC and other matches played there during the summer when the main ground is not being used.

Part of the Nursery is a car park, and the arbours round the perimeter, hired to members for the big matches, remain as a reminder of the days when for the Lord's Week, comprising the University Match and the Eton and Harrow, the Nursery was the social centre of London, sprinkled with club tents from which flags flew, and wherein champagne, salmon mayonnaise and strawberries and cream were the order of the day. It got its name, by the way, because it had been a market garden known as 'Henderson's Nursery', famous, according to Plum, for its tulips and pineapples.

Proceeding clockwise, we flank the Mound Stand, the oldest

public accommodation remaining, before coming on the big modern development which comprises the long row of boxes with bars and seats below and another Members' Friends enclosure above them. Thus we have made the circle, leaving for my Australian's scrutiny the pavilion which we enter from the main door in the rear.

Lord's pavilion, since the pulling-down of the Hotel and members' dining-room to make way for the new Tavern stand, is now the oldest building on the ground. Look at it front on from the field of play and anything of the kind better symbolizing the later-Victorian age would be hard to envisage. There it stands, solid, ample, serene, the epitome of an Empire on which the sun would never set, headquarters of the game above all others that helped to bind it. The foundation stone was laid in September 1889, and eight months later to the day it was ready for the Annual General Meeting.

The only external change since has been the addition of the narrow parapet which protects from the weather the last few rows of seats at the back of the top storey. This did not exist when in 1899 Albert Trott, the Australian who played for Middlesex, hit his fellow-countryman, M. A. Noble, over the pavilion. The ball glanced off a chimney en route, which makes one wonder whether Trott would have cleared the top as it now is. Checking my facts I have discovered that I had long harboured an illusion. Cyril Foley, who played around the turn of the century, wrote some entertaining reminiscences called 'Autumn Foliage', and always found a ready listener in me, maintained – I swear he did – that he was batting at the other end with Trott. Foley said that just before this epochal happening he remarked to Trott that it was so cold he thought it would snow, to which Trott replied he hoped it would as he had never seen any. But *Wisden* says that though the two of them played together that summer for Middlesex Foley did not take part in the match between MCC and the Australians in which the hit was made. Moreover the date was 31 July, at which point in the summer even in England snow is a rarity. Oh dear! But no doubt the conversation took place, on some less momentous occasion.

Personally I have not seen the ball hit into the middle gallery, let alone the top, though I know Keith Miller is credited with having reached the summit, in one of the 1945 Victory Matches, and furthermore was caught allegedly by a member with a wooden leg. Frank Mann hit Wilfred Rhodes into the pavilion certainly twice in an over and probably three times. According to a version told confidently though at second-hand by Ian Peebles the first gigantic blow cracked against the stone-work to one side of a somnolent old member on the first balcony, the second with equal impact the other side. It was in gunner terms a 'straddle'. Whereat the venerable one, with a baleful look towards the field, his peace thoroughly disturbed, got up and departed in a fury, rather as John Willes when no-balled for throwing many years before, mounted his horse and rode out of cricket for ever.

But now listen to a version I recently unearthed. In the *Cricketer* of 7 June 1924 Laurance Woodhouse, who was contributing a regular feature aptly called 'Ruminations', told how he was watching the Middlesex–Yorkshire match on the *top* balcony with his old crony, Freddie Wilson, who was probably reporting the match for *The Times*.

The cricket was fairly quiet, when F. T. Mann came in to face the bowling of Rhodes. 'Ever been up here when a ball was hit up here?' asked F.B. 'No,' I replied. *'Plonk'*, sailing well over our heads, the ball landed on the sixth row from the back of the top tier of Lord's. The cheering was enormous, but it was redoubled and again redoubled when the very next ball came sailing up to the same spot, only with far greater velocity, so great indeed that one nervous spectator decided to take cover down below. He had just time to arrive there simultaneously with another huge drive, which only just missed the pavilion window. Yet once again, and this time from a palpable mis-hit, Mann tried to 'carry' the pavilion. He hit the railings in front of the top tier of the pavilion.

The stories have it in common that two sixes were hit somewhere up aloft of the pavilion, and that a member was driven from his seat. The Woodhouse version rings well to me. Incidentally, the fourth hit he mentions, having struck only the top of the pavilion railing, would have counted four. It doesn't strain the imagination much to hear that the great Wilfred wasn't very pleased, or that he uttered a sharp word to one of his fielders whom he had caught laughing! Yorkshire were in process of being beaten by an innings

– what was there to laff about?

Frank Mann's powers as a hitter are, of course, legendary – though he could play carefully if required. Ronny Aird says he was fielding for Hampshire at Lord's when Mann made an even bigger hit than those described. This one flew clean over the free seats into the Nursery and, the ground being hard, was eventually recovered in one of the arbours not far short of the Wellington Road wall.

Mr Aird is also sure, incidentally, that when Lionel Tennyson took the Hampshire side out at Lord's through the middle gate he was the first man to do so. The different entrances and exits for amateurs and pros were made a permanent gibe about the 'snobbery' of Lord's. MCC maybe were slow to recognize the social implications, but each party was merely using the shortest route to and from their respective dressing-rooms. It was Walter Robins who when captain of Middlesex brought the pros up to change in the amateurs' room; but it made for a bit of a crush, and for a while at least it was popular with none concerned, especially the pros, deprived of the privacy of their own quarters.

Ronny Aird, who came to Lord's as assistant-secretary in 1926, has a long memory for the old characters and for the idiosyncratic happenings of his early days. Sir Francis Lacey, it seemed, assumed so stern an expression over his spectacles when members came to his door that as often as not they thought better of it and retired, much to Lacey's amusement. Ronny had a great affection for the staff, especially George Fenner, who was the first appointed Head Coach until he became crippled by polio, and the Head Clerk, Jimmy Cannon, who after close of play used sometimes to augment his earnings by doing an act at the 'Met' music-hall in the Edgware Road. Ronny had amateur ambitions as an entertainer – he was a member of the Magicians' Circle – and he and Jimmy used to practise tap-dancing on a table. But, talking of entertainers, when the famous George Robey was elected and attended the Anniversary Dinner he turned up mistakenly in a frock coat – a sad case of a funny man trying not to be funny at all.

The only vague parallel I know to the member's reaction at Lord's to Mann's assault was when at Hove Don Smith, now coach at Lancing, was winning a game for Sussex against the clock. The wickets were pitched unusually close to the pavilion, and Smith, pulling violently, kept sending the ball whistling for six, flat and fast, into the members' seats. Despite the good cause the members, afraid for their safety, protested so vigorously that play had to be held up.

To get strictly back to the subject, Lord's pavilion is, I suppose, something of an anachronism in these utilitarian days. No doubt something modern and utterly lacking in charm could enclose more watching members. However, it is an academic point, for who can foresee the moment when it might be economically possible, other considerations apart, for MCC to pull it down and start again?

The Long Room will impress my Australian with its wide panoramic view of the field and, around the walls, its selected treasures. Sometimes the human scene is more interesting than the cricket, as the late 'Buns' Cartwright was acknowledging when a friend asked him why he was sitting behind the sight-screen. 'Because,' he said with a steely eye, 'it's the only place from which I can't see that beggar Bolus'; in fairness to whom let me add that there has been many another staunch England batsman who has not exactly rated top marks for ease and elegance. Brian Bolus – this also gives me a chance to say – has done good service to cricket as captain of Derbyshire – which has never been a sinecure yet, nor ever will be.

Brian is one of not a few modern cricketers who refute the lament of those who say that there is no humour left in the game. He and I have often laughed since over the time when we two and Brian Close were supposed to be the star speakers at the annual dinner of that excellent and, I hope, still prosperous institution, the York and District Cricket League. Unfortunately for us Mr Close was first in the order, and we two waited our turn, first in patience, then in irritation, finally in amused incredulity as the oracle meandered interminably on, in a flow of unco-ordinated reminiscence, until if he had been a more sensitive man he might have noticed that (in the late Lord Birkett's phrase) the audience, receptive enough for the first half-hour or so, had ceased just looking at their watches but, metaphorically at least, were shaking them to see whether they were still going. For myself, I tried to detach myself from the actual situation and to recall Close's hour of honour and glory against the West Indies' fast bowling at Lord's in '63 when his innings of 70 so nearly won the day for England. For that at least he should never be forgotten.

Perhaps the performance at York lasted no more than fifty minutes or so, though it seemed longer; but what after-dinner speaker, anxious to deliver himself of his modest offering, has not known his spirits sink as his glass and all others around him grow empty and another's spate continues to flow unquenched? I hold firm views on the length and style of after-dinner speeches – but . . . as may have been noted already, the subject is not strictly connected with Lord's pavilion. Occasionally, it is true, one hears longish speeches there, in the Committee Room, but at least they are in the afternoon.

Let us then return to the Long Room, preferably when it is empty so that the eye can fully enjoy it. The pictures are occasionally transposed between the Long Room and other parts of the pavilion and also, of course, the Memorial Gallery, for MCC's art collection is now so large that certain pictures, though not the most distinguished and important, are always being 'rested' in the basement.

To the right of the handsome showcase of bats and other cricketana (including the Ashes urn) which forms the focal point of the long West wall hangs one of the best-known of all cricket pictures, 'Tossing for Innings'. The artist is Robert James, the date around 1850, and the bat is shown in mid-air thrown up by one of four young urchins while another is about to make the momentous call, 'round' or 'flat'.

High over the showcase, indeed above the deep decorated frieze that extends the length of the main wall, is the polished oak panel on which are written in chronological order the names and respective years of office of the Presidents of MCC since the first-known incumbent in 1825. There were, no doubt, duly elected Presidents from the Club's inception in 1787, but their identity vanished along with the rest of the club records in the fire that destroyed Lord's first pavilion. This panel is the room's most recent addition of note, and one feels that one day a resting-place for it may be found nearer eye level.

On the far wall the four men gazing out in neat array are, from right to left, and in order of age, Plum Warner, Douglas Jardine, Don Bradman and Gubby Allen. Of these four three have been everything in cricket, players and captains of their countries, selectors, administrators and legislators, holders of the highest offices. During my time their influence off the field has been unrivalled.

To this extent Jardine is in inappropriate company, with the added irony that he hangs between his manager in Australia, Plum, who so hated Jardine's brain-child, Bodyline, and the Don, for whose subjugation it was devised. None of these four pictures has, I think, any great intrinsic merit. Plum is shown half-length, in white shirt and Harlequin cap, much as he must have looked when he led Middlesex as county champions off his beloved Lord's pitch for the last time. With him, as with Jardine, wearing the MCC touring blazer, it seems as though the picture was painted on photographic evidence.

The Don is shown not as the pre-eminent cricketer but shrewd, confident, and with the hint of a smile, through horn-rimmed spectacles, looking just what he now is, a director of companies and a bank, as well as the voice of post-war Australian cricket authority.

Next door, appropriately enough, is the Don's parallel English figure in the councils of the game, as well as his rival on the field, Gubby Allen : the only captain, by the way, who ever won two successive Test Matches against him. Gubby is pictured wearing an England tie, looking out on to the field from the side Committee Room window as he has done for so long, notably in his seven-year stint as chairman of selectors. It is no doubt a fair likeness of the subject in introspective mood, but the artist, John Ward, has not quite captured that blend of charm and determination, that persistence in argument which all at Lord's know so well.

So from the south door we pass, noting John Ward's agreeable line and wash impressions of the three most recent secretaries, R. S. Rait Kerr, Ronald Aird and S. C. Griffith, in the intervening passage, into the Committee Room. Here round these tables, which nowadays take the form of a large fat 'U', most of the substantial cricket issues for all but ninety years have been decided : not only the Laws and all other things touching Marylebone as a club, but the affairs of English cricket in all its aspects, and also those of international import as covered at the annual meetings of the ICC. Though MCC have handed over their over-all responsibilities – implicit though never clearly defined – to the Cricket Council and its adjunct, the Test and County Cricket Board, these new bodies still meet in the old time-honoured sanctum.

As might be expected, much of the modern history of Lord's is expressed by the portraits of the Presidents, Treasurers and Secretaries that look down on the committees and sub-committees and boards and conferences. The treasurership perhaps needs an explanatory word. It is the senior and semi-permanent (unpaid) office, round which, in complement with the secretariat, the management revolves. As an ex-officio member of every sub-committee (of which there are ten!) the Treasurer is the link man who with the Secretary and his assistants dovetails all this effort. Apart from the present Lord Cobham, who held the Treasurership for one year before relinquishing it for wider duties outside cricket, there had been five Treasurers only in this century when J. G. W. Davies took over from Gubby Allen in the autumn of 1976. Of Mr Allen's four predecessors on display in the Committee Room the portrait of Harry Altham is almost the least flattering likeness in the MCC collection, though happily it is now augmented by Edmund Nelson's posthumous portrait of Harry in flannels and Harlequin cap, presented by his son, Dick, with the special request that it be hung in the Indoor School. It is shown opposite page 49.

Harry held the Treasurer's reins from 1950 to 1963, taking over from the ninth Lord Cobham whose work spanned the war years and to either side, 1938–49. Generally speaking, the figureheads at Lord's, in my recollection, have personified a conspicuous charm of manner, and none more so than this tall military figure, who always found time for a word or a smile.

Before this Lord Cobham's treasurership was Lord Hawke's short span of six years which began in 1932 with the death of Lord Harris. Martin Bladen Hawke was truly the founder of Yorkshire cricket, for when he took over the captaincy in 1883 the side was something near a drunken rabble. In his long reign of 27 years Hawke not only brought discipline and self-respect into the Yorkshire XI but in so doing greatly improved the status of county cricketers everywhere. So it is appropriate enough that his is the only Committee-Room portrait in cricket dress. He is wearing the Yorkshire blazer with the white rose on the pocket, and when I see it I often think of the story of the youthful Gubby Allen, fresh to the Committee, making, under Hawke's chairmanship, a spirited address in favour of some cause on which he held strong views.

Gubby, as he talked, was a little disconcerted to notice that Hawke was inclined to shake his head and occasionally mutter, 'No, no – oh, no, no!' As Gubby eventually sat down, Hawke was heard to ask his neighbour, Sir Stanley Jackson : 'Tell me, Jacker, what was he saying?' The word 'martinet' was not coined in respect of Martin Hawke, but he would have seemed a formidable figure on such an occasion. In any case, the young were not expected to make noises in those days! Gubby recalls that when he was elected to the Committee – in 1937 – he was, at 33, six years younger than Guy Jackson, who in turn had almost as many years in hand of the next junior man. Let it be added that Gubby must now have spent more hours in the Committee Room than anyone either before or since, and I would have thought it unlikely that he has ever afterwards been put off his stroke in debate – or, for that matter, elsewhere.

It is illustrative of the breadth of Gubby Allen's services to MCC – and through MCC to the whole world of cricket – that on his retirement two men were appointed to cover the job he did alone. Jack Davies, as I have said, now occupies the traditional office of Treasurer, the money side of which has been taken on by E. W. Phillips under the new title of 'Chairman of Finance'. Ted Phillips is a director of Lazard's, and a man of many City responsibilities, who had for several years chaired the Finance Sub-Committee. Since Davies, ex- of Cambridge and Kent, came more or less straight into office after retiring from a Bank of England directorship no one is likely to challenge the qualifications of either of these to steer MCC affairs in these difficult times. As for Gubby, he is still, as a Trustee, a member of the MCC Committee, and has also been elected to several sub-committees.

It was Gubby's initiative – and Harry Altham's – that resulted in the formation of what was initially called the MCC Youth Cricket Association – the forerunner of the work now done voluntarily by dedicated men on behalf of boys' cricket. He instigated the opening of the doors to honorary membership of distinguished professionals and, later, to the major cricket figures overseas. He was for seven years a notably successful Chairman of Selectors, and was the principal figure, on the English side, as Sir Donald Bradman at GOA's instigation became on the Australian, in the wholly successful effort to stamp out throwing. Since national honour was involved, as well as men's livelihoods, it needed tact and diplomacy of a high order to bring back harmony among the affected parties. Delegates to the ICC were shown great quantities of film of the

45

suspect bowling actions: film that could be stopped where necessary and the resultant 'still' analysed and dissected. It was Gubby's zeal for truth and justice that was the chief motive force behind all this. He killed throwing in 1960 just as Lord Harris and Sydney Pardon had done in their different ways in the '80s.

There are two Committee-room portraits which I suspect most who use the room might be unable to name. One is of Herbert Jenner-Fust, and the other Sir Spencer Ponsonby-Fane. The latter, a figure of rare benignity, would seem to have earned his place in perpetuity since until only a year or two ago he was not only a member of MCC for what was then the record span of 75 years but was Treasurer for almost half that time, from 1879 to his death in 1915 aged 91. A player on the field by day and on the boards by night with the Old Stagers at the first Canterbury Week, one of the three founders and the first Governor of I Zingari, Ponsonby-Fane clearly typified the sort of man around whom the club's high repute in Victorian England was built. For many years he was the oldest link with the past. He knew Lord's from the days when the membership mustered around 300: at his death there were 16,000 names on the waiting-list (a number sadly reduced by war casualties) and the estimated time-lag before election was forty years. That was excessive enough, of course, but they were the days when males were apt to be automatically entered at birth!

In his *Wisden* obituary F. S. Ashley-Cooper records that Ponsonby-Fane, a diplomat by training, 'brought from Paris the treaty ending the Crimean War', was private secretary to the great Palmerston, and Comptroller of the Lord Chamberlain's office; but Ashley-Cooper does not answer the intriguing question why he 'several times' declined the supreme honour of the Presidency. This grizzled patriarch who, among so many other things, was the founder of the MCC Art Collection, may still be vaguely remembered by a few of the dozen or so members still living who were elected before the date of his last visit to Lord's in 1913.

Jenner-Fust's career goes back even farther for he captained Cambridge (without the Fust) in the first University Match of 1827, and was President of MCC six years later at the age of 27. Perhaps he owes his place to having been the youngest of all Presidents: otherwise he seems lucky to hold it if only because for some reason unexplained by the historians he resigned from MCC many years before his death at the age of 98. Talking of links and longevity I recall having a talk at Canterbury in 1946 with a spry, amusing F. A. Mackinnon, 35th chief of the clan, who on the eve of my going to Australia spoke of his tour there with Lord Harris's team of 1878/9. (In the only Test, at Melbourne, he was the middle man in the first-ever Test hat-trick by 'the Demon' Spofforth.) The Mackinnon, likewise then 98, was reckoned an odds-on bet to become the first first-class cricketer to reach 100, and Hubert Preston, editor of *Wisden*, records the old man's reply to a telephone enquiry as to his health : 'I am going to hospital tomorrow – but only for the annual meeting at which I shall preside. I am very well in health – very well indeed. I still do a lot of work in the garden : weeds don't like me at all.' However, the hard, hard winter of 1946/7, in Morayshire as elsewhere, was too much for him, and though he beat Jenner-Fust by a few months he just failed to reach 99.

The member who has been so much longer than anyone else in the recorded annals of MCC is at the time of writing still with us and has furthermore reached his hundred : E. C. Wigan. Mr Wigan has been a member for 77 years, and has just nosed ahead of the Hon. R. E. S. Barrington, the previous title-holder, who died two years ago. Aspirants after the honour won't need reminding that the subscription is waived for all of 60 years' standing and beyond.

The best picture in the Committee Room, and almost in the MCC collection, is of Lord Harris, painted as he was in his late sixties by Arthur Hacker. Below his wing collar is a Band of Brothers bow-tie. His right hand lightly holds the lapel of a double-breasted waist-coat, grey like his moustache. He gazes straight down the room in a steady, appraising way, gently dominating the scene. There, too, hang Stanley Christopherson, most long-serving of all presidents since he held the fort all through the Second World War, and William Findlay, Secretary 1926–36 and President 1951–2, whose urbanity masked, I always felt, a strong reactionary vein. This pleasant likeness was definitely painted from a photograph.

Over the mantelpiece, sitting at a desk covered with papers, is a figure with a pale, ascetic face – Francis Edwin Lacey, the Secretary who brought the administration of cricket quietly, firmly out of its easy Victorian tempo through the first quarter of the twentieth century. When, a practising barrister aged 38, Lacey took office in the new pavilion in 1898 no other part of the present ground was standing, though only a year afterwards the Mound Stand replaced the old tennis and racket courts. There was no special machinery for administering Test Matches either at home or abroad, though the formation of the Board of Control also immediately followed. It was another six years before MCC acceded to the request to set up an Advisory County Cricket Committee. In 1906, after spirited protest at the conditions under which they worked, the Press were provided with a Box over the Professionals' quarters. (They had previously obtained no amelioration except under duress: for the first half-century of Lord's the only recognized representative, Mr Knight of *Bell's Life*, which became the *Sporting Life*, stood all day in the shrubbery beside the pavilion recording the play in his own score-book.) In 1909 the three then Test-playing countries formed the Imperial Cricket Conference, with its headquarters, inevitably, at Lord's.

'Ben' Lacey, so Plum tells us, on his appointment was advised by his predecessor, Henry Perkins, 'Don't take any notice of the ——— Committee.' But MCC now had at the helm a different personality from the easy-going 'Perkino', who was said to have got so drunk at a Club dinner that after a temporary failure of the lights he was observed on the floor going through the motions of swimming, apparently under the impression that he was crossing the Styx. Lacey found the finances in poor shape, took them in hand, and generally put things in order. He personally reorganized the Refreshment Department which – not for the last time – was causing dissatisfaction, and did so to such effect that his stipend was raised from £500 to £700. The MCC minute approving the extra £200 added, 'so long as he shall continue to act in that capacity'. How often in the voluminous records of today's affairs does one notice a similar note of business prudence! He also began the Easter Coaching Classes, and, himself a highly reputable player, proclaimed firm views on the theory of the game.

As to this there is a story of some topical significance. A boy of promise was one day advised by Lacey to alter his grip of the bat. The boy was not receptive, and after practice was summoned into the Secretary's office.

'You know,' he said, 'if you hold your bat properly you'll get into the Eton Eleven this year.'

1911–1976

1. *Right,* with my elder sister, Ruth, now Mrs Edmund Nelson, aged respectively 4 and 2. The horse was soon relegated to the nursery cupboard, superseded by bat and ball. In 1911 Frank Woolley sailed for the first time with MCC to Australia. 1919 saw him installed as my boyhood hero, the very perfection of an all-round cricketer.

2. *Below,* in 1976, the two of us, Frank aged 89, are lunching together in our garden at Sandwich.

3. Founders of I Zingari, the forerunner of all wandering clubs. In July 1845 the tr[i] 'found themselves at supper in the Blenheim Hotel, Bond Street', formed a club and christened it, strangely, in Italian. (*I Zingari* = the gypsies.) On the left is Sir Spencer Ponsonby-Fane (Treasurer of MCC 1879–1915), on the right his brothe[r] the Earl of Bessborough. In the bath-chair is J. Loraine Baldwin – note the IZ cravat, rosette *and mittens*. Painted in 189[?] An original rule of IZ forbade the employ-ment of professional bowlers, who by custom were used to make up amateur sides. The Club thus greatly assisted the development of amateur bowling.

4. H. S. Altham : this posthumous portrait by Edmund Nelson shows him on the playing-fields where he coached so many generations of Wykehamist cricketers. In the background are College buildings and Winchester Cathedral, on which he was a foremost authority. His son, R. J. L. (Dick), presented the picture to MCC with the request that it be hung in the Indoor School.

'Mr Lacey,' came the reply, 'I shall get into the Eton Eleven this year however I hold my bat.'

The year was 1919, and *Wisden* records that in the Eton and Harrow of that first post-war year this 16-year-old went in first for Eton and, having been run out in the first innings without receiving a ball, carried his bat in the second for 69. Thus did G. O. Allen early justify a confidence in his own opinion which so far as Lord's is concerned can only be described as a portent of things to come.

Lacey well merits his continued presence over the committee fireplace. He initiated and organized so much over his 28 years – most of it personally and by hand. For a great deal of his time he had no recourse to a typewriter, and he inherited one telephone – in the basement. On his retirement in 1926 he was accorded the first knighthood ever bestowed for services to cricket, and lived to enjoy the distinction a further twenty years, during which time Plum Warner was similarly honoured, as also was the secretary of Yorkshire and manager of three MCC touring teams at Australia, F. C. Toone.

It is time to leave the Committee Room, our final gaze beside the doorway drawn perhaps to Lord Harris, the dictator of Lord's during his treasurership, which began with Ponsonby-Fane's death in 1915 and ended with his own seventeen years later. He was the keenest of competitors certainly who, like W.G., wanted his pound of flesh. A captain of Eton at Lord's he when bowling retained the ball and ran out a certain unlucky Harrovian called Walroth, an action that might have determined the outcome of a close-fought match which Eton just won. In his old age playing at Lord's against the Philadelphians he is supposed to have had recourse to underarm 'sneaks' in order to save the game.

The professionals took good care to keep the right side of him – did not one of them, after having run himself out at Canterbury, as his lordship bore down on the dressing-room, clamber out of the back window to keep out of his way? But we have Frank Woolley's word that he was the players' best friend. They can indeed all revere his memory today for the fact of benefits being tax-free goes back to the test case of *Rex v* James Seymour, the latter being backed by Harris all the way to the House of Lords which in 1927 decided in Seymour's favour.

Autocrat he certainly was, with everyone at his beck and call in a way barely credible today. Kent Committees (now never completed in under a couple of hours and often nearer three) used to be called for 4.30 at Cannon-street Hotel adjoining the station. If everything hadn't been tersely concluded by five o'clock the last of the proceedings were tidied up as with his retinue he progressed up the platform to his carriage to catch the 5.16 to Faversham. As with W.G. at Paddington I expect the station-master awaited his convenience before blowing the whistle.

Even Plum Warner, most charitable of critics, allows that he could be 'a little testy'. He also wrote that in committee he was 'deferential to the opinions of others, did not force his own views, and was fair and balanced'. When general agreement seemed unlikely he was inclined to adjourn for lunch or tea, saying, 'it helps us to adjust our ideas'. What could never be in dispute was his deep, abiding love of cricket. Though his career was a varied and busy one he wrote in his memoirs, *A Few Short Runs*, 'My whole life has pivoted on Lord's.' When he was abroad as Governor of Bombay he did more probably than anyone to export into India the English enthusiasm for cricket. Lord Harris's famous letter to *The Times* is too well known to bear full repetition here. Plum quotes it verbatim in his *Lord's*. At one point we read :

And my message includes youth, and I advise them to get all the cricket they can. They will never regret it : I might apply to it Mr Jorrocks's commendation of hunting : 'It's the image of war without its guilt and 25 per cent of its danger.' And in my message to youth I will repeat what I said to the half-holiday cricketer : 'You do well to love it, for it is more free from anything sordid, anything dishonourable than any game in the world. To play it keenly, honourably, self-sacrificingly, is a moral lesson in itself, and the class-room is God's air and sunshine . . .'

Mawkish, over-sentimental? Or the language of fine prose? There might be two opinions as to that, but surely there can be no disputing not only a passion for the game but the benevolence of the writer? For me at least this surely, if need be, redeems all.

Continuing to try and convey an impression of the spirit of Lord's and the men who have made it – for the benefit, if you approve the fiction, of my young Australian companion – we must have another look at the likenesses of the three most recent secretaries hanging immediately outside the Committee Room.

Senior in age of service was Colonel R. S. Rait Kerr, known universally as 'R-K', whose span was cut in two by the war. R-K was not everyone's cup of tea, for he could have a curt way with members, and far from not suffering fools gladly at times it was with difficulty he suffered them at all. Still, with Ronny Aird at his elbow this did not so greatly matter, and his merits easily outshone a brusqueness of manner which may have derived from shyness and in latter years from ill-health. R-K was essentially a superb staff-officer who brought to Lord's a military efficiency that became all too necessary to match the difficult times into which cricket was moving when he arrived in 1936. By all account he was a faultless author of agenda and minutes, while on the practical side of the Lord's 'plant' his sapper training was of equal value.

R-K made another inestimable contribution to MCC in the shape of his daughter, Diana, who was recruited directly after the war to the new post of curator, and in the course of her appointment not only looked after and supervised the distribution of MCC's art collection and library but established a unique reputation as an authority on every variety of object that comes under the broad heading of cricketana.

I tried to portray in *SOCP* Ronny Aird's special contribution as the purveyor, through his own personality, of an extraordinary harmony as between all at Lord's : members and secretariat : secretariat and staff : staff and members. Under him MCC was a happy family of a sort impossible now to foster to the same degree if only because the membership has jumped so steeply. Here are some figures : when Ronny went to Lord's in 1926 there were around 6000 members. By 1949 it had risen only to 7500, with a wait estimated at thirty years. A great many members knew a great many other members. In 1962, when he retired, it was still under 12,000, including the fairly recent class of Associates, and there was still a very long waiting list. In the last fifteen years the figure has jumped by sharp stages to 18,000, with associate status abolished and the queue largely absorbed.

It so happens, too, that the wonderful staff which served at the time, say, of my election in 1936 have now departed either to still greener fields or to live in retirement. The last of the old links went with the sudden death last year of 'Joe', brother of 'Dick', sons of 'Old Dick' Gaby who worked at Lord's for a lifetime. There had been either one Gaby or more at Lord's for 116 years. Such gaps are irreplaceable. R.T. retired from the office of Club Superintendent in 1973 and now frequents the pavilion, as an honorary member, a repository of old stories and the idiosyncrasies of bygone members. Joe commanded the main pavilion door, knew more members by name and sight than anyone, and had a genial word with all of them.

Ian Peebles paid a charming tribute to both Dick and Joe among others in a recent *Cricketer* called 'Cricket Upstairs Downstairs', wherein on the subject of members he illustrated how Lord's 'although a respecter of persons has a talent for putting them in proper perspective. When Sir C. Aubrey Smith returned there after many years' absence, a film star, a knight, wealthy and world-famous – he was identified by a contemporary as 'a fella named Smith – used to play for Sussex".'

There were many oddities in the Aird era – and still are some, but they are not so easy to identify since the pavilion is apt to be either terribly full or disappointingly empty. Many old-'uns, and indeed the now middle-aged whom he favoured, may recall the little man who took up his station near the Long Room door on to the field at the boys' matches and consolingly offered a bag of sweets to dismissed batsmen on their return. In cold print it might be wondered whether this Mr Haddock's motives were all that was to be desired, but one look at his simple, smiling face must have disarmed suspicion. What response he may sometimes have had from young hopefuls out for small scores at the sight of this unexpected and probably unwanted offering is more questionable.

Billy Griffith after eleven years under Ronny Aird as joint assistant-secretary with Jim Dunbar took over the secretaryship in 1963 and held the reins for the twelve momentous years that followed. During this time the 'administrative tail' at Lord's grew vastly in size and scope with developments of the utmost significance both on the field and off. On the cricket side the three one-day competitions, making their successive bows, altered the general shape of the first-class game involving long debate – and, for a secretary therefore, an interminable succession of minutes and agenda. There was also a new state of things in that the amateur ceased to be : all were now dependent cricketers.

More crucial than all this from the secretary's point of view was that MCC voluntarily abjured their ancient status, universally accepted though never put into words, as the instigators, administrators and arbiters, of everything in the world of English cricket as well as the permanent hosts and organizers of the International Cricket Conference. Now there was to be a British constitution for cricket with a democratic flavour; the Cricket Council at the top, comprising in its turn the three essential bodies, the Test and County Cricket Board, to control what its title implies, the National Cricket Association, to co-ordinate and encourage every form and facet of cricket short of the top class, and MCC themselves, officially now only the law-makers. They had 'started it all' – 'the Advisory', as it was called, for county cricket, the Board of Control for Test Matches, the MCC Youth Cricket Association and the MCC National Cricket Association – these latter, subdivided into county organizations, now brought together under the NCA.

But for all that this meant in secretarial terms the most testing aspect of Billy Griffith's time was the almighty rumpus that became known as the D'Oliveira Affair : first the cancellation of MCC's tour to South Africa because their Government had said that Basil D'Oliveira, the Cape Coloured who had emigrated here, would be unacceptable as a member of our team; then the last-minute abandonment of the South African tour to England on the plea of the British Government. Friends took up irreconcilable positions on this most controversial event in cricket since the Bodyline tour, and there was that dreadful meeting at Church House, Westminster, wherein the MCC Committee had to fight off votes of no-confidence in their handling of the business. Church House, indeed ! The general spirit was not overflowing with Christian charity, nor would the general standard of debate (though with an exception or two) have commended itself to the illustrious forerunners of those chiefly concerned whose respective impacts on Lord's I have been talking about in this chapter.

Billy Griffith, though he had a fine war record and won his DFC on D-Day as a lieutenant-colonel in the Glider Pilot Regiment, was and is essentially, like Plum Warner, a man of peace : what more

53

ironic than that each should have been closely involved in the biggest two rows ever to darken the face of cricket?

I have many happy pictures of Billy in my mind's eye: as a Cambridge undergraduate of the famous sporting generation of the '30s in the congenial atmosphere of Mr Goggs's wine bar behind Leicester Square where in the fashion of the day we used to drink quantities of hock-and-seltzer – a mild enough quencher in all conscience: of his return to the dressing-room at Queen's Park, Port-of-Spain – utterly exhausted, having been pressed into service because of injuries as opening batsman, and answering the call with a hundred in his first Test – the heat was so humid and intense that the sweat was coming through the front of his pads, something I've never seen before or since: of his brilliant wicket-keeping as George Mann's vice-captain in South Africa where for two Test Matches he was preferred to Godfrey Evans: of his brief years as *Sunday Times* cricket-writer and a summer Sunday at Bolton Abbey in Wharfedale where he was so over-burdened with work for other papers that for the one and only time in my life I ghosted a Test report, I think for the long-deceased *Daily Graphic*.

John Ward's water-colour, done shortly before his retirement, shows him looking up from his desk with the tired expression that he often indeed could not disguise. It was the only defect of his qualities that he loved Lord's and cricket too well. However, though he spent many hard months of his retirement slogging away at a recodifying of the Laws, there he is now at Arundel, taking the utmost pleasure from the game, running the cricket at that most beautiful of grounds on behalf of Lavinia Duchess of Norfolk, looking distinctly younger than when he left St John's Wood the best part of three years ago.

There are many others known to fame who have either decorated Lord's in the past or who do so today, to whom or about whom my young friend might have liked to talk. We might have seen Doug Insole hurrying about on the business of the TCCB whose chairman he now is; or George Mann, chairman of Middlesex, or John Warr, who represents the Australian Cricket Board in England; or a hundred and one other cricket notables to whom Lord's and the Long Room is a focus in summer. But there is a limit to what can be digested at one visit, so let us leave the pavilion as we came in, pausing only to admire the likeness of the man who 'bestrode the game like a colossus', who won men's hearts for cricket in a way unknown before, but for whose career even this pavilion might not be standing, rich alike in treasures and history.

Archibald Stuart-Wortley's picture, a signed print of which commands the wall beside my desk as I write, shows W.G. in the moment before he begins to shape the stroke. The left shoulder is forward, the eyes bright and steady above the dark, square beard, and beneath the MCC cap of red and yellow. The bat is slightly raised equally ready to play back or forward, though the left leg is a foot in front of the crease with the toe of his brown boot slightly raised. So a forward stroke, whether punitive or otherwise, is the likeliest outcome. W.G. was 42 when the painting was done, and the lissom lines of youth have given way to an ample frame. He isn't fat but looks as though, in the modern phrase, he'll soon have to 'watch it'. No doubt he must have done, for those thousand runs in the May of 1895 that finally sealed his fame, the last of them made at Lord's, were still five years into the future.

The peculiar cocking of the toe was a 'W.G.-ism' that caught on among a certain sort of gentry, to the peculiar fury of Charles Kortright of Essex, reputedly the fastest bowler of his day. W.G. could do as he liked, but if anyone cocked a toe in the direction of 'Korty' he pursued only one ambition, to land a full-pitch on it in the quickest time possible. Kortright might have cried, as W.G. is reputed to have done in some moment of argument – 'I *can't* have it, and I *won't* have it.'

This is no place, nor am I the authority, for a dissertation on the moral principles of W.G. Stories spread of his being a bit sharp : of pointing up into the sun and observing to the young man he was bowling to, 'Look at they ducks' – whereupon the victim is duly dazzled and bowled out. There are many such – to which there seemed more point, no doubt, if they were attributed to the Old Man. There's no doubt he was an enthusiastic practical joker. I would only add that I never met anyone who knew him and did not greatly like him. As I wrote on the occasion of one of his anniversaries in the *Daily Telegraph* :

I prefer to think of him as a devoted country doctor, who during a match in which he made two hundreds stayed up all night because he had promised to see a woman through her confinement : who at Christmas bade the parish poor bring two basins which were filled by him and his wife, one with roast beef and vegetables, the other with plum pudding.

He was a legend beyond compare in his lifetime, yet never lost his humility, his love of a joke, the common touch. Is not this a sure explanation for the affection in which he was held by so many generations of Englishmen?

But the Mecca and those who have made the game what it is have exercised their spell long enough. It's time we moved out into the country.

4
Echoes from Sussex

The Antient Town of Rye and the Saffrons Ground at Eastbourne loom large, both of them, in my recollection, so let us next make a hypothetical journey thither from Sandwich across into Sussex, taking in a few other points of interest along the way.

First call along the coast must be the Crabble Ground at Dover, unique in shape with its pavilion and members' area perched high above the field, clamped as it were to the steep chalk cliff, and making, of course, a marvellous vantage point. Dover first lost its Week, and for the moment also its remaining match is in abeyance – the pitch has been poor and support variable. Yet the scale of the ground and its attraction, to say nothing of past associations, make it a proper rendezvous for first-class cricket.

The feat that comes first to mind when I think of Dover is Kent's brilliant victory over Gloucestershire there in 1937, at which, naturally, I would dearly like to have been present: 219 Kent made in 71 minutes, averaging 9 runs an over. Les Ames recalls that the outfield was lightning fast, and that Gloucestershire bowled their overs at commendable speed, considering the punishment. *Wisden* shows that they delivered 21.2, and that the runs were got by Ashdown (62 not out), Woolley (44), Ames (70) and Watt (39 not out). Alan Watt was a lovable rustic whose murderous hitting was pure village-green stuff. He fairly sailed into the off-breaks of Tom Goddard, who no doubt, as usual, was grumbling cheerfully.

There was once an occasion, by the way, when Tom found himself captaining Gloucestershire, and was soon wheeling away. After an hour or two of toil he was heard to complain : 'Why doesn't the silly beggar take me off?'

My companion should hear of another piece of hitting at Dover which I did see, and which of its kind was scarcely less extraordinary. It was in 1968, and it involved Gary Sobers, no less. In the fourth innings of a county match, with Kent pressing for the Championship, Gary won the game for Notts by making 105 not out in 77 minutes in light so utterly drear that one feared not for the batsman, who seemed to be seeing the ball as though batting in his native Barbados, but for the fielders as the ball flew to all points of the compass, often in the air at great speed and almost invisibly out of the background of the trees that ringed the field. Colin Cowdrey was out of the Kent team, injured, and we looked on together, fascinated and amazed. Surely he must miss or misconnect soon? But he never did. It was as though an infallible radar was at work. It was uncanny.

And, by the way, how Frank Woolley would have enjoyed it! The old man on his annual summer visits from his home in Nova Scotia saw his modern equivalent bat from time to time. His standards have always been exacting but Sobers lived fully up to them, and nothing in the modern game gave Frank more pleasure than to watch him play.

Talking of genius we come next, a few miles down the coast, to Folkestone, memorable to me for the 2nd XI match between Middlesex and Kent wherein Denis Compton and I in 1936 put on 100 together for Middlesex, after which he proceeded forthwith into the county side, and took his swift sure steps to fame: an England cap the following year, the first of his hundreds against Australia the summer after that, and so on.

There was a Folkestone Festival in the '30s wherein the cricket was reputedly light-hearted and the evening amusement even more so, with a fancy-dress dance that elicited the unusual both in costume and behaviour. 'Crusoe' once went as Sir Julien Cahn, and Frank Mann, one-time captain of Middlesex and England, as a Lyons waitress or 'Nippy'. A vast figure in black bombazine, white pinafore and cap, he is said to have penetrated to the women's loo, emerging seconds later to cry, 'I've flushed a couple off the nest.' Apocryphal? I'm not sure. There was a gaiety about the cricketers between the wars that can scarcely be imagined of those of today.

But there was one confrontation in a Folkestone Festival match between two of the world's greatest cricketers that was very far from comical, and it is still remembered by survivors of the game. Learie Constantine decided to settle a grudge of a personal kind against Walter Hammond and when at the close of the 1928 season the latter came in to bat for an England XI against the West Indies 'Conny' promptly let fly very fast and very short. Hammond, magnificent player though he was, never, as they say, 'fancied' the fastest bowling, as he was to show especially in the Old Trafford Test of five years later. That was the occasion when the West Indians (for the one and only time in a Test in England) in the persons of Constantine and Martindale attempted a version of Bodyline which was frustrated by a combination of Douglas Jardine's skill and courage and the extreme docility of the pitch.

Now at Folkestone Constantine added to the peril by overstepping the crease not by a few inches but by a yard and more. The scene in a Festival game was wildly out of context, and Hammond ended it as quickly as he could by very obviously throwing his wicket away to Griffith, bowling from the other end. What 'got into' that hot-blooded but normally fair-minded West Indian, I suppose, will never be known.

If my Australian friend and I now proceed, hugging the coast from Folkestone, we find ourselves flanking Romney Marsh, in another likewise famous sort of sheep country, and by way of a vexatious profusion of right-angle turns arriving via the Landgate in the medieval town of Rye. There is a pleasant cricket ground at Rye lying at the edge of the marsh below the town, but we are concerned rather with the delights of the famous links and the comforts of the Dormy House. Rye has been acclaimed the best winter course in England, and its rights to such a title (not that the membership would concern themselves in the matter) are not easily to be gainsaid. Rye is a true links, its close-cropped turf and, especially, greens of a nature that would announce their identity to an old habitué at once if he were suddenly deposited there 'blind' by helicopter or parachute.

The course is as full of character as the place itself. There are two starting-points, at the 1st and 10th – a great bonus this in the case of a highly popular club – and however hard it has rained earlier in the day one returns with shoes as dry and clean as one started. You can see a lot of golf from the windows of the club-house which in an unostentatious way is extremely comfortable and with a very good table. It used to be simple to a degree, with ham and buttered eggs the regular speciality. Now the choice has been stepped up with no diminution of quality.

One identifies several people particularly with Rye, for instance R. H. de Montmorency, my father-in-law, though he was dead

long before my marriage to Ann. 'Monty,' of whom I shall have
more to say, was a great Ryeite and also one of the founders of the
Oxford and Cambridge Golfing Society whose headquarters and
spiritual home is here. At the Camber end of the course in the last
of the row of Coastguard Cottages lived Leonard Crawley, my
colleague on the *Daily Telegraph* for almost quarter of a century,
and his wife Elspeth. In some small exchange for much hospitality
I offered once or twice, when he himself was still in the hunt, to
help him, by reporting as 'Our Special Correspondent' the final
rounds of the President's Putter. In 1950 Leonard after the 16th in
the semi-final was two up on P. B. ('Laddie') Lucas, that glamorous
figure who, among other distinctions, played for Great Britain in the
Walker Cup while still a freshman from Stowe, won a DSO and bar
and a DFC as a fighter pilot, became an MP and ultimately forsook
politics in favour of the Chairmanship of the Greyhound Racing
Association. Leonard disliked the one-shot 17th on the grounds that
it was flukey. In consequence he sometimes played it indifferently
and now missed his three, the left-handed Lucas being therefore one
down on the 18th tee. He cut his drive now into the deep pit that
looks rather like a bomb crater. Crawley hit a beauty down the
middle. By the grace of God, Laddie found a good lie and pushed
a long iron somewhere quite close. Leonard's second, straight as an
arrow, just went through the green, and he lost the hole to a 4.

He played the 19th perfectly, but Laddie laid another long-iron
second close, holed his putt for a 3, and so, against all the odds,
just got home. Nothing very extraordinary in this, you may say,
and nor was there. I recall it, however, for Leonard's attitude in
defeat which he took with Olympian detachment, having nothing,
he felt, with which to reproach himself. He was a perfectionist as
regards all games, with sound and rigid views as to how the ball
should be hit. In his prime as a golfer – so they say who should know
best – no one *struck* the ball better, whether amateur or pro. It was
this that gave him the utmost pleasure. He liked to win, naturally,
but it was the method that mattered. Leonard would have been
sympathetic to the man who, protesting to his opponent about the
latter's appalling luck, got the bland answer: 'Are we playing *how*
or *how many*?'

I owed my position as cricket correspondent of the *Daily Telegraph* to him in that in early 1946 the first Lord Camrose after

reading an essay he wrote on Douglas Jardine gave him the choice of two jobs, the cricket and the golf. With a wife and two children just growing up Leonard felt that cricket would too often keep him away from home. So he opted for golf, and on discovering from a chance meeting with me that I was available kindly put my name forward.

In a later chapter, with the author's permission, I shall give the substance of a letter which *The Times* printed at the height of the Bodyline row from which the temper of the piece on Jardine that impressed Lord Camrose may be judged. The journalist in the owner of the *Telegraph* must have rejoiced at discovering a games-player who was an expert on his subject – or, rather, on two – who was more than happy to speak his mind.

This he proceeded to do as our golf correspondent for quarter of a century, attracting the majority of the swelling public for golf as the sporting pages of the paper gradually expanded (with the easing of newsprint restrictions) to something like their pre-war size. I wonder, by the way, if any game has been better served by its chief writers than golf was when Bernard Darwin, Henry Longhurst and Leonard Crawley were all in action together.

My old colleague has a way of putting things that was all his own whether talking or in print. There is a rich sprinkling of sporting allusion and simile – such as this summing-up in the case of someone who had been gravely ill: 'Oh, yes, it was very nearly Close of Play.' That could only have been Leonard.

After a foursome one day at Rye his partner, a mighty fellow who had fortified himself against the cold with a great many sweaters and scarves, was apologizing for his indifferent perform-ance. Leonard said, 'My dear Robin, say no more about it. This is a very difficult game. In any case – ' poking him in the ribs – 'you can't play it dressed up like the Pope.'

He, by the way, when it was cold, was inclined to wear a sheep-skin jacket and gloves which, with the dignity that characterized all his movements, he took off and handed to his caddy before each stroke. The ritual completed, and the club selected, one saw in action that slow, superbly rhythmic method, the stroke so perfect in execution that the ball seemed almost impervious to cross-wind. He was very straight and very long, and there was no more perfect swing, whether amateur or professional, in the world of golf.

Leonard had his own names for people, some of them, like mine, distinctly bizarre. I was 'Lord Sockem' – because when we were comparing our respective remunerations I am alleged once to have said : 'Oh, I sock 'em for expenses.' When I was staying away, letters so addressed to friends' houses caused both confusion and hilarity. Naturally, in case this libellous nickname got back to my lords and masters, I had ever after to be even more scrupulous than before in rendering my accounts.

Men of strongly expressed opinions cannot expect to avoid animosities, and in a few cases Leonard seemed positively to nourish them, while at the same time his friends were endeavouring to smooth the ruffled waters. But the frictions weighed but lightly against the friendships for which many and not least myself have good cause to be grateful. In particular he has always been kindness itself to the young.

It is generally a sign of affection when stories collect round a man, and those surrounding Leonard are legion. For instance, there is the saga of the teeth which were always being left behind. They were retrieved from the call-box at the RAC, and from Tulsa, Oklahoma. The station-master at Leuchars where he alighted from the sleeper for St Andrews was under instruction to see that they were not wafted north to Aberdeen. Once when in France he was told that the Duke of Windsor would like to see him he hurried to the locker-room and extracted them from his ball-bag. Donald Steel, his Boswell, is the chief repository of Crawleiana, and I hope one day he produces the same sort of nostalgic biography-cum-anthology as Peter Ryde has done of Bernard Darwin. I write in the past tense, by the way, for Leonard's public appearances now are infrequent. In retirement, however, he is still firing off epistolary salvoes, as well as occasional pieces for the *Field* and the *Telegraph*. He does so from a cottage alongside the church at Worlington – 'They've only got to pop me over the wall.'

The town of Rye perched high above the dunes and marshes is patently a haven apart, as is the links that lie some two or three miles out to the south on the sea side of the Camber road : individual places attracting special people such as John Vidler, Ben Travers, E. F. Benson, Bernard Darwin and a host more. Both the Golf Club and the Dormy House which snuggles just inside the

Landgate that bounded the old town have always been convivial haunts – as to which a rather ridiculous story comes to mind which will not suggest, I hope, that an undue consumption of alcohol was the rule. Not so. It concerns Monty Ravenhill who certainly did himself better than most. It was said that Monty's car knew the way home from the Golf Club to his home at Playden without prompting from the driver. One dusky evening, bearing its owner and two of his companions, it stopped at the level-crossing for the passage of the Ashford train. The following exchange is then related to have taken place :

'Straordinary well-lighted village we've just passed through.'

'Yes, and did you notice the first house was on fire?'

Monty will be recalled by some as the most genial of drones with, between his teeth, a habitual long cigarette-holder which oscillated unpredictably through about 90° like a tiller unattended : for this and his being the father of the very lovely Lorna who married Dickie Twining. After the briefest of war marriages Dickie was killed in North Africa, whereupon Lorna lost herself in tireless service. L. F. Ellis in *The Welsh Guards at War* gives Lorna Twining a paragraph to herself. He says :

All who served in the 3rd Battalion in Africa and Italy know that after Captain Twining was killed looking for his lost patrol at Fondouk Mrs Lorna Twining went out to minister to her husband's battalion and others in the 1st Guards Brigade. They all know this and bless her. There were many other ladies who served the army in mobile canteens, but there were very few who served with one formation throughout a whole campaign, and who arrived with such consistency when 'tea and wads' and the other extras she brought were just what were wanted most by men who were having a hard time.

J. L. S. Vidler, Harry Altham's contemporary at Repton and Oxford, presided over the Dormy House as its secretary after his retirement from the Prison Service to which he brought a reforming spirit and broad humanity which combined to make him an unrivalled authority on penological matters. I shall have a little more to say of him when we come to consider a few eminent all-rounders.

It was apt to be a select company which after dinner gathered round the fireplace at the Dormy in the late '50s when in his years of retirement Darwin lived at the club. We had dined well, too, during the reign of Mrs Elliott who as cook-housekeeper was granted quite a licence in the way of bustling everyone into the dining-room sharp at 7.30, and also of wearing the club ties of some of the societies who came down at week-ends. Someone had given her no less distinguished a one than the Oxford and Cambridge Golfing Society – after which, if I remember aright, the idea rather caught on.

Until very recently the presence of Ben Travers maintained Rye's literary associations which centred on Henry James and the Bensons, E. F. and Arthur. A little sketch by E.F. gives an inkling of what a precious fellow James must have been – 'an acquired taste' surely even in those mannered days. 'E.F. had been playing golf and James met us after our game at the club-house and gave us tea in an ecstasy of genial nebulosity as to what we had been doing. "Some be-flagged jam-pots I understand, my dear Fred, let into the soil at long but varying distances. A swoop, a swing, a flourish of steel, and a dormy." '

Even for a man of letters Henry James was more than ordinarily absent-minded. Benson tells how James one day saw advancing down the High Street a woman whom he knew that he knew but whom his racked memory failed to identify. To his dismay she made a beeline for him across the road and said : 'I've had the rest of it made into rissoles.'

'And then in fact,' he said, 'the cudgelling brain ceased, for I recognized my own cook and knew that she was speaking of the leg of lamb I had eaten hot and roast on Monday and cold on Tuesday.'

There is much of Rye in Benson, and it is a temptation that must be resisted to linger with both. Now that the indestructible Ben Travers has left Watchbell Street for the Garrick Club the only tangible link with the literary people, so far as I know, is the window in the south transept of Rye church commemorating E.F.'s brother Arthur, formerly Master of Magdalene, Cambridge, who in his spare time wrote, surprisingly, not only the words of 'Land of Hope and Glory' but a profusion of sentimental novels, and thus acquired a devoted and rich American fan.

As correspondence between them ripened she attempted to

At the County Cricketers' Golfing Society's annual meeting at Worplesdon : Percy Chapman, eminent England captain and cricketer (no one before or since has got near to his *six* successive Test victories over Australia) ; R. H. de Montmorency, my wife's father, personifies the scholastic sportsmen scattered throughout this book ; great amateur golfer, Blue also for cricket and rackets, Eton house-master ; on the right is Charles Ambrose, distinguished golf artist with oils and pencil between the wars.

Sir John Masterman : a mellow study during his provostship of Worcester College, Oxford ; all-round sportsman, academic, at the hub of MI5 in war-time, University vice-chancellor, author — and friend to generations of undergraduates.

7. G. O. Allen : on his 50th birthday, 31 July 1952, after making a hundred for The Arabs against Sir William Worsley's XI at Hovingham Nor was it his last — he got 143 not out for the Free Foresters against Cambridge the following year. After becoming a selector in 1955 he played no more.

8. 'Old-fashioned leg-hit'? The score-book confirms that the Arab needed runs against time in our annual match against R. M. Stow's XI in front of the boys of Horris Hill School : behind the stumps an Oxford all-rounder and ex-Bradfield housemaster, A. J. N. Young.

bequeath on him a large part of her fortune. Arthur Benson found a happy way out by diverting her benevolence towards his college, which benefited astonishingly, as all Magdalene men must know. Benson never met the American lady but it is fitting that at least her name is recorded in an inscription beneath the church window.

From Rye it is a brief run to Hastings where the Central ground lives up to its name, bang in the middle of everything and almost literally on 'the front'. The ruins of the Castle make a free vantage point from which to see the cricket. Playing there on tour with Dulwich Cricket Club when very young I made a hundred which settled the match, and so atoned for having bagged a pair at Ashford the previous day – an unusual sequence of stark failure and success which, strangely enough, I exactly repeated when playing in Germany against the Rhine Army many years later.

Sir Home Gordon and Arthur Gilligan and Les Ames in turn put their energies into a September Festival at Hastings which for a while ran a reputable second to Scarborough. But the cricket, in the nature of modern festivals – as distinct from the older variety – was by definition unmemorable. The summer's chief attraction at Hastings was generally Sussex *v* Kent, and there are those who still remember a sparkling and prolonged exhibition of batting there by K. S. Duleepsinhji which was a prophesied sequel to the meeting between these two sides at Maidstone earlier in the summer.

Kent in dry weather caught Sussex at Mote Park on a pitch suspiciously wet at one end – a phenomenon which, plainly, defied nature and in the opinion of Sussex had been engineered for the benefit of 'Tich' Freeman. Sussex duly capitulated by an innings, whereupon Duleep, a man slow to wrath, said, 'They are cheats – wait till they come to Hastings.' Since the year was 1929 one may assume surely that at this range of time no sore feelings will be awakened by this story for which, just conceivably, as I like to think, there could have been an innocent explanation.

However that may have been, Duleep at Hastings sailed into Kent with a rare relish – and in particular into 'Tich'. On the first day he made 115 in 100 minutes, which was just an appetizer for what came afterwards. In the second innings he scored 246 in $3\frac{1}{4}$ hours. Towards the end *Wisden* says that 'he did not play quite so well . . . giving indeed two hard chances, but for the most part he was completely master of the Kent bowling'. On the face of it this seems scarcely an over-statement! Sussex had their revenge by 167 runs, though without having things all their own way, for the aggregate was 1451 runs for 36 wickets, a figure only once exceeded in a county match. Nor did Freeman come too badly out of it – considering the run-scoring, nine for 239 was no mean return.

In terms of forcing batsmanship, though, this was the rapier at work rather than the bludgeon. Duleep's batting must have been the most celebrated performance at Hastings since Jessop's onslaught on The Players of the South there in 1906. Home Gordon once pointed out to me the chapel on South Terrace behind the pavilion, the face of which Jessop is said to have peppered. In all he hit five balls out of the ground, but several, perhaps many, of the 30 fours he hit that afternoon cleared the boundary rope and would in later years have counted six. As it was, he made 191 off the Players' bowling between 2.15 and 3.45, and my old friend Henry Grierson saw the end of it. According to Gerald B odi ibb in his admirable book, *The Croucher*, Henry 'was staying on holiday at St Leonard's and hearing that Jessop was batting dashed off in an old horse bus. As he arrived at the turnstile a ball landed among the hansom cabs parked where the bus station now stands by the Town Hall.' It's a prodigious carry.

The recital of these feats provokes a thought. It has often struck me that there is almost a specially clear Sussex light – a translucence in the air scarcely matched elsewhere. Whether or not this is true, I'm sure that the roll of outstanding batting performances on the grounds of Sussex compares well with any other part of the country. Think of the fearful plunder wrought in their day by Ranji and Charles Fry, and how when William Gunn and Arthur Shrewsbury opened the innings for Notts at Hove most of the rest of the side reputedly went down for a bathe. Did not Duleep make 333 there in a day (without the need to divest himself of a sweater) against Northants, and thus inspire a degree of bathos in an agency report which sticks in the mind after all but half a century. There were two features to the cricket at Hove yesterday, we were informed. One was the splendid batting of K. S. Duleepsinhji who in five and a half hours scored 333, etc. etc. The other was the wicket-keeping of Bellamy who 'failed to concede a single bye'. How many, one asks oneself, would have passed the bat?

Eddie Paynter once made 322 at Hove and even cut half an hour off Duleep's time of a few years before. Then there was Harold Gimblett scoring 310 for Somerset at Eastbourne, and various prolific associations between Ted Bowley – what a *felicitous* player – and John Langridge: John not perhaps all ease and grace but a wonderfully dependable accumulator. In Hugh Bartlett's great year, 1938, when he made a hundred against the Australians at Hove in 57 minutes, he was a consistently prolific scorer on his home grounds, as, both before and after the war, was George Cox. Of course, bowlers got their chances too, especially when there was a touch of sea fret around. But when a high-class batsman was in on a day of sun and soft breezes he really was in.

But it's time we descended upon Eastbourne which is half an hour's drive westward via Bexhill, Cooden Beach and Pevensey. Passing Cooden and its golf course, part links, part pasture, I may recall to my Aussie friend that Lionel, the third Baron Tennyson, died in the hotel there one morning, the newspaper at his bedside open at the racing page. Was he flushed with success or bemoaning 'another wuddy loser'? Never mind. Lionel Tennyson was a Corinthian figure, a man of the Regency perhaps, with an insatiable appetite for the pleasures of life, and a sportsman full of daring and courage. Technically maybe he was not a Test Match cricketer, yet he was perfectly cast as England's captain in '21 following the long succession of Australian victories chiefly brought about by the fast bowling of Gregory and McDonald. Lionel's response to the challenge was to lead England to two favourable draws which stopped the rot, and to emerge with a batting average for the series of 57.

When one comes to exemplify the triumphs of temperament in our 'beautiful, complicated game' the case of the Hon. L. H. Tennyson (Hampshire and England) in 1921 is a sure stand-by.

5

Cardus's Scoop

The Saffrons! A fragrant name for a benign ground which, summer by summer, is host to more games of cricket, of divers sorts, than almost any in England. I knew it first in August 1930 when, at the age of 23, I escaped from the chore of sub-editing in the *Evening Standard* office, in company with Peter Aitken, who was similarly engaged, for a fortnight's cricket holiday.

We played, the pair of us, for Eastbourne in half a dozen two-day matches that year, each game following the other without respite. MCC, the Harlequins, Old Malvernians, Uppingham Rovers, Old Eastbournians, Bradfield Waifs, Repton Pilgrims, Hampstead, Yellowhammers and Cryptics were some of the clubs which used to perambulate the south coast, calling in at Eastbourne on the way. The cricket was very good, and the Eastbourne CC a match for most, with Kenneth Harding, one-time of Sussex, as our captain and several more with some first-class experience turning out from among J. L. Bryan, F. C. Quaife (the pro), J. G. Wagener, C. H. Knott, H. L. Wilson, J. C. Masterman, P. G. van der Bijl, and others who were drafted in from time to time.

Peter Aitken, younger son of Lord Beaverbrook and brother of Max, was primarily a lawn-tennis player, and good enough to qualify for Wimbledon; but he got by also as a cricketer, and he got by with plenty to spare as a companion in the evening hours. Like everyone else he stood in dreadful awe of his father, who, as like as not, woke us with an uncomfortably early telephone call endeavouring to keep an eye on things from afar. 'Yes, Father,' would come the answer to that rasping, quick-fire Canadian volley. 'I had an early night. Got twenty-five yesterday, and they seem very pleased with me. Yes, having a great time. Yes, I'll make sure . . .' etc. etc. Poor Peter! He was always in one scrape or another, 'accident-prone' as would be said today. Compared with his brother, who had a brilliant war in the RAF, he must have been a sad disappointment to Beaverbrook from early manhood until his early death in a boating accident in Denmark. But in his youth he was a loyal, amusing friend.

It was at the Saffrons that I first met Harry Altham who brought the Harlequins, and in two days annually gave to all concerned a perfect exposition of the arts of captaincy. It was an education to see the intelligent thought and care that Harry gave to the situation generally and to each member of his side in particular: to bat against first-class amateur bowling, directed by him, was an exercise in all the skills one could muster, and was a challenge which made any success well worth savouring. Nor was our own captain, Kenneth Harding, outclassed by comparison.

The most famous match that ever was, or will be, played at the Saffrons was, of course, that between Archie Maclaren's XI and the Australians of 1921, which ended in the first defeat suffered by Warwick Armstrong's great side, just after the conclusion of the Test Series they had won so handsomely. The story has been recounted too often to bear a complete re-telling – though mostly, it is true, by one observer destined soon for fame, Neville Cardus. The occasion could not have been better devised for the most romantic of all cricket writers – a challenge thrown down to the Invincibles by a cricketer once great, now rising 50, who had not been seen on a first-class field since the summer of 1914. He would pick a side to beat them, he said, and an amateur one at that, chiefly from Cambridge. In his *Autobiography* Cardus tells how he, the recently appointed cricket correspondent of the *Manchester Guardian*, received in advance a note from Maclaren suggesting he came down to Eastbourne. The postscript said: 'I think I know how to beat Armstrong's lot.'

This invitation put Neville in a quandary, for since first he, a ragged urchin, could raise 6*d* to pass through the Old Trafford turnstiles Maclaren had been his hero before whom even Reggie Spooner and Johnny Tyldesley paled to shadows. 'He had an aristocratic face; he walked the grass as though he lorded it . . . He lighted a fire in me never to be put out.' But simultaneously, he writes, in these last days of August Surrey and Yorkshire were playing a vital championship match at the Oval, while his own Lancashire were engaged at Leyton. His News Editor pooh-poohed the idea of watching these amateurs, and told him bluntly that his duty lay in London.

But the pull of Maclaren prevailed. And then what? His side were skittled before lunch for 43, and by the Saturday evening the Australians had made 174 and taken the first of Maclaren's second-innings wickets for 8. Cardus makes a fine story of his own humiliation preceding final triumph, as well as of the match. On the Monday morning he packed his bag, 'sent it to the railway station', and called in at the Saffrons to while away an hour before the one-o'clock train took him to London and the great happenings at the Oval. In particular, he took this last look because Maclaren had gone in himself overnight to hold the fort. One final glimpse he must have of 'the finest Roman of them all' confronting the fire and fury of Gregory and McDonald.

Alas, the finest Roman was bowled by McDonald with the first ball of the day, and the young reporter, sick at heart, turned towards the gate. His dejection was complete. But still some extra sense bade him stay, and he began to hear the bats of Aubrey Faulkner and Hubert Ashton making sweet music over the sparsely-peopled field. Their stand burgeoned and Cardus forgot his train (though not, presumably, his bag) and throughout the sunny afternoon enjoyed the long partnership between these two splendid cricketers, the grizzled South African and the youthful undergraduate; and after Ashton left for 75 the dominant Faulkner carted the Australians all over the field until, having forced Armstrong to post three men in the outfield, he at last made his only mistake. Not since the 1912 Triangular Tournament, said *Wisden*, had Faulkner played such an innings as his 153. So the Australians had to make 196 to win, and overnight lost Collins for 25.

Let me turn now to a remembrance of the third day's play not of Cardus's but of a participant (and one of the three survivors among the two sides), Gilbert Ashton, who in 1964 contributed to the *Cricketer* a fascinating account, of which this is the latter half:

Then came the third and most dramatic day which will live long in the memory of those who played, and perhaps of those who watched. Carter, the night-watchman, was brilliantly caught in the box off Falcon, Bardsley played what seemed a perfect forward defensive shot, and was bowled between bat and pads by Gibson. Macartney followed, clean bowled by Falcon, and at lunch the score was 93 for 5.

We were now in with a chance. Tension was mounting, word had got round, the crowds were pouring in. Only Maclaren remained as calm and unmoved as at lunch time on that first day. Andrews and Ryder were together. They started to attack. Runs came faster than they had done before in either Australian innings. Falcon, tiring rapidly after another great spell, was taken off in favour of Faulkner. 140 for five. It all seemed over. Suddenly Ryder slashed at a good-length ball from Gibson, still bowling superbly, and was caught in the covers. The ball took an age to come down. Andrews, who had looked horribly secure, was bowled by Faulkner. Gregory LBW Gibson 0. The game had swung again. Then came Armstrong, their last accredited batsman, to face his first crisis for many a long day. He looked ill at ease. He was anxious not to face Faulkner. He played no sort of shot to his first ball from that bowler, a loud appeal for LBW rent the air. Not out. An exactly similar ball, an exactly similar shot, a quiet but firm appeal and the Umpire's hand went up. Fittingly, Gibson claimed his sixth wicket by bowling the last batsman, Mailey, for 0. The match was over. The Australians had been beaten – by 28 runs.

Did the Australians treat the match light-heartedly? I do not think so. Only Ryder in the second innings, when the game was very much in the balance, threw his wicket away by a rash shot and he may easily have been deceived by the flight of the ball. No, the Australians had been squarely, if improbably, defeated and generously acknowledged afterwards that they had fallen to a better side. That, of course, was an exaggeration. It was a freak result. Another example, perhaps unsurpassed, of the uncertainty of the game of cricket. But in that particular game they had certainly been matched in every department, bowling, batting and not least in fielding and captaincy.

Gregory, tall and menacing, a formidable and intimidating bowler, and so often a terror to English batsmen, never struck a length and was hit for 50 runs in nine overs in the second innings. Macartney, sturdy and short in stature but strong and compact, the most brilliant batsman I've seen, so quick on his feet and, like Hobbs, so superbly balanced, was not at his best.

He was always a delight to watch or to field against, for one never knew whether a half-volley would be played early or late, straight or square.

McDonald bowled magnificently in both innings with his superb action and beautifully rhythmic run up to the wicket : the finest fast bowler I've seen, not excluding Larwood and Lindwall. His bowling came very quickly off the pitch and he made the new ball swerve very late.

Armstrong, a formidable figure of a man, was past his prime as a batsman, but as a bowler his length was always immaculate and in the summer of 1921 he had mesmerized the English batsmen. He could only be successfully played by a batsman who like Faulkner was prepared to use his feet. His top-spinner fizzed off the wicket like a fast bowler.

But my own abiding memory of the game will always be of the imperturbability of Maclaren. He had given the side hope when all seemed lost, courage and inspiration. At the end, calm and dignified, he led his side off the field. It was his farewell to cricket. He had kept his word.

The survivors, by the way, are now reduced to only three : Gilbert and Hubert Ashton, and 'Nip' Pellew. The crucial catch given by Ryder that took such a long time to come down was safely taken by the writer, Gilbert Ashton, eldest of the three brothers who played in the match and captain of the talented Cambridge side of 1921. Six catches were held altogether by Maclaren's side, curiously enough all by Ashtons, Hubert catching four and Claude one. In addition to his batting skill Hubert was a very fine close fielder–which makes it the more extraordinary that despite making 357 in six completed innings against the Australians that summer he was not chosen for a Test match.

Hubert was the best bat of the Ashtons, but Gilbert's part in the initial recovery deserves mention here, irrespective of my gratitude for his allowing me to republish his account. He went in at 8 for two on the second morning, having been duly flattered by Maclaren saving him overnight. Soon it was 20 for three with Geoff Foster gone, and Hubert joining him. Another wicket then and the miracle must have been doubly impossible. But now Gilbert, against Gregory and McDonald, made 32 of the 40 which the brothers put on for the fourth wicket, showing in so doing that the fast bowling could be safely played. Armstrong separated them, Gilbert disregarding Hubert's advice not to try and hook him. Thus the way was paved for the great counter-attack by Faulkner and Hubert.

The fielding of Maclaren's side (with the venerable captain standing at first slip throughout and having scarcely a ball to take) was brilliant, by all accounts, and must have inspired the *three* bowlers to superhuman effort. Perhaps the most extraordinary thing about the game was that it should have been won despite the bowling strength being reduced to three by Walter Brearley having pulled a muscle when batting on the first morning.

Neither Falcon nor Gibson is much remembered now, but both were bowlers of Test Match potential if their lives had followed different courses. Gibson was an Etonian with a fine flowing action, medium in pace, an outswinger basically, whose playing days after coming down from Cambridge were spent in the Argentine. Michael Falcon, a Harrovian, devoted himself to running the Norfolk side for many years, and appeared on and off for the Gentlemen between 1911 and 1927. I played once with him close on his 64th birthday in a Festival of Britain match for George Mann's XI against his old county at Lakenham, and it was easy to see what a superb action he must have had when he was shattering the Australians in the game of his life. Falcon at Eastbourne had seven for 67 in the first innings, Gibson six for 64 in the second. Faulkner's leg-breaks and googlies in the two innings accounted for five for 63. What help Brearley could have given this trio is open to conjecture. At 45 his days as a fast bowler were far behind him. However, as I remember him teaching boys how to bowl at the Lord's Easter classes on chilly spring days long afterwards, ruddy-faced and every inch a son of Lancashire from his bald head to his boots, he was an apostle of fitness. No doubt he would have obliged his old crony, Maclaren, by 'putting them there' and so afforded them some relief.

The Australian side, incidentally, was identical with that which had played in the last Test except that Ryder displaced Pellew – a change that cannot have affected the strength. If my younger readers are sceptical of Gilbert Ashton's view that the Australians took the match with proper seriousness I would only add that to those who saw them play half a century ago it is hard to imagine them playing any other way. The common idea today that for a touring team only Tests 'matter' is quite a recent heresy. Of this game Arthur Mailey told me more than once how acutely nervous Armstrong was on going out to bat in the second innings : 'shaking like a great jelly' was the phrase, if I remember aright.

As to Cardus's account my suspicious mind slightly doubts the decision to desert the match, unless perhaps play started at 11.0 – consider that the score was 8 for two when Maclaren was out to the first ball of the day and 60 for four when Faulkner joined Ashton. And he misread his *Wisden* when he talked of Surrey being simultaneously engaged at the Oval against Yorkshire : in fact a more momentous contest was in progress at Lord's, the second of the famous Championship-deciding matches between Middlesex and Surrey. Yet he was plainly present to record what he describes as his only scoop, and it is as well for cricket history that he was. Like many another devoted raconteur he never scrupled to stretch the literal truth if by doing so he could embroider a good story. These were all time-worn, and after frequent repetition he no doubt came implicitly to believe the decorated version.

There was, for instance, his marriage – an event that is inclined with most people to remain tolerably clear in their minds. Cardus tells how he went to Old Trafford in the course of duty one morning, how Makepeace and Hallows came out to bat, and opened with care, whereupon he repaired by taxi to a registry office to wed Edith Honorine King. While he was away 'and had committed the most responsible and irrevocable act in mortal man's life', Lancashire had increased their total by exactly 17 : Makepeace 5, Hallows 11, and one leg-bye.

When this endearing item appeared in his *Autobiography* a keen cricket student, Geoffrey Copinger by name, took it upon him to check the facts, only to find, of course, that they could not be verified. It so happened that these famous players only went in together once in June, against Sussex, when Makepeace made 4 and 24 retired hurt, Hallows 109 not out and 0. Makepeace was out of the side for a month or more, Jack Barnes took his place, and the regular pair did not bat again together until August!

Rumour then had it that Neville in fact was married in the depth of winter, but to research further would serve no useful end.

It's a splendid story whether the glad event happened in spring or autumn – or, for that matter, in 1920 or 1922. But I expect he got the year right for it was, of course, an Australian summer!

The truth is that in his later years my old friend was inclined to hold the floor – often indeed entertainingly. In *Who's Who* he listed Conversation as the first of his hobbies, but if it were not to be a one-way exercise the other half had also to be a tough and unyielding competitor. And what a ripe and colourful background from which he talked! I cannot presume to speak of his place in the world of music, though I know that one of the achievements he looked back upon with most satisfaction was undoubtedly the weekly hour-long musical programmes which were broadcast throughout Australia during the war. He brought many thousand Australians to an appreciation of music, just as, both in England and Australia, the rich imagery of his cricket writing – heavily adorned with musical allusions – brought a new public to the game. The tactical side of cricket meant little to him, the refinements of technique not much more. His fascination was with the expression of character in action.

He saw styles and attitudes in terms of background and personality – and in particular made affectionate heroes of the old northern professionals. He conveyed in literature of his own unmistakable stamp the poetry of McDonald's run-up and delivery, the utter dedication of a cock-sparrow like Emmott Robinson, the impish genius of George Gunn. What a game is cricket that it can bring to fulfilment from the slums of Manchester and Sydney men of the artistic quality of Cardus and Mailey! I make no apology for recommending once again Arthur Mailey's *Ten for 66 and all that*. As for Cardus he has left a corpus of 24 books on cricket and music severally or in conjunction. His *Autobiography* will be a social document so long as cricket is played and music remains for mankind the food of love and the spirit.

It was natural, of course, that after Neville's death (in early 1975, in his sleep, aged 85) his Memorial Service should be a musical event – if there were to be a service. The doubt lay in his lack of religious conviction. In youth he had been a positive atheist, but his position had certainly shifted later. So John Hester, a friend of mine since Pusey House, who was then Priest-in-charge of St Paul's, Covent Garden, the church adjacent to Neville's club, the Garrick, and by tradition connected with the arts, agreed to a service there, and some 700 attended.

At its beginning Father Hester said he had only once met Sir Neville Cardus, by my introduction, at Lord's where we three had sat together watching on the first pavilion balcony. He had gathered then that Neville's position might be compared with that of Jowett, of Balliol, who said to Margot Asquith : 'My dear, you must believe in God despite what the clergy tell you.' This, I think, was the only overt reference to our Lord in the service apart from a prayer commending his soul and a final blessing. Otherwise I suppose the proceedings could be considered an oblation to St Cecilia, the patron saint of music, and a lovely offering it was. The chancel was entirely filled by the Royal Philharmonic Orchestra, James Loughran of the Hallé conducting Elgar's Serenade for Strings, and Mozart's Piano Concerto in A Major, played by Clifford Curzon, and the Clarinet Concerto. Interspersed we had Miss Wendy Hiller declaiming Francis Thompson's immortal lines 'At Lord's', and a reading from Dame Flora Robson and a tribute by Alan Gibson which caught the Cardus flavour perfectly.

This is how he began :

Since we are in a church I thought it proper that we should have a text. Hear then these words from the prophet Blake. (I am not sure whether Blake was one of Sir Neville's favourites, though he has recalled how enthusiastically he would join in 'Jerusalem' in his days with the Ancoats Brotherhood.) Blake wrote, in 'Auguries of Innocence' :

> Joy and woe are woven fine,
> A clothing for the soul divine;
> Under every grief and pine
> Runs a thread of silken twine.

On an occasion such as this, joy and woe are inseparable companions : thanksgiving for such a life, sadness that it has ended. But more than that : it was the mingling of joy and woe that made Sir Neville such a writer – the sensitivity to the human condition, not least his own; the ability to observe it and to communicate what he saw, with detachment and yet with passion. His books are full of humour : rich comedy, sometimes

76

almost slapstick, and yet he keeps us hovering between tears and laughter.

Gibson ended :

Joy and woe are woven fine. They are not alien, they are complementary, 'a clothing for the soul divine'. And in another part of that poem, Blake says :

> It is right it should be so,
> Man was made for joy and woe
> And when this we rightly know,
> Safely through the world we go.

I am not sure whether Sir Neville Cardus would approve of that as an epitaph : but he is probably too busy to bother just now, arguing with Bernard Shaw.

Or Archie Maclaren, or Thomas Beecham, or C. B. Fry, or indeed anyone whose wing he could clutch. Alan, needless to say, performed the always difficult task of speaking a Eulogy to a congregation of friends of the dead one with proper gravity but withal occasional shafts of wit. At the end of a movement, in subfusc and the scarlet and black hood of an Oxford MA, he mounted the pulpit and arranged his notes, only for the music to start again. Whereupon he came down the way he had gone up until the final movement had really ended. When I sympathized afterwards with him for misreading the umpire's signal he said : 'Oh, I knew it wasn't the finish, but in the non-conformist conventicles of my youth the pulpit was always provided with a chair and I thought I'd wait up there. I'd forgotten your Anglican ways.'

Talking of the hereafter, here is a ridiculous story of the clergyman who died and was duly wafted aloft. There he saw another old cleric sailing by on a pink cloud with a maiden of great beauty. 'Ah, Fontwater,' he cried, 'I'm so glad you've had your reward.' 'She's not my reward,' came the reply, 'I'm her eternal punishment.' There may be theological flaws in this little gem but at least it has a respectable pedigree, having been recounted by Sir Alec Douglas-Home, as he then was, at a Forty Club dinner.

We've strayed a bit from the Saffrons, so let us return, in a manner of speaking, with a footnote on Maclaren. During the Tests of 1930 part of my job, aside from writing a Test piece for the earlier editions of the *Evening Standard*, was to act as go-between with Maclaren who had been engaged to pen, from time to time during the day, sage thoughts which I collected and passed on to the telephonist.

Maclaren (like Cardus) seldom stopped talking, and there he sat in box or stand, a figure of awesome dignity, white hair showing below the brim of his black Homburg hat, and with an IZ tie, disquisitioning to a bunch of selected cronies. Patiently I would wait for the oracle to draw breath. Then when my presence was too obvious to be ignored further he would say: 'Oh, there you are. Well, there's absolutely nothing to say.' It's not for me to decide whether I've always treated my various amanuenses with more consideration than I had from Archie Maclaren, but I think I can say I've tried to. Four years later with Charles Fry, when the Australians next came, I was luckier. By that time I had been promoted to the main editions, sharing the space with the great man, who was unfailingly kind and helpful. He orated a great deal, too – but then he could talk and write simultaneously.

And now a further recollection of Eastbourne, and, strangely, one not unconnected with music. Though the Grand Hotel has long ago priced itself out of the market so far as cricketers are concerned it was once the favourite haunt for all teams visiting the Saffrons. Many a convivial evening have I enjoyed there, occasionally perhaps ruffling the ecclesiastical calm of the big lounge which was the original Palm Court of the Grand Hotel of broadcast fame: where Albert Sandler and his orchestra played mellifluously away to old ladies bending over their crochet, and their venerable consorts, comfortably replete under their dinner-jackets and stiff evening shirts. For that matter I have had recourse to the popular recipe for clearing the eye before cricket next morning: an iced shampoo from the hairdresser and a pint of Pimms.

There was a memorable night at the Grand during the County Week – it would have been around 1930 – when Duleep was the centre of a respectful circle, talking in that very quiet, very modest way of his: a gentle, charming man if ever there was one. Did he put the weight consciously on one foot or the other when he was waiting to receive the ball? The answer was neither – or, if you like, each in turn. He said he aimed to be pressing just slightly first on the ball of one foot, then the other, so causing a barely percept-ible rocking motion. That way he found he could move more easily either forward or back as the length dictated. Could he say how early he judged the length of the ball and so decided on the stroke? Yes, he aimed to decide at the earliest possible moment, 'because if I've made a mistake I have time to change my mind'. Was he good at picking the googly? Well, he always tried to do so from the action, 'but when the light is good I can see from the seam in the air which way it is spinning?' Duleep's keen Oriental eye gave him an advantage over ordinary mortals, but some batsmen of Aryan stock will say the same thing. I have a hunch that either Hobbs or Hammond – and I can't be sure which – never trusted their read-ing of the hand. They tried to determine the direction of the spin by watching the seam in the air. Failing that they played the ball off the pitch.

The modern players, or some of them, who like to regard them-selves as highly sophisticated, are inclined to disparage their pre-decessors as belonging to an Age of Innocence. To my generation it's rather funny to think of men like Hobbs, Hammond, Hendren – to say nothing of Duleep, Fender, Jardine, Bev Lyon and Walter Robins – as innocents abroad. When a young googly bowler said to Pat Hendren, 'You can always pick my wrong-'un : how do you do it?' the little man replied, 'I watch you putting the ball into your hand.' Whereafter, following this kindly tip, I expect the young man had the sense to adjust the ball in his fingers before turning to start his run-up.

Duleep had all the ingredients to make as great a captain as he was a cricketer, and would surely have led Sussex to the Champion-ship if his health had not failed him. They were indeed running for the title in August 1932, and I recall being at Cheltenham and see-ing the grief of his team when the news came that he must drop out of the match against Gloucestershire. They knew that consumption had sent him to Switzerland for a spell some years before. Though he again made some sort of a recovery the match before this one at Cheltenham proved to have been his last for Sussex. My last sight of Duleep was a few weeks earlier when in the second of two Test Trials held to inspect the candidates for Australia he complemented the 128 he had scored in the first one by making 92 not out at Cardiff : a nice treat for the Welsh.

Another snatch of the talk that evening at the Grand comes back. He was speaking of Maurice Tate who, 'great-hearted' as he was popularly, and rightly, described, like all famous cricketers needed sympathetic handling. Maurice by now had come to husband his strength for the times when it would be best rewarded. Duleep said if he asked him at the start of an innings how he felt he'd always say, 'Me, skipper? I'm fine.' His captain got the information he wanted more subtly. 'I used to wait two or three overs and then have a look at the footmarks. If he was really putting everything in he'd already begun to dig a hole with the front foot. Then I knew we were all right.' Maurice Tate, by the way, was attached to the Eastbourne club as second professional for a while before the first war.

My most recent memory of the Saffrons is of a marvellous match-winning hundred there scored by Colin Milburn to win the match for Northamptonshire : 141 not out he made out of 201 for no wicket, with Roger Prideaux keeping him admiring company at the other end. They needed just under two hours' batting, and Milburn's hundred, in 78 minutes, was the fastest of the summer in the County Championship. It was a hot, sunny August day in 1967 and, according to my report, Milburn

having got the measure of the bowling, the fours simply flowed. It was one of those innings of which one might say one scarcely had to watch, only to listen. Wilfred Rhodes would have enjoyed it. Milburn played all the strokes, but his signature, so to speak, is the square hit on the off-side, played with the utmost felicity of timing off either foot. Of his 24 fours (to say nothing of a six) most flowed in that direction. Like Denis Compton in his day he is a great teaser of cover-point . . . In this form it is hard to think that there is no room for Milburn in the England XI.

As fate had it this square, strong, cheerful and eminently likeable young man was destined to play for England only twice more before a car accident robbed him of an eye and English cricket of its most exciting young prospect.

This glamorous hundred by Milburn, by chance, exactly celebrated a century of county cricket at the Saffrons. But, of course, the game is infinitely older in Eastbourne than that. It goes back at least to 1738, and ample records exist of other eighteenth-century games played on various grounds there.

Why 'the Saffrons'? Simply, it seems, because the land was put to growing the yellow-flowering plant that was in demand for dyeing and medicinal purposes. Likewise Larkin's Field adjoining, identified for some of the best croquet lawns in England, and in the farther distance for a preponderance of buttercups, was named after the town's saddler, who in the eighteenth century grazed there the cattle from which he got his hides. Nowadays preparatory school-boys disport themselves on Larkin's Field while on the Saffrons the summer's fixture-list contains the best part of two hundred matches. A focus for cricket indeed.

6

Harry Surtees Altham

As I have said already it was on the cricket field at Eastbourne that I first got to know Harry Altham, and so it is at this point in my itinerant reflections – though Lord's and Oxford would have been equally appropriate staging posts – that I may conveniently try to give some sidelights on a remarkable man. For this purpose I have read again much that was written about him when he died, at the age of 76, on 11 March 1965, and, of course, the memoir which Hubert Doggart devised and edited called *The Heart of Cricket*, which the *Cricketer* published two years later.

These writings, as might be expected, combine to give an admiring picture of a man held by a singularly wide range of people in an unusual degree of respect and affection. In the obituary written in the factual, anonymous vein generally adopted by *Wisden*, however, I notice for the first time what can only be described as a howler. The second paragraph of the piece begins: 'Altham collaborated with E. W. Swanton in a book, *The History of Cricket* . . .' To put the thing in perspective let me just repeat the author-relationship between us as I described it in *SOCP*. The first edition of *A History of Cricket* (note the indefinite article) was written by Harry when I was a boy. It was twelve years later, in 1938, that he honoured me by asking *me* to collaborate with *him* in a Second Edition. This I did, and so continued with three subsequent editions, as the junior and subservient partner, until the last appeared in two volumes some three years before his death.

When at Desmond Eagar's behest I wrote an essay on H.S.A. which was sold for the benefit of Hampshire Youth cricket I chose for a title 'The Compleat Cricketer'. And who indeed had better claims to be so called? First he was a player of first-class attainments. Second, he was a captain of extraordinary perception, though he had no chance of exercising this particular skill either at Oxford or with Hampshire for whom he played only after the Winchester term was over. Third, he was an assiduous and highly successful coach to many generations of boys and undergraduates. Fourth, he was a historian, indeed *the* historian if one evaluates the scope of his researches, let alone their quality, with that of any rival. Fifth, he was an orator, of charm and distinction to every variety of cricket audience. Sixth, when his time as a house-master was finished he became the chief pioneer in bringing the game by means of new organizations to youth generally. Seventh and last, again in the later years, he threw himself into the administration of cricket both with MCC and with Hampshire. As President of Hampshire he was, at his death, in his nineteenth year of office. At Lord's he filled the all-embracing post of Treasurer for thirteen years and was President in 1959/60. Do not these seven faces of a cricketer compel the adjective 'compleat'?

But if such a catalogue suggests perhaps 'a one-track mind' remember that he was for twenty years the highly successful house-master of a great school. He was in his day probably the foremost authority on Winchester Cathedral. He was a lover of the classics and knowledgeable about prints and pictures, cricket and otherwise, about silver, philately, and chinoiserie. Hubert Doggart has told how 'he would describe with immense pleasure the day he bought the thousand-year-old Chinese horse' which decorated his drawing-room. His war record was notable, not the least for his luck in surviving all but four years as an infantry officer on the Western Front. He served with the Fifth Battalion of the 60th Rifles, and emerged a major with DSO, MC, and three mentions in dispatches.

Obviously, if he had wanted one, Harry could have had a head-mastership. Repton springs naturally to mind. But I do not think he ever came near to making the break from Winchester. His roots had grown so deep there. The school, and all things Wyccehamical, were so near his heart that he could not bear the thought of separation. Perhaps, too, his own over-modest estimation of his talents helped to dilute schoolmasterly ambition. I am thinking of the letter of thanks he wrote me in 1960 following the publication of *The Compleat Cricketer*:

I can only say quite simply – thank you, old friend, but may Clio forgive you for the distortion of the portrait into far more than life-size. You know as well as any man how much cricket has meant in my life, but only I know how much more it has given

to me than I can ever possibly have given to it : and only I know
how basically second-rate a chap I am.

This is a self-evaluation with which none who was ever close to him
would concur.

Harry – as must be evident from this bare chronicle of interest
and achievement – had a rare *zest*. It was a favourite word of his,
quoted in a well-worn phrase of Andrew Lang. But his greatness lay
less in what he did than in the kindliness he showed in all his deal-
ings and in his friendships, especially with the young, the enthusiasm
he radiated for all their hopes and activities. He understood the
hearts of boys.

There was an intensity about his love of life and people that age
would not quench. Jim Hornby, then headmaster of Bramcote,
recalls how late in life Harry, on a visit to the North, addressed on
the same day first the sixth form of a grammar school, next the
members of a county cricket club, and finally the inmates of the
city gaol. It's a sure bet that he struck the right note on all three
occasions. It was not in his nature to slow down, and it was on
another speaking visit to the North that he died, by an odd quirk
of chance in the house of David Wilson, nephew of Rockley Wilson
whose library at Winchester, I believe, first sparked the idea of his
attempting a history of the game.

Harry, so his last host tells me, had travelled up to Rotherham
at the pressing invitation of John Hampshire, with whom he had
struck up a friendship during one of the coaching courses at Lilleshall, to talk to the Rotherham Cricket Society. Hearing of this visit
the Sheffield Cricket Society 'cashed in', and David Wilson therefore picked him up at his Rotherham hotel on the morning after.
Motoring to Sheffield they stopped to see the site of the old Darnall
ground shown in the well-known print, and also the Hyde Park
ground where 16,000 once turned out to see the All-England XI.
Cricket, of course, came to Yorkshire via Sheffield, so this little
pilgrimage must have been much to Harry's taste. How sad he
would have been, though, to know that the cricket life of gaunt,
grimy Bramall Lane, so rich in history, had but a few more years
to run !

In Sheffield the first call was to the Cathedral, followed by a
refresher at the wine-merchants of which Norman Yardley was in

charge, and a sociable lunch, with Norman also present, at the Sheffield Club. On the way home the pair of them stopped at a bat-making workshop 'where Harry enjoyed himself enormously'. After a rest at home, with the aid of a tennis-ball, he gave a net to David's son (and my Godson) Christopher, aged eight. In due course under Norman Yardley's chairmanship he 'talked as well as he always did about the history of cricket to the Sheffield Cricket Society'. A nightcap and a bath was the prescribed end to the strenuous day. His bath was run for him, and when he failed to emerge was found dead on the bathroom floor. His end had come suddenly and peacefully as it might have done at any time, for he had had a warning a year or two before. Could his last hours, I wonder, have been more characteristically spent?

Harry Altham was the product of a family with a distinguished tradition of service – of a kind we may dwell on for a moment since it shaped the public school and university generations of his day, so large a proportion of which perished in the 1914–18 War. Harry's grandfather was Major W. S. Altham of the 83rd Foot, and his father likewise proceeded from Winchester and Sandhurst into the Royal Scots, of which he duly became Colonel. In Lieutenant-General Sir Edward Altham's career, as it was sketched in *The Times* obituary, can be traced characteristics reflected strongly in that of his son. Born in the year before the Indian Mutiny he was only 22 when appointed adjutant of his regiment. Having served in South Africa he passed through Staff College, but promotion was slow in the afternoon of the Pax Britannica and he was 40 when he returned to the Cape as assistant military secretary to the Governor-General and Commander-in-Chief. In that capacity he compiled the Intelligence Manual which formed the basis of opera-tions when the Boer War broke out in 1899. Though he saw action throughout South Africa and became full Colonel in 1903 he was put on half-pay for a while, during which he contributed military articles to the Press, and notably the *Morning Post*.

Harry's father was 58 at the outbreak of the Great War, wherein he successively took charge of the administration on Salisbury Plain, went to Gallipoli to organize the transport and supply services at Mudros, filled staff jobs in Egypt, and finally spent three strenuous years as Quartermaster-General in India before retiring in 1920 at the age of 64. By now he was KCB, KCIE and CMG; he had

85

collected in the Great War eight mentions in dispatches.

The last 23 years of General Altham's long life, at Winchester, he devoted to his old school and to the Church. His elder brother, Altham Surtees Altham, was a priest of Anglo-Catholic convictions which he communicated to the younger Edward. The priest had 'a great capacity for love and happiness' which he spread widely in a ministry that lasted 55 years and included no fewer than four curacies and five livings, mostly in the diocese of Exeter. The General in his retirement served on diocesan committees and chaired the Winchester branch of the Church Union. But Harry inherited, if not the high churchmanship, not only his father's energy and organizational ability right through to old age but also through his paternal grandmother a strong literary association. For she was a sister of the poet, Elizabeth Barrett Browning, and Robert Browning, that enigmatic figure whose bones rest beside those of Chaucer in Westminster Abbey, was therefore her brother-in-law.

When *The Barretts of Wimpole Street* was produced in 1930 the General was one of twelve grandchildren who protested vehemently in *The Times* against the portrayal of Mr Barrett, with the result that the character was modified by the playwright, Rudolf Besier. The author of the *Morning Post*'s military articles must have viewed with special pride those early essays of Harry's in the *Cricketer* which he amplified into *A History*.

So much for the General : enough surely to see whence emanated Harry's capacity – in Hubert Doggart's words – to communicate to the young his own vitality, optimism, convictions and his simple belief that life was there to be lived with zest, honour, purpose and courage.

Clearly he possessed from youth up the attributes of leadership. Equally he was lucky in that Repton cricket in his day was so strong. Harry was given his colours in 1905, by J. N. Crawford whose record supports the claim many times made (by H.S.A. not least) that he was the best-ever schoolboy cricketer. Harry's record over his four years in the XI was competent rather than spectacular, and I dare say that a just verdict was that of the great Charles Toppin of Malvern in *Wisden* when he rated him more the made than the natural cricketer. This is borne out by the fact of his not getting a Blue until his third year, Oxford being thus deprived, according to his contemporary, Dick Sale the elder, of an outstanding captain. However, Harry was one of the four members of his 1908 Repton XI who played for their counties that same August, and in his first match for Surrey, against Leicestershire at the Oval, he made 35 out of 67 in less than an hour. 'Showing no sign of nervousness he played as coolly as if he had been taking part in a quiet game at school,' said the *Morning Post*. Only Tom Hayward, with 39, got more. Harry's 47 in the second innings of the University Match of 1911 did much to win the match, but otherwise he did not accomplish much either for Oxford or Surrey.

The innings of his life was played in 1921 at Canterbury for Hampshire, whom he now assisted in the school holidays. It was Frank Woolley's benefit match, and Frank still remembers the innings with gratitude for it prolonged a game which otherwise would have ended on the second day. As it was, Kent won by eight wickets only on the third evening. Hampshire had batted first on an awkward pitch, and collapsed against Woolley and Freeman for 68. Kent accordingly acquired a long lead, Godfrey Bryan (179) and Lionel Hedges making 208 together in a couple of hours. They seemed set for an early victory when Harry took command. He made 141 without a chance in $3\frac{1}{2}$ hours, and though there is no need to accept the later claim of Gerry Weigall – always prone to superlatives, whether of praise or censure – that it was the finest innings ever played at Canterbury save for 205 by Bradman, a comparison which was also made with Maclaren's 226 in 1896 is easier to appreciate.

For Harry's batting was founded essentially on classic principles, with high back-lift, a predominant top hand, left knee well bent in the forward stroke, and head thrust over the line of the ball. He thought himself a better bat, incidentally, in his late thirties and early forties than before because he was then stronger on the onside. By then he had given up county cricket. Schoolmastering allowed him only a few weeks in August. The fact is that like many others he would probably have developed into a very fine player but for the war and the calls of his profession. What is sure is that many years of coaching gave him a knowledge of the techniques of the game in all its aspects, not only batting, that was second to none. Since there are those who set their faces against coaching at cricket on the ground that it produces cricketers of dull uniformity, and since Harry was always vehement in its defence, I may here pause to quote an ample and convincing reply he made to the denigrators of coaching in an article he wrote for a text-book sponsored by Gillette:

The whole of cricket history challenges them. Was not William Beldham, greatest of all batsmen in the Hambledon era, coached by Harry Hall, the gingerbread-maker of Farnham? Did not W.G. always look back with gratitude to the coaching he had when a small boy in the family orchard net from his Uncle Pocock, and to his formidable mother's insistence that if he concentrated on playing straight he would go one better than even his greatly gifted, but unco-ordinated, elder brother E.M.? Were not the very foundations of Australian cricket laid by Lawrence and Caffyn, who stayed behind to coach in that country after our first two tours there? And, to come down to today, would not Sir Leonard Hutton agree that the foundations of his batting were laid in the Headingley nets, and Messrs May, Cowdrey, Dexter and Sheppard say the same about the coaching they had at their schools? 'Ah,' comes the quick rejoinder, 'what about the greatest of them all, Sir Donald Bradman? He was never coached, and look what he was and did.'

The answer to that, I think, is that Sir Donald was a phenomenon from which it is dangerous to argue. First, he had extraordinary gifts of eye, speed of reaction, and physical co-ordination; second, he had, and I may add has, an exceptionally astute analytical mind, coupled with icy concentration and relentless determination. What he did in fact was to coach himself by watching, analysing, and then by unremitting practice, even by himself, working out what he wanted to be able to do with the bat, exactly how it should be done, and then getting down to doing it until he was satisfied – and Sir Donald is not easily content. Surely, too, it is significant that he, the outstanding 'natural' batsman of his own, or perhaps any, generation, should also be the author of one of the best coaching books ever produced. Clearly Sir Donald believes that there is a technique in cricket which in fact pays, and one that can be both taught and learnt.

Nor is it surprising when we look a bit closer at the problem. The basic background is the plain fact that cricket is not a natural

game : we walk, we run, we write, we drive, we ride 'full
chested', but cricket, whether batting, bowling or fielding (except
in pure defence), must be played sideways. If we pick up a club
or a bat – the words are in fact synonymous – our natural instinct
is to grip it more tightly with the bottom hand to swing it cross-
wise; but that is exactly what you must not do at the crease if
you want to stay there; you have got to hold on with the top
hand, and swing it not across but down the line of the ball.

To play a forward or back stroke right means mastering what
is very far from being a natural movement, but master it you can
if you are shown how, and master it you must if you are to be
able to stay at the wicket long enough to exploit whatever natural
ability you have for hitting the ball : and when it comes to attack,
what a reinforcement to that natural ability it is when the coach
explains that the wider the half-volley you want to drive, the
more you must turn the back of the left shoulder on the bowler
and lead with it out and on to the line : that the secret of all
driving lies in the initial dip of the left shoulder, and that, if you
want to cut securely and effectively, you must just pick your bat
up high, and that you cannot do that if your right elbow is tucked
into your side; even in the 'natural' cross-bat strokes the young
player will not unaided realize that if he is to play them safely
and effectively he has got to get his head on to the line of the
ball, and then keep it still, and that the ball should be hit with
a whip of the arms and hands, and not by any heave of the body.

It is just the same with bowling and fielding. However naturally gifted a boy may be, he can only make the most of these gifts
by being helped to understand the right techniques, and
encouraged to persevere in practising and mastering them. To
take two simple examples – how many young bowlers realize unaided the importance of keeping their left shoulder pointed at
the target as long as possible in the act of delivery? And how
many young fielders automatically 'get down early', stay down,
and watch the ball right into their hands?

I could continue on these lines almost indefinitely; suffice it
to say that in every department of the game there are basic
principles which all the great players have in fact observed far
more than they have ever disregarded. But to coach boys in
them should never mean that we turn out 'robots' playing on a

uniform pattern. The end product will inevitably vary within wide limits according to a boy's 'make-up', whether of physique, temperament, or that indefinable something which we call 'ball sense' : the worst of all coaching sins is to stop a boy from hitting, still more from wanting to hit, the ball. But the more he can be helped to hit it right, the better chance he will have of going on hitting it.

Harry himself was a superb coach because not only did he 'know it all' but because his own enthusiasm was so evidently communicable. Thus he brought the best out of the generations he taught at Winchester, and also after his retirement out of those he taught to coach in the MCC Youth Cricket Association classes at Lilleshall. It is with this wider activity that he made the most lasting of his contributions to cricket. He had been elected to the MCC Committee in 1941 when his house-mastership of Chernocke had still six years to run. By 1948 that highly demanding episode in his life was over, and on September of that year he and I instigated a productive correspondence in the *Daily Telegraph* following the wholesale English defeats at the hands of Bradman's Australians.

A national scheme for the encouragement of youth was Harry's answer, and when in the following year he chaired the Cricket Enquiry Committee at Lord's (one of the several investigations set up to examine the health and future development of the game) a recommendation to this effect was its most important outcome. Hence the MCC YCA which, started with a capital grant of £15,000 from the Club, was thenceforward run on a county basis, and later transformed into the present National Association of Young Cricketers.

The NAYC is one body catering for boys of all ages; the English Schools Cricket Association – in one way complementary, in another a friendly rival – is the other. Into the work of ESCA also Harry threw himself, functioning for seven years as its President. In short, most of the present concentrated organizational activity on behalf of boys' cricket can be traced back to his grasping of the nettle in 1948. Yet he would be the first to point to the help that has come from other quarters, in particular from Gubby Allen, his successor as Treasurer of MCC. The Cricket Enquiry, from which the rest sprang, was in fact Gubby's brainchild.

It was one of Harry's regrets that he never went to Australia to see a Test series, but I suppose it was the next best thing that he chaired the Test selectors who chose the team that retained the Ashes in 1954/5 and in so doing, under Len Hutton's captaincy, won a series in Australia for the first time for more than twenty years. As it happened 1954 was a summer of almost unparalleled wetness and the initial visit to England of the new State of Pakistan suffered grievously from the weather, so what for Harry was a ridiculously overdue Sabbatical could have been ordered more happily. However, the 'end product' was achieved, and to him must go a due proportion of the credit for the unexpected, adventurous and, of course, triumphantly successful choices of Tyson and Cowdrey.

Of Harry's work as a schoolmaster others have written from first-hand in *The Heart of Cricket*, notably Jim Hornby and John Gammell. To one who spent an occasional night or two in Chernocke, as I did, now and then, his lively interest in all his boys – and certainly not only the more gifted – whether in work or sport was transparent. 'If you are really to find yourself,' he used to say to his new boys on their arrival, 'you must lose yourself in something bigger : in your house, in your school, and in the people in it. For, after all, the thing that you really go to school to learn is not how to play games, or even how to pass exams, but how to live, and living means sharing with and giving to others.'

Though his house was highly successful by the concrete criteria of cups and scholarships, what they were mattered more than what they did. I recall the surprise with which he once received my enquiry as to who prepared the boys of his house for confirmation. Without, of course, disparaging the chaplains ('the pros', after all) in any way, how could I possibly think he might have entrusted the matter to anyone else?

Harry was 71 when, on the nomination, according to tradition, of his predecessor, Lord Portal of Hungerford, he became President of MCC. Having been Treasurer since 1950 he knew the ropes as well as anyone – the historical background, the personalities, the procedures, the chain of command, and so on. And it was as well the head man was so exceptionally qualified for 1959/60 proved an exceptionally eventful and contentious year. When he took office feelings were unusually tender following the throwing troubles on the MCC Australian tour just ended. On the County front the echoes of the post-war boom had faded some time since and MCC were accordingly asked by the counties to initiate yet another enquiry.

In May 1960 South Africa left the Commonwealth and so automatically debarred herself from the Imperial Cricket Conference (as it was still called) due to meet as usual under the President's chairmanship in July. As if this were not enough to tax Harry's diplomacy the South Africans, who chanced to be touring England that summer, had brought with them in Geoffrey Griffin a blatant 'chucker'. Moreover, though the unfortunate young man had been called for throwing innumerable times by several umpires, the South Africans persisted in picking him again for the Lord's Test. There the inevitable happened, after which for the remainder of the summer Griffin was not chosen, and the ordeal for all concerned was mercifully suspended.

There followed in July the most momentous of all ICC meetings, with Sir Donald Bradman and W. J. Dowling representing Australia and every country sending its top brass to debate the throwing business. Harry's chairmanship earned the praise of all, but how willingly would he have forgone the plaudits in exchange for a peaceful Presidency! There was trouble, too, on the home front in the form of a book by Jim Laker, or, rather, a ghosted one under his name – considered to be so scurrilous that the MCC Committee withdrew his honorary membership. (It has since been restored.) One way and another it must have been with relief that he handed over to one of his earliest pupils and most distinguished of Wyke-hamists, Sir Hubert Ashton.

Less than five years later Hubert was making the address at the Memorial Service to his old friend in Winchester Cathedral, with every stone of which he was familiar. The congregation was recommended to the words of the Prophet Micah: 'What doth the Lord require of thee, but to do justly, and to love mercy, and to walk humbly before thy God.' And if they thought them apt as relating to H.S.A., many present must have applied them in their minds equally to his devoted widow, Alison, who as I write, in her 87th year, is still hale and insistent on keeping dusted and tidy the side chapel behind the Cathedral high altar which serves as his memorial.

In *The Heart of Cricket* there are, of course, many stories told by and about Harry. Let me end by repeating one related by George Cox since the situation and the remark must have appealed to him. Returning together to Winchester one evening from a day's cricket at Hove, George and Harry came to Tillington. This is George's description :

I said, 'There's a lovely cricket ground up there. I've seen a Medici print of a cricket match and you can tell it's Tillington by the coroneted church tower behind.' 'Let's go,' said H.S.A., and although it was getting towards dusk we turned right to the church and were directed up through the village.

There on the left, as we neared the top of a rise in the Weald, we saw the little cricket ground with its small pavilion up on the right and the men of Tillington in the middle, standing, as in an old print, in shirt sleeves and braces, against the skyline, and the great line of the Downs in the background. There was no movement on or off the field. It was one of those lovely still evenings in May and but for the chuck-chucking of a blackbird in the hedgerow and an occasional comment from cover-point all was quiet. We stood entranced – for quite a while – neither of us speaking. Then a small boy got up from the long grass where he'd been watching with his friend and passed in front of us.

I said, to find out what match was going on, 'What game is this ?'

He looked aghast at me, and then he looked at H.S.A., future President of MCC, past England Selector, Historian of Cricket, and in the voice of a true son of the Sussex countryside replied, 'CRICKET.'

George Cox was a cricket enthusiast close to Harry's heart, and so, too, though of a very different temperament, was Walter Robins. When in the spring of 1965 Harry died, Walter – or Robbie as many knew him – wrote me from home to Barbados where I was watching the Test series between the West Indies and Australia. Having registered his pleasure that the Australians looked to be in for a beating (as duly happened), Walter said he had been to Lord's to watch his Godson, Patrick Compton, son of Denis, being coached in the Easter classes, and he found the conditions 'abominable', both under cover and outside. He let himself go with characteristic gusto :

> To think that since 1908 the Rugby Union over the years has lent £400,000 at 2% to enable clubs to buy their grounds, and here we are at headquarters with £300,000 in securities, re-developing the corner-site, putting up a 17-storey block of flats in order to finance the rebuilding of the Tavern and Boxes. Alas, so far there is no thought of building a cricket school for clubs and boys to practise in during the winter; but if they did what a memorial it would make for H.S.A. – the greatest of them all. So far at Lord's we have the Grace Gates, the Harris Garden, and the Warner Stand, but in my humble opinion Harry very quietly did more for cricket than any of them.

Walter's final claim for Harry is indeed a large one. But no one would dispute that an Indoor School (which was indeed part of the major development plan of 1970) would have been his most fitting memorial. However, better late than never. The new MCC Indoor School is about to open its doors as I write, and Harry's full-length portrait in flannels decorates what will be for ever known as the Altham Room. On one side it gives out on to the viewing gallery for the indoor nets, while from the window on the other one sees the green grass of the Nursery and all ages busy at practice the summer through.

7
Eminent All-rounders

The writing of such a chapter as this fulfils my first test in that it gives me pleasure. The man who can play games well as a preparation or accompaniment to achieving success in the sterner things of life is entitled to our admiration. There is also the undoubted fact that in these highly competitive days there is more compulsion on the average mortal to specialize in every form of activity, sporting and otherwise. Thus time may show – though let it be hoped not – that these words are something of a tribute to a dying breed. My modest terms of reference are that (with one exception) these men must be, or have been, known to me. Nor is even this qualification in any way inclusive. Moreover I have already said a good deal about Harry Altham and other figures of distinction, while to C. B. Fry, the greatest Corinthian of all, I paid my humble tribute in *SOCP*. Tuppy Owen-Smith, who must be very high on any such list, I shall reserve for my Oxford chapter.

I begin with a figure of world acclaim much interested in cricket – not that he was himself a notable player. When I came back from the MCC tour of Australia of 1958/9 my editor, Colin Coote, said: 'Would you care to meet Monty? He's very interested in what happened in Australia, and he'd like you to go down to Hampshire and see him.' When I called his number it was 'Montgomery speaking' two seconds after the bell had begun to ring, and arrangements for a visit were crisply made.

My first thought was that the reigning President of MCC, who was Lord Portal, was going to nominate another great war-leader to succeed him, and I was therefore selected to give him a briefing on what had been an unexpectedly unsuccessful tour. I even lightly (and perhaps with slight malice aforethought) mentioned the idea to one or two great men of Lord's who received it with consternation, and not surprisingly. Monty would certainly have ruffled a few feathers, which might have been no bad thing. But, as I was to discover, he knew very little about cricket – too little indeed to realize how much there would have been to learn in a year's tenure of the game's highest office.

Harry Altham was then Treasurer and I recalled his telling me how, soon after the war, Monty wrote to Hampshire (of which Harry was President) saying he intended to come down to see a certain day's play. He would arrive at 11.20 and trusted that the teams would be lined up ready for his inspection. But the great showman picked the wrong man in Harry, who said in reply that only a royal visit carried with it a formal presentation of teams. He was sure, however, they would be glad to meet him in their dressing-rooms. And this is what happened.

Monty's house at Isington Mill when I kept the appointment was, of course, a great fascination, and luckily cricket didn't play a very big part in our conversation. It was easy enough to imagine, meeting him in his advancing years, what a tonic in North Africa his unshakable self-confidence must have been to men of all ranks, hard-pressed and with the experience of bitter defeat. I wonder, by the way, whether in a pre-battle briefing of officers he really did utter the words: 'Our Lord said – and in my view rightly . . .' Having a bishop for a father he was much inclined to quote the scriptures.

Unfortunately, though H. H. Montgomery must have been a capable cricketer – he had the misfortune to play for Cambridge in every match of the season except the University Match – little in the way of subtle appreciation of the game filtered down from father to son. Monty saw it as a simple, uncomplicated exercise wherein everything boiled down to leadership, as may be judged from the following letter – sent while he was staying with Sir Winston Churchill at Chartwell – during the ten years or so through which our periodic correspondence lasted:

Chartwell,
Westerham,
Kent.
30th August, 1964.

My dear Swanton,

I was greatly interested in the comments contained in your letter dated 28 August. I must confess that I did not understand the part played by the Chairman of the Selectors. But the analogy you suggest about the C.I.G.S. (now the C.G.S.) and a Commander-in-Chief is not a correct parallel.

The C.I.G.S. recommended a suitable C-in-C to the Prime Minister, because it is a political appointment. For instance, my appointment to the Eighth Army, and later to 21 Army Group, was made by Winston Churchill – who was Minister of Defence and also Prime Minister.

A C-in-C, or Captain, having been appointed, he chooses his own team. A C-in-C in the field is a very powerful person. I chose my own staff, and my own generals, and the C.I.G.S. (the Chairman of the Selectors) never disputed my wishes. I was always given what I asked for by the War Office – so long as I was successful and won my battles (my Test Matches). Of course if I had lost battles things would have been different; indeed, I would most probably have been sacked myself; however that never arose because I made it a habit to win my Test Matches!

I now understand the immense importance in the past of the Chairman of the Selectors in the cricket world. But it may be that the whole structure, the whole machinery of selecting teams for international battles, requires revision. Should not the M.C.C. appoint the Captain?

Is there a need for anybody else? I would have thought that the M.C.C. and the Captain could do the job themselves – the Captain choosing his own team. In fact, I would abolish the Selectors; with a group of that sort, all having different opinions, the final result will always be compromise – and that is the beginning of failure, the way to lose battles.

Let the Captain choose his own team, turning for advice to the President of the M.C.C. and the Secretary of the M.C.C. as necessary.

To sum up I would have the Captain appointed by the M.C.C. He chooses his own team, turning for advice to the President and to Billy Griffith. The Selectors are 'out'.

What have you to say to that?

Yours Sincerely (signed)

Montgomery of Alamein

P.S. You are at perfect liberty to quote me whenever you like – if, of course, you wish to do so.

As from: Isington Mill, Alton, Hampshire.

There have been times no doubt when we would all have liked to abolish the selectors and pick the England XI ourselves – even without the President of MCC to help us. But there have been few captains, if any, who would either want or would be confidently accorded such a responsibility. The Australian captain is never even on the selection committee.

When I tried to explain some of the technical clues Monty was inclined to lose interest and say, 'I know about batting. I went in first for St Paul's and was *vewwy* successful.'

How successful? Thanks to some kind research by W. St P. M. Hancock, the Bursar of St Paul's, I have a mental picture of Monty's cricket in 1906, his last summer, when he finished top of the averages (37.2) and was described as 'a fine bat with a beautiful shot past cover . . . Has made an energetic secretary.' That is not hard to credit. However, 'his ground-fielding leaves room for improvement, and he also tires very quickly in the field'. This might well be the only time his stamina was ever brought into question! High hopes were entertained for him in 1907, but by then he had passed into Sandhurst, and that seems to have been almost the end of his cricket, though he played a little in India. Monty, by the way, was one of those whose schooldays, according to his memoirs, were happy ones. 'For the first time in my life leadership and authority came my way' : he was captain of the Rugby XV.

And what was Monty's best innings? A nice touch here – it was his 87 against London County wherein, when W.G. came on to bowl, Monty 'hooked his slows to the boundary with great persistency'.

Greek meeting Greek! I suppose this may have been Monty's first encounter with fame. Granted that W.G. was in his fifties, he had recently taken eight wickets against the first West Indian side to come over, and he was the last man in the world to 'let up' against schoolboys.

After we had had a very good lunch on this first meeting – with a glass of wine for me, water for him – I was shown the treasures both inside the house and out : notably the two caravans, one which had been with him from Alamein to the German surrender at Luneberg, the other, distinctly more elaborate, probably used by Rommel. It had a bath and shower, and Monty's habit, he said, was to sleep in the bigger and work in the smaller caravan. He moved out for only two people, the King and Winston. No common-or-garden MP ever got near his tactical HQ, let alone the caravans.

In front of the caravans was the original notice-board which was at once set up on the precise spot proclaiming that at Luneberg on 4 May 1945 Monty had received the surrender of 'All German Armed Forces in Holland, in North-West Germany including all islands, and in Denmark'. He told me how a night or two later the board disappeared, and so he ordered the mayor of Luneberg to be sent for. The mayor was apologetic but in the circumstances there was little he could do. He would make enquiries. Monty continued: 'I told him, "If that board is not back in position in twenty-four hours you will be shot." Of course, I wouldn't have shot him: but he didn't know that. Next morning the board was returned.'

To stick for a moment to eminent men of the world who have had sporting connexions, Lord Home of the Hirsel in his memoirs *The Way the Wind Blows* has said something of himself as a school and undergraduate cricketer. According to his contemporary, Gubby Allen, he had a lateish out-swing and pace off the pitch, and though he didn't get a Blue he came as near to it as going with the 1926 Oxford side on tour. He is the only British Prime Minister to have played first-class cricket, and when afterwards the Tories were in opposition made the ideal President of MCC in that he knew quite enough about cricket yet was not too close to the politics of it.

Lord Home's successor as Tory leader, Edward Heath, is, of course, renowned as a yachtsman, is an enthusiastic supporter of Kent cricket and did at one time dabble with golf. A bag of clubs was to be seen when Ann and I went to Chequers for the dinner-party he gave to bid farewell to Sir Robert Menzies on what proved to be his last visit, and it was as a member of Royal St George's that Mr Heath when PM brought to Sandwich his Jap opposite number, Mr Tanaka, and some of his entourage. He said later that after the golf the talks atmosphere, which had been rather frigid, went with a swing.

The secretary of St George's, Brigadier Geoffrey Walker, with the ultimate in tact advised me and the only other fellow-member who had been taken prisoner in the Far East in advance that the Japs were coming in case we might wish to keep away. General Billy Key, who commanded the 11th Indian Division in Malaya, did so. I on the other hand was not going to miss my golf, and in the smoking Room suddenly found myself being bowed at and shaking hands with Tanaka in person. I believe his is quite a common name in Japan – in any case it was not the occasion to enquire whether he was related to the Tarsao camp-commander who had the reputation of being the worst on the Burma–Siam railway.

In view of Prime Minister Tanaka's subsequent disgrace, involving charges of corruption, it would be churlish not to mention that on his visit to Sandwich he was conspicuously open-handed, giving presents to his opponents and their caddies as well as to the club itself. In the ladies' room – part of an institution the membership of which is wholly male – we are reminded of him by the figure of a geisha girl looking out, perhaps a shade self-consciously, from her glass-case at our wives and families.

Another holder of high office, the late and much lamented Lord Cobham, one-time Governor-General of New Zealand, led Worcestershire, and was a violent hitter. Looking at what is now the Frank Woolley stand at Canterbury it is hard to imagine anyone hitting clean over it, as he did, reputedly having the ill-luck also to smash the windscreen of his car parked behind. Charles Cobham also bowled very slow off-breaks and was one of only two men who to my knowledge gave the ball such a tweak that one could hear the buzz – he's in good company, for Arthur Mailey was the other.

The late Duke of Norfolk, another man of power of a different sort, was so widely respected for his life of service that his favourite diversions, cricket and racing, were positively lifted by his association with them. I have told in *SOCP* of the unique impact he made in Australia and West Indies.

One of my earliest acquaintances with a man of affairs who was also a sportsman dates from the start of my time at the *Evening Standard*. My room – shared with Eckersley, the greyhound forecaster, and Maplesden, the lawyer who in theory had to vet every word that went into the paper but in the rush of editions was generally one or more behind – was next door to that of the grandees of 'The Londoner's Diary'. At the head of this galaxy was Bruce-Lockhart, author then of *Memoirs of a British Agent* and of much else since including the *Diaries*, edited by Kenneth Young, which to an old Beaverbrook employee make fascinating reading.

The diaries are sprinkled with his golf, but he was always coming in to me and exchanging gossip on Rugby football. He was scrum-half in the famous Fettes XV of 1904/5 and an exact contemporary of the great K. G. McLeod, whom he idolized, and of another pre-first-war Scottish international, Moir Mackenzie. They were the days when as many as six Fettesians played for Scotland against the first All Blacks: no wonder that at Cambridge a pair of red Fettes stockings was said to be a passport for a Blue! When Bruce talked of Fettes and the game north of the border, Balkan politics, the Russian revolution, all the rest of his stock-in-trade were forgotten, a Scottish lilt came into his voice and a sparkle to his eye. He was one of a company of older men who went out of their way to help me as a young journalist.

Kenneth McLeod I met in his late middle-age at the Cape where he lived, still a magnificent figure of a man and with the charm towards the younger generation that was so characteristic of his own. Talk of all-rounders! What about him? He would probably have been picked to play Rugby for Scotland as a schoolboy but his headmaster forbade it. As it was he got a Scottish cap as well as a Blue as a freshman, and though he gave up the game on coming down from Cambridge he had already established himself as one of the greatest of centre threequarters. He won the 100 yards twice in the University Sports and dead-heated a third time, and played twice for Cambridge at Lord's. For Lancashire his fielding and at times his hitting were legendary. He was nicknamed 'Grunt' – or that's how the Scots seemed to pronounce it, for his second name was Grant – and he gave up football to please his father after his brother L. M., a double Blue and International only slightly less talented, had died at Cambridge of the then dreaded appendicitis. *A Hundred Years of Fettes* proclaims K.G. as the supreme athlete in that he performed brilliantly at all while troubling about none.

Still in the world of letters let it not be forgotten that Sir William Collins, who commissioned this book though, alas, he did not live to read and advise me on it, was a Corinthian Casuals player at football, a Wimbledon lawn-tennis player, and an extremely good bowler at Harrow where he was two years captain of the XI. I like to remember that we led opposing sides in the annual Vincent-Square battle between the Authors and Publishers. Billy was as admirable an example of 'the complete man' as one could hope to find.

Two of the most successful dramatists of the last forty years have it in common that both have written a play or film about a Test Match, and both in *Who's Who* list their recreation simply as 'watching cricket'. Ben Travers, still hale and writing at 90, and Terence Rattigan have, it is true, been more patrons than players, though Terence followed father and uncles into the Harrow XI. What was not in the family tradition was getting in one year and being left out the next, and he was said hardly to have been forgiven until, scarcely down from Oxford, he suddenly came up with *French Without Tears*.

Not long ago, having spoken to a college society in Oxford, I was asked by the secretary if I could confirm with Rattigan a tentative agreement to address them. But no luck. He wrote me a frivolous note : 'Do you seriously think I'd have the temerity to follow you? It would be like doing a *pas seul* after Nureyev, or going in to bat after 100 in 85 minutes by Don Bradman. Never fear. I only choose to speak to audiences without previous stars in their eyes, like the Bermuda Ladies' Dramatic Society.'

I come now to three men for whom games were a relaxation in lives of rich fulfilment, G. R. Girdlestone, J. C. Masterman and J. L. S. Vidler, friends of one another and all in their later years well known to me. Gathorne Girdlestone, born in 1881, was ten years the senior of the other two, so we may give him pride of place. He was one of the great pioneers of orthopaedic surgery who used the grim lessons learned with the RAMC in the first war for the benefit of cripples after it. He and a colleague, Sir Robert Jones, started a national campaign which culminated in 1920, long years before the Health Service was thought of, in the Central Council for the Relief of Cripples. Gathorne's work was centred on the Wingfield Hospital at Oxford, the city of William Morris, later Lord Nuffield, who became his admirer and patron.

The combination of Gathorne's professional skill and Nuffield's millions, and the consuming drive and energy of them both, made Oxford a famous centre for orthopaedic treatment and research. When the second war came the Churchill Hospital arose, largely designed by Gathorne, as a complement to the Wingfield-Morris to which was attracted a brilliant Spanish surgeon, called Joseph Trueta, who became Gathorne's No. 2.

Gathorne was a strikingly handsome man, whose presence made

a positive impact wherever he went. He was deeply religious, and used to take me to hear Evensong at New College and afterwards dine in Hall. We also played golf at Frilford, I, 25 years younger, struggling to keep up. He played golf, as he did everything else, briskly and passionately. His philosophy on the links was quoted by J. C. Masterman in his autobiography *On the Chariot Wheel*: 'When you have a critical putt to hole it is the most important thing in the world; after you have missed it nothing could matter less.' He won a golf Blue in the days when the University Match was a one-day affair decided by singles, and built a house at Frilford for a retirement with Ina, his wife, that he was destined never to enjoy. For he died in almost full harness at 69.

Anyone who wishes to criticize the Honours system can think of many deserving cases who have been neglected. Gathorne was an uncompromising fellow who put a few backs up in his time, and that could have been a reason why he had no official recognition outside his profession. Perhaps something was offered and declined. At any rate, no one in my experience gave his talents so unsparingly and devotedly to the service of his fellow-men.

Much the same could be said of John Vidler in the field of penal reform, wherein he also was a pioneer whose work lives after him. Nor were his efforts ever officially recognized. He was a contemporary at Repton of Harry Altham who gave him his colours and afterwards played with him for Oxford. John was one of the seven members of the Repton side of 1907 who subsequently played first-class cricket. This was a vintage time both for Repton and for Oxford. He was also a golf Blue and in late years captain of Rye.

John's progressive ideas were first seen at Borstal, from which he graduated to Maidstone Gaol. Though I never saw him in these environments it is not difficult to imagine his methods and easy to believe their success. He was the most natural, unaffected, straightforward person imaginable, whose manner towards a prisoner would be exactly the same as to anyone else. In his obituary notice for the *Cricketer* J.C. described him as in the best sense 'classless', and with a wonderful power of making contact and creating sympathy. In *The Times* it was said:

To serve under him was like living with a dynamo on one side and a volcano on the other. He made outrageous demands on all his staff and they loved him for it. After his retirement he returned to his beloved Rye, where he played golf, running the Dormy House Club rather in the way he ran Maidstone Prison.

I can testify to that – also that the Dormy was never more popular than during his time there.

Of all those mentioned in this book whose careers bear testimony to the value of the *mens sana* ideal no one has exemplified it over a long life to greater effect than John Masterman, known universally as 'J.C.'. His fascinating *On the Chariot Wheel* has been so recently published that for many of my readers a précis of his career will be superfluous. Yet I refuse to deny myself the main facts before turning to his sporting prowess. J.C. on the strength of a First in modern history was appointed to a Lectureship at Christ Church in 1913, but was ordered a change of scenery in Germany for a year, and at the swift onset of war the following August failed to get out in time and accordingly with many other English unfortunates was interned at the famous Ruhleben Camp for its four-year duration.

Between the wars he was a don at Christ Church, and as such saw a highly distinguished band of Englishmen through the history school. When the second war came he made up, with a great deal to spare, for the service he had been unable to give in the first. Behind the bare reference-book entry 'Major (Local) and specially employed' lies the story of the 'turning' of the entire German espionage network in Britain to serve Allied ends by the system (which he had the prime share in perfecting and administering) known as the 'Double Cross'. Back at Oxford in 1945 J.C. became for fourteen years Provost of his old college, Worcester, during which time he served as Vice-Chancellor of the University. The reputation of Worcester (so those whose opinions most merit respect informed me) reached a new peak during his Provostship, towards the end of which – unlike his friends Girdlestone and Vidler – he was honoured with a Knighthood.

Well into his 71st year J.C. had surely earned a retirement devoted to writing and to the performance of those honorary functions for the public good which descend and stick like burrs on men of his capacity. But now he was offered an entirely new field of work as 'Adviser on Personnel Matters' to a large collection of industrial companies in the Birmingham area known as the 'Birfield Group'. For six years this concern had the benefit of J.C.'s unrivalled judgement of men and his capacity to induce harmony and friendly relations. He developed a high respect for the chairman of Birfield, Herbert Hill, whom he described as 'one of the truly great men' he had known, and despite his modest account it is clear that this last active phase of his working life was no less successful than any other.

It is almost certainly true that over the span of more than forty years John Masterman exercised a stronger influence over the University of Oxford in general and the undergraduates connected with Christ Church, Worcester, and Vincent's Club in particular than any other man, and it is clearly the case that despite his busy life he found time to play a wide variety of games. No doubt then his views on the value of the all-round character are predictable, but his own example at least gives them unusual weight. He is quite unequivocal.

He thinks the taunt more commonly heard today than of yore that games are a waste of time needs denying with all possible emphasis :

I do *not* think we pay too much attention to athletic success; I believe that games help the development of character and assist the growth of scholarship. In a word I am a whole-hearted supporter of those who believe that men should develop as what used to be called 'all-rounders'.

I can see a certain Harry Surtees Altham trilling contentedly on his harp as he comes upon these words in the celestial library.

J.C.'s athletic career should be an encouragement to those who might be supposing that one so highly gifted could easily reach the top at whatever form of activity took his fancy. It was not like that with him at all. Indeed, though he became an international at two games and first-class at three others, the only Blue he got was for athletics (he won the high jump for Oxford in 1912). After the war he played lawn tennis and hockey for England, and at the age of 45 achieved in the course of a week an improbable treble, scoring a couple of goals at hockey against Cambridge, and competing both in the President's Putter and the South of England Squash Championships.

He was scarcely a 'natural' in any of these games or for that matter at cricket where his run-up to bowl, knees and elbows at stiff angles, fingers splayed, rather resembled an agitated spider. It happened that I played cricket, golf and even hockey with him (I for Dulwich, he for Hampstead), and there was a strange angularity about his performance at all three. What was equally evident was a thoughtful and highly determined and competitive approach, whether on the cricket or hockey field or on the golf course. He was elected a Harlequin, and pulled his full weight when in his late forties he undertook a strenuous tour of Canada with MCC. His mother lived at Eastbourne, and I treasure the memory of happy days playing in his company at the Saffrons.

I must say something of another all-rounder I was fond of, of a rather different type, Glyn Hughes, the doctor and rugger personality always known as 'Hughie'. He was renowned chiefly for two things, his record in two wars, as a young man in the first and a comparatively old one in the second, and his long service for the Barbarians, that great and unique wandering club which for so many years seemed to revolve around his personality. But he was a familiar figure also in the golf worlds of St Andrews and Sandwich, and with the Lucifers, and he did much voluntary work of an administrative kind over many years for his fellow-doctors.

Service in fact was the keynote of his life, and I have known few men more widely admired, and with such good reason. In the first war as a young doctor he won the DSO and bar and the MC, and in the second, rising to be brigadier, a further bar to the DSO and was also created CBE. As DDMS, Second Army he was first into Belsen and his encounter with Kramer, the notorious camp commandant, made some of the most terrible evidence at the Nuremberg trials. Most communicative of men as a rule, Hughie could not be drawn on Belsen, and it was only after his death, reading the first-hand report of Richard Dimbleby who went in with him, that I fully realized why. Thirty years later it needs a strong stomach to take this passage in Jonathan Dimbleby's absorbing biography of his father.

Hughie toured South Wales with the 'Baa-Baas' Easter after Easter, first in 1912 as player, then as hon. sec., finally as President.

In 1972, 60 years on, the side in its last match and on what proved
to be his last tour strove to pay him a final compliment and
miraculously succeeded. They actually ran up – and against New-
port at that – their all-time record score of 60 points, the final try
bringing the tally to 60 being scored under the posts. Thereupon the
kicker made sure he missed the easy conversion that would have
spoiled the story.

The list of those I saw first engaged at Lord's and Twickenham
who have come to distinction in wider fields is a long one, and a
few examples must suffice. In the rugger world Wavell Wakefield
and Carl Aarvold come at once to mind, both captains of Cambridge and England who gave their services, respectively, to both
Houses of Parliament in one case and finally as Recorder of London
in the other.

George Abell never quite got as far as an international cap but
the breadth of his activities was wider than most, for he played
cricket for Oxford and Worcestershire, was captain of the OURFC,
and also had a hockey Blue yet withal took a First. This was the
prelude to a distinguished career in the Indian Civil Service that
culminated in his being Private Secretary to the Viceroy in the years
prior to independence and partition. Then followed a new career in
the City first as adviser and then a director to the Bank of England.
He occupied his final three years, before retirement allowed him to
accept honorary posts in the world of education, as First Civil
Service Commissioner. Was ever a knighthood better earned, or
games prepare a man for richer achievement?

Jack Davies (J.G.W.) has it in common with Abell that he
collected a cricket Blue and a first and was also a director of the
Bank of England. MCC are now lucky to have his services as
Treasurer in succession to Gubby Allen. Jack played long and
successfully for Kent, and incidentally reached the heights of an
international trial as a centre-threequarter for Blackheath, but is
always remembered as the man who bowled Bradman for a duck.
It was on a fair May morning at Fenner's in 1934, and though the
pitch was as flawless as ever Jack, in 'sneakers' as usual and with
sleeves flying loose, was bowling his off-breaks round the wicket.
The Don pushed forward, possibly playing for just a shade of turn,
and the ball hit the off-stump. Such was the victim's reputation that
the undergraduate crowd greeted the event with an embarrassed

silence, almost as though someone had committed some sudden gaffe
in a cathedral. Don mounted the pavilion steps with a wry smile,
saying, 'I reckon it must have slipped out of his hand.'

Talking of Bradman, here is a little-known fact that is evidence
of his extraordinary eye and speed of reaction. One Australian
winter in the mid-'30s he decided to take up squash. Ian McLachlan
(father of I. M. and A. A.) was rated a good player, yet Don beat
him within a few weeks of starting. He then went on in this first
season at the game to win the South Australian Championship.

More recently at Cambridge three other cricket figures, University and county captains all and Test players, have achieved a wider
fame. David Sheppard since I wrote of him in *SOCP* has passed
from the Suffragan bishopric of Woolwich to the see of Liverpool,
one of the most challenging jobs in the Church of England.

Hubert Doggart, who gave David his Blue, himself picked up
five Blues, for cricket, soccer, rackets, fives and squash, as well as
a reputable second in History. He was captain of four of them, a
distinction surely unrepeatable. After running both cricket and a
house at Winchester – a taxing double, as all have found who've
tackled it – he is now Headmaster of King's School, Bruton.

Mike Brearley, the third in this little category, was not so versatile
as Doggart nor so fine a bat as Sheppard but academically excelled
them both. In fact Mike brought off a first and an American fellowship – which makes it all the more laudable that in the winter, after
leading Middlesex with conspicuous success (Gillette and Benson
and Hedges finalists 1975, Championship 1976), he has chosen to
devote himself to the care of young people who are emotionally
disturbed.

Now all the dramatis personae of this chapter are, or have been,
either famous or fairly well known – and if that encourages a
further taunt of 'name-dropping' I need scarcely say I am wholly
unrepentant. Yet, of course, as I say, the field is a vast one, and
everyone who has read this far can think no doubt of other and
perhaps even better candidates. Equally they will know of others
who've been a shade less in the public eye – especially perhaps
among the dedicated, uncomplaining fraternity of schoolmasters.

From among these I select to bring up the rear, so far as the
moderns are concerned, an old friend who is not the least of the
products of Cranleigh. Vivian Cox, having been the big Pooh-Bah

at school, went up with an Exhibition to Jesus, Cambridge, in the mid-'30s. More than ordinarily good at every game, he had played two years at scrum-half for the English Schoolboys with his Cranleigh contemporary (who went on to play with much distinction for England) Jeffrey Reynolds, and so was an obvious candidate for a Blue even in those days of bounteous talent. When Vivian trotted out as a freshman to play for the 'Varsity against Blackheath he was the only man among the backs who was not then or very soon to became an international. He got star 'write-ups' but was rated too brilliantly individual to make the best link with Cliff Jones and Wilf Wooller, so he contented himself with playing for the OCs and for Surrey, and then, turning to hockey, won a Blue and played four times for England in the same season.

Early in the war when my Gunner battery were making a show of defending the east coast against the Führer our rugger XV came back one day to headquarters much cast down at having suffered a crushing reverse at the hands of a naval side for whom 'a little old beggar with a beard' apparently made rings round them. Shortly afterwards I was visited by the culprit, Ordinary-Seaman Cox, who was one of a trawler minesweeping crew. He soon rose above that, finding himself on commission manning the Admiralty War Room, sailing with Churchill (after Pearl Harbour) to Washington and setting up his personal map-room at the White House. Roosevelt next had his services as naval attaché, in which capacity he designed and operated the White House map-room, where the major staff meetings are still held.

Action next. Vivian was chosen for Admiral (soon Lord) Fraser's staff, and in that capacity was on the flagship on various Malta and Arctic convoys, saw the sinking of the *Scharnhorst*, then took part in the Pacific operations in the Philippines and at Okinawa which culminated in the Jap surrender in Tokio Bay.

He went first after the war into films, producing Alec Guinness, Trevor Howard, Yul Brynner in, among others, *Father Brown, The Prisoner* and *The Long Duel*. Disillusioned with films – 'Wardour is the only street in the world on which both sides are shady' – he was recruited by David Emms to the staff at Cranleigh where he spent ten of the happiest years of his life.

Vivian retired at 60 but only as far as the Mermaid Theatre, in the invigorating atmosphere of which he is now producing and managing in alliance with Bernard Miles. Such is the full life of yet another all-rounder : it is fresh in my mind since I proposed his health in his year as chairman of the OC dinner.

I started the chapter with one Monty and I end with another Monty, the father-in-law whom I never knew. I told in *SOCP* how it was not until after he retired from his Eton house-mastership at the age of 55 that R. H. de Montmorency could play any top competitive golf, though earlier, just once in 1921 at Hoylake, he emerged from schoolmastering to represent Great Britain against the United States in the immediate precursor to the Walker Cup and suffered honourable defeat at the hands of the immortal Bobby Jones. It was after his retirement that he took a British side to tour South Africa, and did other things which he had denied himself earlier such as playing in the Open and Amateur Championships. Aged 56 he reached the last eight of the Amateur, but it was probably even more notable that at the half-way mark in the Open at St Andrews only Bobby Jones of the amateurs stood in front of him. Monty had sailed through the two qualifying rounds and began 74, 75 before the fifth and sixth rounds inside five days found him weakening a little. Even so with 309 he finished seventh amateur, and was there at the death, with Jones carried shoulder-high off the home green amid such scenes as had not before been seen on a golf course, his score of 285 being by six strokes the lowest winning score ever recorded. Bernard Darwin called it a 'stupendous feat' and was so full of his play and of the excitement of the crowds that, for once, he could not spare a word about Monty.

Bernardo generally did, and the tone was uniformly laudatory. He 'was blameless and trustworthy to an almost incredible degree even for him; he never put a foot wrong'. By all accounts – and there were many – he must have been one of the steadiest, straightest golfers ever, and, though strangely allergic to foursomes, everyone's choice as a foursomes partner. At one time, by the way, he held the amateur record for three courses, Rye (71), Stoke Poges (68) and Worplesdon (70). He also held two important offices in the game, the Presidency of the English Golf Union and of the Oxford and Cambridge Golfing Society, which he had helped to form.

The photograph of Monty with Percy Chapman opposite page 64 tells more of his nature surely than I can hope to do at second hand. Many of the comments after his death at the age of 67 are likewise revealing. Newspaper space was less precious forty years ago, but it is still significant of the powerful impression he made on people that the obituary notices of her father in Ann's cuttings-book add up to more than 150 column-inches.

There was the Eton connexion to be recorded – 27 years on the staff and a long and successful house-mastership; then the games including the winning of Blues for cricket and rackets as well as golf. (He was said to have been recommended by W.G., and if so the Old Man must have been pleased with his protégé's scores of 25 and 62 at Lord's, with a couple of wickets thrown in.) Much was inevitably written about his golf, but so much of the tribute was personal and clearly written from the heart. 'He was a kindly and intensely hospitable man, of a simple and straightforward character which commanded affection,' wrote Bernard Darwin.

Who could hope for a better epitaph?

8
A Few Old Buffers

In my earlier years as a club cricketer – I suppose I strictly mean until the outbreak of war in 1939 – variety and humour were added to the scene by a number of old fellows who seemed pretty ancient to us then – how they would appear on the club scene in these days of limited overs and everyone doing the hundred yards in even time is unthinkable. More's the pity. They did little harm in return for the labour of managing innumerable sides and clearly extracted vast pleasure from the game. Their cricket pedigrees were varied, ranging from some who had once been very good players to a few who never had been, and never could have been.

Of the former sort Hampstead was something of a repository, and my first recollection of the type takes me back to Bognor. We used to enjoy family holidays at Felpham nearby, propelled there by Dr Edwards aforesaid in his rather grand De Dion Bouton. Arthur Goodall used to run the Bognor side which at times would include a Gilligan or two, and in my later teens a place was sometimes found for me. The MCC colours of red and yellow were then seldom worn round the neck but often round the middle, the flannels of this generation being thus kept up. The sash was maintained in place by loops and was knotted at the front.

Hampstead in August used to progress clockwise round the south coast, with Bognor near the end of the run. I can see behind the stumps 'Father' Beaton, a walrus moustache almost brushing the bails, and with his sash or 'square' spilling out so that it covered most of his bottom. Old Beaton was the ultra-respectable father of two beautiful daughters much in the news as Bright Young Things of the '20s, and a son, Cecil, making his way as a society photographer. There was also a much more orthodox son, Reggie, who played for Hampstead, was an RAF officer and died young. George Hickson was of the Hampstead red-and-yellow company, a genial man who for the charitable purpose of endowing a hospital bed started a club, which he called the Purchasers, with a tie of verdant

Mistress. 'Your master is somewhat upset that you should have given him out LBW.'
Butler. 'I 'ad no option in the matter, my lady. I might 'ave overlooked a limb or two, but the 'ole body overlapped the wicket.'

This cartoon, reprinted by kind permission of *Punch*, I discovered inserted in one of Neville Cardus's personal scrap-books.

green, gin and tonic (i.e. white and very pale blue). To be elected you had to have 'bought it', so to speak, by doing something unusual, bizarre or ridiculous. Word went round the cricket world, for instance, that Tom Pearce had been elected as having been the only county captain in 1948 to bowl out the Australians in a day. Essex did so at Southend – for 721! Freddie Brown, a congenial chap after the founder's heart, now runs the Purchasers.

There were two Georges, Hickson and Hewetson, great friends who seemed always to be laughing. George Hewetson was one of the deafest men I ever met at cricket but was said never not to have heard when asked to have a drink. He must have had a radar system in his hearing-aid. An alternative version had it that when he saw anyone talking to him he simply said, 'Thanks very much, gin and tonic.' Count Hollender (also with two lovely daughters) was there chiefly on social grounds, and the side were strong enough to carry one or two such. For there were several class performers around, such as the Atkinson brothers, N. S. M. and B. G. W., both of whom played for Middlesex as also had Leonard Burtt, Arthur Tanner and, a little later, the current President of MCC, 'Tagge' Webster. 'B' Atkinson, by the way, is credited with one of the most extraordinary hits ever made at Lord's. In the Middlesex–Surrey match, which used to mark the climax of the county season, he executed an overhead tennis smash at a bouncer, sending it high over the head of Alf Gover, the astonished bowler, into the pavilion seats for six. 'B' was an institution as a master at Edinburgh Academy, a splendid bat who used to get 1000 runs for the Grange, and then 1000 more for Hampstead and others during the school holidays.

Before getting back to my old buffers – the word being used, as will be appreciated, in a wholly respectful sense – let it be recorded that no club in England can have fielded so many distinguished players over the years as Hampstead. F. R. Spofforth ('The Demon'), A. E. Stoddart, who once made 485 for Hampstead in a day, though exactly why he committed such an enormity I never heard, and Gregor MacGregor, all of early Test Match fame, head the list. I am proud to have played in the '50s for Hampstead, as I had earlier done for the club of comparable lustre south of the river, Beckenham.

H. D. Swan and T. H. Carlton-Levick I wrote about in *SOCP*, both buffers of the first order and the former *comfortably* the worst cricketer I ever saw. There was also Stanley Colman, of the mustard family, who ran The Wanderers and whose portrait still hangs in the Long Room at the Oval. Whether he was ever much good I'm not sure, but my recollection is of seeing him in the changing-room being bound up from ankle to crutch by his Jeeves. Varicose veins, perhaps.

Then there was Lord Ebbisham, father of the present peer, who as Sir Rowland Blades managed to combine an active life in the city of London – and indeed the office of Lord Mayor – while playing a lot of cricket, much of it for Sutton. His great ambition – he was an exceptionally slow bowler – was to take 100 wickets in the season and it was said that matches were sometimes hurriedly arranged in September in order for this annual milestone to be reached. J. C. Masterman used to tell how, encountering 'Rowly' during the winter, he put the time-honoured question. Had he done it yet again? Once the old boy seemed less pleased than usual to have been asked, and after saying 'yes' added after a pause that he might have taken the last two or three on the beach.

Billy Williams was a robust and upright old fellow who sported an MCC cap as well as a sash and also a clipped white moustache. He had bowled for Middlesex in his youth before reverting to leg-breaks, but his chief achievement was, as a moving spirit on the Rugby Union, to urge the purchase of Twickenham. The ground was considered too remote from London to be suitable as the game's headquarters and was scathingly referred to in its early days (before the first war) as 'Billy Williams's cabbage-patch'. Very late in life Billy, who was something of an old buck, was cited as co-respondent in a divorce suit, and was said to be highly indignant when the case was dismissed.

But of these old fellows of my youth none stands out more clearly than E. Shirley Snell, a figure of great dignity scrupulously turned out, whether on the field or off, and indeed known by the somewhat dubious title of 'the best-dressed man in London'. It fitted him perfectly that he was in Rothschild's: one felt the most crucial secret of City or State would be safe behind that suave, grave demeanour. Shirley's life-long interest, however, was not banking but Incogniti, for which distinguished club he played first in 1910 and last, at the age of 71, in 1953! He was many years on the committee and match-manager for 22 – which, of course, was far too long seeing that he was 28 when he was elected. Nor, strictly speaking, had he ever been much good.

When I knew him the chief characteristic of his bowling was width, and in the early days of the Romany Club when he played for me I used sometimes, much to his pleasure, to get through the conventional three overs at least expense by giving him the new ball. By the time a couple of young batsmen had decided that the stuff was every bit as guileless as it seemed, with luck he would be putting on his immaculate sweater and the faded Incog cap of purple, yellow and black. The secret was to get him off quickly, which he never minded, even if by chance he had taken a wicket.

In his early days he was, it was said, something of a martinet as a match-manager, and woe betide the candidate who offended his strict sartorial sense, or who failed to mind his p's and q's either on the field or off. But at heart he was a kind man, of the sort that in any club is worth his weight in gold, happy to play anywhere at the last minute, carry his bag for miles, and arrive early, and *expect* to bat No. 11. At Lord's he always sat in the same seat, on the left beneath the Committee Room window, where I would seek him latterly each summer scarcely thinking he would have survived the winter, living alone in a bachelor service-flat in Hallam Street. He seemed to regard me in a way as his protégé, always flattering about my work on radio and TV and in the *Telegraph*. Frail as could be, he saw through the summer of 1965, and died in the autumn aged 83.

One wonders sometimes what these Swans and Ebbishams and Shirley Snells would make of the worst of the cricketers of today, with their long, greasy hair, grubby flannels and the apparent contempt for club colours which reaches the point of a strange, inverted snobbery. (Note I did say the worst of the moderns, not quite the generality, though I would not suggest the standard of turn-out is other than indifferent.) Perhaps their chief reaction would be one of mystification at the lack of self-respect, to them clearly implied in complete indifference to appearances. They had inherited a natural acceptance of the established order. Pride of nationality, of school and club was, for them, automatic, and with this came a consequent regard for convention and good manners.

Having said as much I must add that I am far from un-appreciative of the virtues of the young denim-clad generation today. They may be scruffy, but in general they are wonderfully considerate to one another, and also to those other people who are prepared to accept them as they are. As for snobbery, they scarcely know the meaning of the word.

There was one venerable figure from the golden period of amateur cricket, 'Buns' Cartwright, who never lost touch with young cricketers and who would have echoed these last sentiments, I think, up to his death at 87 last year. From time immemorial, first as secretary and then as president, he was the guiding spirit of Eton Ramblers. Apart from all else he was a far from conventional figure himself. It is unusual, after all, to see emerging from White's or the Bath Club a man in a London suit, with carnation, umbrella, a cloth cap and blue 'sneakers'.

'Buffer' does not in any way fit the eccentric personality of Colonel Cartwright. Old other things will occur to those who knew him. There are several appellations of variable politeness beginning with 'b'! Buns was seldom known to withhold any remark that came into his mind. Often he hit the nail on the head with cruel accuracy. Often he said outrageous things, not seriously meant. Authority was anything but sacred to him, in any sphere.

Buns broke upon the cricket scene in the Eton XI of 1907, from which date comes his first recorded comment. The afternoon before the Eton–Winchester match the visiting Eton team were taking tea with the headmaster of Winchester's wife, sitting nervously on the edge of drawing-room chairs and waiting for someone to break the ice. Young Cartwright did so, pulling out a handkerchief, mopping his brow, and exclaiming, 'Gad, ma'am, I'm sweatin'.' Whether or not this brave sally put everyone at their ease Dick Twining, his contemporary and the narrator of this little story, did not record.

Buns, like others who fought in the first war and by the grace of heaven survived, never followed a profession or business career – though they were the first to the colours when the call came again in 1939. While not exactly rich they had enough, as bachelors, to scratch very comfortably along, swelling the profits of the London clubs, playing various games with the utmost spirit in their due season, watching them at Lord's, Queen's Club, Twickenham and elsewhere, and, of course, following the horses at Newmarket, Ascot and Newbury. A limited existence, to say the least, but one can see how it might be drifted into, after the horrors of war, and how, once accepted, a man without special qualifications or aptitudes might continue to opt for the easy life.

But I malign Buns Cartwright, to the extent that he served at one time as a judge's marshal, and also between the wars did fulfil another definite function and a highly responsible one. For when F. E. Smith became Lord Chancellor he appointed the gallant major (his rank retained from service in the Coldstream Guards in World War One – the continued use of temporary rank being then a regular custom) as his Patronage secretary. Though scarcely noted for his interest in things ecclesiastical, all church livings of which the Lord Chancellor was patron thus became Buns's concern. With his beetling brow and fierce military moustache he was a formidable figure at the best of times. How he must have seemed from the other side of a desk in the palace of Westminster to nervous young curates under inspection for preferment is, at this range of time, a comical thought. No doubt Buns fulfilled his duty as conscientiously as might be – but it was, on the face of it, a peculiar appointment.

Picking up Buns in his flat one evening to go round the corner to the XL Club dinner at the Hilton – he never missed either this or the two MCC dinners, the Anniversary and the dinner to the touring side – I counted 23 items of headgear hanging in the hall. More than half of them were decorated with hat-bands of various club colours. If on a hot day at Lord's he took off his jacket one would expect to see that a Panama hat with an MCC hat-band and a Rambler tie was complemented with IZ braces. The Australians, on his visits down under following MCC, were intrigued, to say the least, by his sartorial variations, which prompted illustrated interviews in such papers as the *Sydney Sun*. There was even a picture of him shaving, braces and all. This reminds me that *The Times* a few years ago took a photograph of him at Ascot in full fig (the sneakers perhaps for once discarded), and failed to identify him in the caption. They were surprised by a brisk demand for prints of a splendid picture. He was a man full of peculiarities, one of which was that he never owned a car : so how many hundred thousand miles he travelled in other people's is anyone's guess.

As a cricketer Buns got near enough to an Oxford Blue to be elected a Harlequin. I recall him as a rugged competitor both on the cricket field and the golf course. I doubt whether he ever met Stephen Potter; if he had I'm sure that the pair of them might have swapped experiences in the subtler fields of Gamesmanship. Buns was always a good friend and a bad enemy; a shrewd sporting judge and critic. He was at his best in the long annual letters accompanying the Eton Rambler fixture-card, which he used kindly to send me, with news and gossip of the great company of Ramblers of his time – literally thousands of them covering his 70 years of membership. If Shirley Snell was the best-dressed man in the city, Buns was just about the best-known man in the West End.

Needless to say, stories about him are endless : he was, as I say, a bachelor, but far from unappreciative of feminine company. A young cricketer once returned from a holiday in the South of France, saying: 'Who do you think was there but old Buns. Yes, and Mrs Buns too. She was charming.'

Now to a sketch of an utterly different sort of person though he had in common with Cartwright a deep affection for cricket. Sir Home Gordon Bt was likewise an Etonian, though he was no cricketer of any sort or kind. Born in 1871 his memory went back to a visit to the old Prince's ground in Belgravia where he was taken, before his seventh birthday, to see the 1878 Australians – the very first team to come here apart from the Aboriginals – play the Gentlemen of England. In 1880 at Lord's he was presented to W.G., and later that summer he was also taken to see the first of all Test Matches between England and Australia at the Oval. Thereafter until his death at the age of 84 the abiding passion of this extraordinary little man who never had the physique to be a player was watching cricket. These were ususual credentials for one who, in addition to being a publisher, from his schooldays on practised cricket journalism, and set himself up as a statistician. His *Cricket Form at a Glance* purported to give the batting, bowling and fielding figures plus details of teams played for, number of Tests and Blues, and hundreds scored, for all who appeared in first-class cricket over two seasons even though in only a couple of matches. The first edition began at 1878 and ended with 1902, a second took things on to 1923, and yet a third, in paperback, told the story from 1878 to 1937. A note on the cover announced that all royalties would be allocated to cricket charities by the Committee of MCC.

In his book of memoirs, *Background of Cricket*, Home Gordon quotes Lord Hawke who in his foreword to Herbert Sutcliffe's *For England and Yorkshire* described him as 'the greatest statistician of the day, nay of all time'. Hawke 'then declared that the brain reels at the incredible toil of my encyclopaedic computations, but that they were a labour of love. That is true, and they were also comprehensive, for after publishing the life figures of 3687 cricketers,, inclusive of every one who had played in any two of these seasons in first-class cricket, only a minute number of accurate omissions were forwarded to me by correspondents.' The book also contains lists of all the runs and wickets for and against every county in the championship over this 60-year period.

Others were distinctly less complimentary about Home Gordon's value as a statistician and I think Irving Rosenwater's judgement, as the leading present-day historical researcher, may be safely accepted. He says:

Home Gordon's figures were always extremely impressive to behold, but too rarely stood up to careful examination. There was a lack of science, and he was much more clearly an able gossip than an able statistician. His figures today are virtually never quoted because his inaccuracies have been proven time and again. He does, however, occupy a genuine niche in the story of cricket if only for the remarkable span of his watching experience. And he did claim to have got Jack White into Percy Chapman's side for Australia!

All in all, and one way or another, the Bart claimed a good deal. Nevertheless he earned full marks for industry, and for tackling such a vast job at a time when the game was far less closely documented than it is today. There were not so many rivals looking over his shoulder, quick to pounce upon error.

He was, of course, what would now be called a 'cricket nut' of the first order, a busy, vivacious, garrulous, good-hearted midget of a man who was enormously friendly with everyone and loved to be in the know. By many he was held in affection; others were irritated that one so ludicrously ignorant of every technical aspect of the game should have so much to say and moreover find many in authority apparently prepared to listen to him. On the face of it, it was strange that Plum Warner gave him a weekly platform on page one of the *Cricketer* which he filled with an egregious mingling of fact and fancy under the title 'In the Pavilion'. But, after all, the *Cricketer*, which never had a penny to spare, got the stuff for nothing, and at least they had a willing, not to say eager, contributor.

Home latterly attached himself almost exclusively and almost permanently to Sussex, but with his trim, minute figure, short, thick moustache, invariable red carnation and unmistakable cackle he was a familiar figure wherever the game was played. His particular friend was Peter, or Percy, Perrin, a fine bat in his day for Essex, and throughout the '30s one of the Test selectors. For seven years running the job was done by a triumvirate of Warner, Perrin and another little man busy for cricket, the ruling spirit in Lancashire, Tommy Higson.

It was a strangely incongruous alliance, the 'squeaking Bart', as he was sometimes called from the high pitch of his voice, and this rich East-ender, a head and more taller than Home, who in a low growl scattered aitches all over the place, was at his ease in any company, and was, incidentally, by repute an outstanding shot. He was said to be invited to the Sandringham shoots and to be a favourite with King George V, for whom blunt, earthy characters such as Pete Perrin and the railwaymen's leader, J. H. Thomas, apparently had a fascination.

'Anyone got a fag?' Perrin would ask gruffly. If no one obliged he added, 'Then s'pose I'll have to smoke one of mine,' brought a tin of tobacco from his pocket and rolled his own cigarette.

Like Buns Cartwright, neither Perrin nor Home Gordon was known to own a car, but the deficiency was made up by another extraordinary character called Leslie Hindley, who drove the pair of them round England, from ground to ground, in a large open tourer. Hindley was a lugubrious-looking fellow who, whether in London or the country, always wore a bowler hat. Whether he knew anything about cricket I cannot remember, but his pursuit of the game was insatiable. On one day Home records they saw the finishes of three games, at Leyton, Lord's and the Oval, and after the last one drove to Vincent Square to see whether anything was going on there. Here now is 'a nut' to beat all comers, on the evidence of Home Gordon's book:

Never allowing a servant into his room, he cleans it himself. In it, apart from some pieces of carving he has collected and a complete series of every modern postage stamp, are the cards of every cricket match he has seen, the itinerary of every motor run he has taken, copious diaries, the programme of every play and concert he has attended – he was once pupil and subsequently instructor at the Academy of Music – every crossword puzzle published in the *Daily Telegraph*, five barometers and innumerable notebooks compiled on any subject . . . Motoring, he takes

a despatch-case in which there is the drum-stick of a fowl, choco-
late, various cricket reference books, maps and his daily paper.

He had never drunk alcohol, tea or coffee, and the height of his
ambition was, according to the Bart, to cut his (Home Gordon's)
hair.

Yes, we had our eccentrics in the '30s all right.

Long prior to his peregrinations with Perrin – when indeed the
latter was piling up runs for Essex – Home, as I have said, was very
friendly with Lord Hawke, who chaired the very first Test selection
committee, in 1899, and thereafter served until 1909 inclusive. Add
the tie-up with Plum Warner, and I suppose it may not have been
such a presumption as it seems at first glance – though it scarcely
smacks of modesty – that he should declare : 'It would be affectation
to pretend that I have not been in closer association with a majority
of successive selectors than anyone else.'

Home Gordon was an institution, around whom all sorts of
stories circulated, including, I suspect, many rumours whispered in
his ear by people just for the fun of seeing how they progressed.
Sussex on retirement became his home, and cricket and the county
club the centre of his existence. He went almost everywhere with
the side and indeed in an expansive moment was actually presented
with his county cap by Arthur Gilligan. He was photographed wearing it, sitting in a team group, the expressions on the faces of the
players being not all of unalloyed joy at the sight of the recruit to
their ranks. In his obituary *Wisden* records this unusual award,
adding that it was 'an old one belonging to A. E. R. Gilligan'.

One can see him at a remove of forty years promenading the
boundaries, spruce, button-holed, high-pitched and more than a
little absurd. At Horsham he was supposed to have gone into the
ladies' loo by mistake, and to have been shooed out by a large,
furious woman towering over him. Crusoe claimed to have been an
eye-witness of the scene as Home backed nervously away, making
nasal, placatory noises which only increased her indignation.

'Get out, you horrible little man.'

'Thaank you.'

'How dare you come in here?'

'Thaank you.'

'I shall report you to the police.'

'Thaank you.'

No doubt the story was fancifully embroidered as it went the rounds.

Once or twice in the first week of August I would see the Bank-holiday match between Sussex and Middlesex at Hove and then motor across for the second match of the Canterbury Week, giving a lift to Home Gordon. It was thus I was first introduced en route to the Dormy House at Rye where he was a member – as he also was of the Golf Club, of which indeed, though no sort of player, he was once captain. It may well be that it was on one of these journeys he told me a story illustrative of his publishing instinct. When he was the proprietor of Williams and Norgate he published Lord Hawke's memoirs, entitled *Recollections and Reminiscences*.

Though the book was as pedestrian as the title it did well enough to encourage Home to order a reprint. Then one fateful day he saw the evening paper headlines announcing Hawke's speech at the Yorkshire AGM wherein he said he hoped to God the day would never come when a professional would captain England. 'At once,' said Home, 'I picked up the telephone, got on to the printers, and was just in time to cancel the new edition. It was as well I did, for after that speech we didn't sell another dozen copies.'

I suppose of all maladroit remarks in the cricket world this one of Hawke's just about takes the biscuit. It has often been claimed in explanation that since in those days sides were invariably led by amateurs all he was trying to put across was that he hoped the day would never come when there was no amateur good enough to play for England. A pity then that the noble lord did not say so, for the phrase has been used ever since as evidence of the crippling snobbery supposedly surrounding cricket.

So much for Home Gordon and his companions, except to add there is no one living to whom this sketch could give offence. Though married twice Home Gordon had no issue, and the twelfth Bart – the title dating back to Charles I in 1631 – was the last.

The nearest parallel I can think of to his place in cricket was that of another small man of Sussex in the world of Rugby football, Major R. V. Stanley, known as 'Uncle'. Though never in residence and never a player – he was the Magdalen College organist – 'Uncle' Stanley for a spell on either side of the Great War more or less ran Oxford rugger. He was elected to represent the University on the

Rugby Union and from this actually gravitated to become, for just one season, an international selector.

Who remembers *The Lady Vanishes* and the conversation in the train between Basil Radford and Naunton Wayne when one of them talks rather slightingly of someone and is rebuked by the other?

'Steady on, old chap, he did play for the Gentlemen.'

'I know – but only once.'

My characters seem rather to have declined from buffers to butts. Ah, well, there used to be room on the games scene for oddities, though in these super-serious times they seem scarcely to have a place. Some of them did much good, and none much harm : and they were often a source of such humour as nowadays we have to look hard to find.

9

First Tours

If the *Evening Standard* had not changed their minds my first visit overseas would have been with Douglas Jardine's MCC side to Australia on the most momentous of all tours in 1932/3. As a result I would either have been 'made' as a cricket correspondent many years earlier than was the case or, I suppose, if my picture of events had not appealed to my editor my employment with Beaverbrook Newspapers would have terminated there and then instead of continuing almost until the war.

Bruce Harris, the lawn-tennis man preferred to me at the last minute, as I have told in *SOCP*, sent home a version of the Bodyline row supporting Jardine's tactics and on arrival home found himself for a while both principal cricket and lawn tennis correspondent. Accordingly, poor Swanton, who had been reporting Tests at home the previous three summers, was selected to do so only when Harris was required at Wimbledon or to follow the Davis Cup – an affair in which, thanks to Fred Perry and Bunny Austin, we then had a close patriotic interest.

The fact was I was useful to the paper chiefly as the Rugby football correspondent, and though my rejection for Australia was a great disappointment there were compensations, including my being able, in the latter part of the summer of 1933, to get seven weeks' leave to go with Sir Julien Cahn's team to Canada, USA and Bermuda. A tour of a very different colour!

If it is true that much of the pleasure of life lies in anticipation on the one hand and memory on the other, there is nothing, for a cricketer, to beat the preparations for one's first tour abroad. Getting the glossy literature from the shipping line, holding the promise of, in this case, a week or so of earthly – or, rather, marine – paradise: the tour brochure containing the itinerary, including such romantic names as the Heights of Abraham, Niagara Falls and Long Island: being measured for the team's blazer: going through the formalities of obtaining one's first passport: such things stimulate the imagination for the pleasures ahead.

It may well be wondered why Julien Cahn invited me to join the party, considering he had a regular ready-made first-class side quite sufficient for his purpose. However, I had for a year or two taken up a Romany side for a week-end match at his home, Stanford Hall, and I shared rooms in the Temple with Ian Peebles, who had played irregularly for him hitherto, and was obviously a highly desirable acquisition. I expect it was also thought I might help to publicize the tour – which I did in the *Cricketer* and the *Illustrated Sporting and Dramatic*. The tour was also the subject of the first of the two contributions I have made to *Wisden*.

The addition of Ian and me brought the strength of the team to fifteen, on top of which came Julien's wife Phyllis, a charming person popular with everyone, and two or three of his in-laws. The party foregathered on the eve of departure for a great luncheon at Claridge's where I recall the room had been given a cricket décor for the occasion. No expense spared!

The occasion, as it turned out, made the headlines since J. H. Thomas, then Dominions Secretary, used it to utter some strong comment on the Bodyline tactics adopted by England the previous winter in Australia. In his position he had been concerned at the diplomatic level – a matter on which I shall have more to say in my next chapter. Jimmy Thomas was a warm character on whom it is a temptation to digress – which I shall do to the extent of quoting briefly from his notice in *The Dictionary of National Biography*. When Macdonald's Labour government fell in 1931 and he formed a National government with full Conservative support Thomas was one of the four Socialists to stand by his leader, and so retained office. But, like the others who adhered to Macdonald, he was ostracized thenceforward by Labour generally and in particular by the NUR whose lifelong servant he had been. The Union even deprived him of his pension. As R. C. K. Ensor wrote, 'in his unhappiness he developed a proneness to intemperance', and Peebles recalls that the Cahn champagne had loosened his tongue that day at Claridge's. A few years later as the result of a judicial enquiry following a Budget leak Thomas had to resign, and when he surrendered his seal of office to Edward VIII he is said to have remarked, according to Ensor, 'Thank God your old dad is not alive to see this.' There was much sympathy for Thomas in this crowning misfortune, for his Commons statement declaring that he had not consciously betrayed any secrets was generally accepted. The verdict of Baldwin, by then Prime Minister, was: 'I don't think Jim deliberately gave anything away. What he most likely did was to let his tongue wag when he was in his cups.'

Cannot most of us think of friends who, when not strictly sober, just might have unwittingly broken the rules in some such way?

Talking of Edward VIII's 'old dad', and of his friend, the Dominions Secretary, there was an irreverent twist to the last words attributed to George V on his death-bed: 'How is it with the Empire?' The alternative version from the simple sailor with a fondness for music-halls and the less sophisticated pleasures of life was, 'What's on at the "Empire"?' We may dismiss no doubt the fanciful notion that the great King-Emperor, aiming to pay a last tribute to the one game common to all his myriad subjects, the cementing bond as many would say, asked the final rhetorical question: 'How's that, umpire?'

This was the side which sailed off from Southampton on 11 August 1933 aboard the *Empress of Britain*: Sir Julien Cahn, R. C. Blunt, P. A. Gibb, G. F. H. Heane, C. R. Maxwell, D. P. B. Morkel, H. R. Munt, F. C. W. Newman, I. A. R. Peebles, T. B. Reddick, R. W. V. Robins, S. D. Rhodes, E. P. Solbé, G. F. Summers and myself.

Apart from the captain it was a formidable collection, headed by two England bowlers in Robins and Peebles, and two other Test cricketers of note, Roger Blunt of New Zealand and Denys Morkel of South Africa. Paul Gibb was later to be designated as of Cambridge, Yorkshire and England. George Heane and Stewart Rhodes shortly became joint captains of Notts before George, known as 'Farmer', took on the job alone. Maxwell in his time kept wicket for three counties, Middlesex, Notts and Worcestershire; Ray Munt played for Middlesex ('but only once!'), 'Lofty' Newman for Surrey, Tom Reddick for Middlesex and Notts, Philip Solbé for Kent, Geoff Summers for Surrey, and I (*three times*) for Middlesex.

All except Ian and me were employed in some way by Cahn, mostly in his vast hire-purchase furnishing business. Newman was his private secretary and right-hand man in respect both of business and cricket. Morkel sold him his motor-cars and was set up in what became the firm of Morkel and Carnill. Munt looked after his wines and was soon well established in the trade. He was not quite the cricketer most of the others were, but I recall his being upgraded once by the Canadian Press in a way that caused us some amusement. Poor Ray after a day's play at Toronto had the misfortune when having a shower to slip on the soap and knock himself out – which prompted next day a headline suggesting all sorts of possibilities : ENGLAND BOWLER RENDERED UNCONSCIOUS.

I have given some idea of Julien Cahn's own cricket in *SOCP*. Researching, however, in Sir Home Gordon's statistical compendium I notice he gives the first-class career bowling figures for his fellow Bart as two for 193, average per wicket 96·50. He persuaded every touring team except the Australians to play against his side on his own superb ground at West Bridgford, only a mile or so from Trent Bridge. He played himself on these occasions, possibly creating a record by making his initial first-class appearance at the age of 48. Perhaps he had another claim to distinction, of a sort : I cannot believe that a *slower* bowler ever found his way into *Wisden*.

Julien was hilariously pleased if he got out a famous player, as occasionally occurred as a result of sheer fatigue, or a preposterous catch, or even maybe as a return for hospitality. Duleep I seem to recall was once a victim.

Cahn, by the way, was much addicted to the practical joke, the cruder the better : what was euphemistically known as the 'whooppee cushion' might have been invented specially for his benefit. It was simply an inflatable bladder which when surreptitiously inserted on a chair and sat upon by an unsuspecting victim emitted a resonant, unmistakable sound. Imagine then old H. D. Swan, large, ponderous, captain of a team of notables, at the end of a cricket lunch, thanking the directors of the shipping firm of Elders & Fyffes, whose team we were playing, for their hospitality and no doubt slipping in a phrase or two about their splendid part in transporting teams across the seas to strengthen the bonds of Empire.

As the peroration ends Alan Hilder, at Cahn's instigation, slips the blown-up cushion on Swanny's chair, and he sits down to a deep echoing reverberation. The Elders & Fyffes team, a bit over-awed by the occasion anyway, look momentarily embarrassed as the face of the victim registers first horror and then mystification until Julien Cahn's burst of laughter reveals the enormity of the joke. The height of vulgarity? Of course. I can only add that it seemed very funny at the time.

Julien Cahn used his great wealth to give more happiness to more people than many millionaires. Nor did I ever hear that he was less than generous to any of the cricketers he employed. If they showed any business ability they prospered quite irrespective of their use to him on the field. There were many stories circulating around this highly unusual sporting figure including some which suggested that every now and then he needed someone at his elbow who would say firmly, 'But you really mustn't do that.' (Come to that, which of us would maintain he might not have benefited at some time in his life – or indeed often – from the advice of some candid friends whose judgement he valued? Not I, by a long chalk.)

An instance of this occurs to me in Cahn's case. He was not a member of MCC in the '30s, and Plum Warner, always favourably disposed to anyone doing service to cricket, was prominent among those who thought that, in view especially of all the tours abroad that he had financed, he should be elected under the rule which allows men in special circumstances to be brought forward out of their due turn. At that time Cahn was president of Notts and as such arrived at the Grace Gate in his Rolls-Royce to see his county play Middlesex. The rule, then as now, is that members of visiting clubs are given the courtesy of the pavilion but must pay the charge for ground admission, in those days a shilling. Cahn refused to pay, whereupon the gateman, leaving the car at the gate, sought direction from higher authority, to wit the secretary, Billy Findlay. On the instructions of Findlay the car and its occupant were admitted and the matter would no doubt have ended there had not Cahn in the Long Room informed anyone interested how he, whose efforts for cricket cost him £25,000 a year, had been insulted. Thereupon the move for his election was promptly forgotten. All because of a shilling!

Thank heaven he got in shortly before his sudden death in 1944, or Phyllis Cahn would hardly have given MCC first call on the wonderful cricket library which he, in turn, had acquired from F. S. Ashley-Cooper. The sad bungling whereby many valuable books were not claimed by MCC and subsequently were put up to auction and vanished was no fault of hers.

Cahn's first appearance at 48 was less odd, in the circumstances, than the break between appearances of the Rev. R. H. Moss, a

member of the Oxford XI of 1889, who though giving much help
to a struggling Bedfordshire early in the century when vicar of
Woburn seems not to have played in another first-class match until
he suddenly popped up for Worcestershire at the age of 57 in 1925.
It would be pleasant to think that after the game he returned to
his parish in the glow of success, and it is true that in the only
three overs he was allowed he collected a wicket – and that of
Gloucestershire's top scorer, Capt. M. A. Green. However, he made
2 and 0, and *was not persevered with*. Alec Bedser surely would
have been more sympathetic to aspiring experience! The best that
can be said is that he lived another thirty years in which to reflect,
and perhaps inform his friends, that in his second and positively last
innings for Worcestershire he was bowled out by a then promising
youngster named Walter Hammond. The parson's victim, Mike
Green, afterwards manager of two MCC teams abroad, came to a
cruel end, bent so crooked with rheumatoid arthritis that he could
see nothing but the ground as he shuffled one foot agonizingly after
the other.

But to return to the tour. The voyage on the gleaming white
Empress of Britain gave me a taste for ships that I've never lost,
though all that I can positively recall of it was certain clandestine
evening visits by some of us to the tourist class at the instigation of
a young man on his first visit to America. With a companion he
was going to have a look around the States, having resigned his
army commission, and he was wasting no time. The bird-life, he
rightly maintained, was superior on the lower decks. His name was
David Niven.

Sailing up the St Lawrence to Quebec, and getting as we glided
through an inkling of the task that Wolfe accomplished in scaling
the heights, with Montcalm, all unconscious of his presence, up
above, we had a quick glimpse only of the city, but time enough
to register an insular surprise that everyone seemed to be speaking
French. Our first matches were at Montreal, played on matting
stretched over turf in the midst of a stadium, and we, who were
bearing the cricket flag in unfamiliar territory, supposedly enthral-
ling all and sundry by our performance, very nearly met with an
initial defeat. Apart from the fact that our captain could not bear
the thought of losing at any time, this would have been a highly
unpropitious beginning. Yet there need have been little surprising

about it. We were confronted by several able bowlers, West Indians employed on the railway, and scarcely any of us had played on matting before.

The names of those bowlers stick in my mind after more than forty years but I must withhold them because of the rumour – which might well have been baseless – that one of them had just emerged, fit and raring to go, from a gaol sentence for having kept a disorderly house. However this may be, he and his pal were too much for our star-studded batting side after we had bowled out All-Montreal for 103. I was not selected for this game, but watched the mounting crisis with Julien Cahn, whose acute anxiety quickly communicated itself to the rest of the party. It would have been overstretching it to say that defeat would have meant no wine at dinner, but there was a very clear relation between the team's success and the cordiality of the atmosphere. With five or six out for about 50 Cahn turned to me. What could he do? Luckily I had heard frequently enough from the hero's own lips how Ian Peebles had saved a tricky situation in a Test on the mat at Johannesburg by batting $2\frac{1}{2}$ hours for 26, and I suggested he should be promoted from No. 11 to face the crisis. He was and did : we scraped home by two wickets, and thereafter when Cahn was anxious for advice he was inclined to ignore his Test cricketers and the other wise men of the entourage and, to their amusement, come to me.

We went on to the capital city of Ottawa, staying at the splendid Château Laurier overlooking the Ottawa River which forms the boundary between the states of Quebec and Ontario. In 1933 Quebec was 'wet' and Ontario 'dry', or at any rate dryish. Consequently there was always a string of taxis at either end of the bridge across the river ferrying thirsty customers across and bringing them back replete. Sad, the reader may well think, that this is my prime recollection of the first city of the Dominion, and I can only say in extenuation that it was 44 years ago and that *Wisden* confirms that we played cricket every single day.

In the grounds of Government House, Ottawa, where W.G. once played, Ian and I batted together, the situation being complicated (or not) by our having had a squabble of some kind and accordingly being temporarily 'non-speaks'. We got 50 apiece, and it's safe to say it was the only partnership in which I was ever involved that was conducted in complete silence.

The best ground and the best cricket were at Armour Heights, Toronto, where we encountered Norman Seagram, distiller and cricket philanthropist, and the likes of Billy and Clark Bell, good players both, of whom only the former survived the war and became one of the chief instigators of the newly-formed Canadian Cricket Association. We played at Hamilton, at Ridley College, St Catherine's – Upper Canada College and Ridley were the foremost cricket-playing schools – and at London, Ontario, saw the stupendous wonder of Niagara, and then crossed the border into the USA.

Our American opponents in Chicago and New York were largely expatriates with a good sprinkling of West Indians. The games were a pleasant interlude preceding the sterner contests ahead in Bermuda, and though we heard with some concern that a few months earlier Don Bradman had been got out in Chicago four times for under 50 we weren't seriously extended. The Australians were certainly playing XVIII of Illinois on each occasion, but I recall the story of W.G. being asked which of his innings he had most enjoyed. Maybe with tongue in cheek he is said to have replied that it was his 400 not out against XXII of Grimsby, adding that all 22 fielded out and the grass was very long!

Thanks to the efforts of a few – and notably of John Marder, the former President of the USACA who died recently – cricket is today gaining modest ground though without coming near to the standards reached before the First War when the Gentlemen of Philadelphia were a match for the strongest of the counties with a bowler of world class in J. B. King. Not many know that the first tour by English cricketers overseas was that to the USA in 1859, sponsored by the provision merchants, Spiers and Pond.

I have told in *SOCP* of our hectic, action-packed week in Bermuda. It may have been, so to say, a small pool but at least we were big fish therein, the first side from England ever to visit the oldest colony: the bunting, the speeches, the carriage processions round the packed Prospect ground, after the manner of royalty, the noise and drama of the cricket, made unforgettable memories. Incidentally, and very much by the way, the pleasure of riding behind horses in an open carriage is much dependent on the way of the wind. The aroma can be powerful.

We won the key match against Somerset, the island champions, by three runs (85 to 82) thanks to a marvellous running catch across the sight-screen by that great character and stout-hearted cricketer, 'Farmer' Heane of Notts. It could, however, have been claimed that we won thanks to an illegality which perhaps after nearly fifty years can be safely revealed. When the game started, Cahn having won the toss, I was 12th man. However, we were soon in trouble and our captain had also had a look at the fast left-arm bowling of Arthur Simons, who on a coconut mat stretched over a concrete base was whistling round the batsman's ears alarmingly to say the least. Perhaps it was the four leg-byes which Paul Gibb nodded involuntarily off his head that persuaded him he might enjoy watching this match rather than playing. (He was 50, after all.) Anyway, Cahn, with the game well under way, scratched his name off the order of going in and inserted that of Swanton at No. 8. Not many of my readers will need reminding that a captain must nominate his team before the toss. I scored five and held a catch, and we won by three !

After the last game – wherein we were again lucky to preserve our unbeaten record – and the final junketings we climbed aboard the *Queen of Bermuda* looking forward to a quiet 36 hours' voyage to New York. We were scarcely out of harbour when the crew began to secure everything that could be secured, and we were soon being tossed around by a genuine full-scale hurricane. The stewards were as ill as we were, and we heard afterwards that the great German liner *Bremen* had hove to, to ride out the storm. The *Queen of Bermuda* staggered through it, and, two nights and a day later, deposited a party of purged, distinctly *piano* cricketers at New York.

As they have shown other touring sides since – including MCC under Len Hutton – the Bermudians are no mean cricketers, especially on their own coconut-cum-concrete pitches. It was lucky for us that wrist-spin was a closed book to them, as also it had been to our earlier opponents – to the extent that in twenty matches Walter Robins took 90 wickets for six runs each and Ian Peebles 70 almost as cheaply. Alma Hunt, an all-rounder, who once took part in a West Indian Trial Match only to be told afterwards that it had been decided he, as a Bermudian, was ineligible for the forthcoming tour, was the leading player, and it is he who comes annually to the International Cricket Conference at Lord's as Bermuda's representative. So much for my first tour.

Of all the memories that haunt this old cricket traveller there is nothing to beat the first sight of Table Mountain looming square and vast out of a misty dawn as the mail steamer brought him on the last smooth lap of his journey to the Cape. For me this land-fall a few days before the Christmas of 1938 was momentous as marking the start of many tours accompanying MCC teams abroad – to all the Test-playing countries indeed and almost all the grounds, save those of Pakistan. Three months before, it seemed that my free-lance expedition with Hammond's team which I was then planning could never be, but Neville Chamberlain had returned from Berchtesgaden with his umbrella and a scrap of paper to the ignorant delight of me and most of my friends. So MCC had sailed in October and here I was, due to be whisked north in the Blue Train to Johannesburg where the First Test was about to start on Christmas Eve : where I was to give my own first Test broadcast, the first on cricket sent back to England by a BBC correspondent, and the first ever heard in South Africa.

There was another first in connection with this trip, for it was the first time MCC had attempted to muster England's full strength for a tour abroad other than that to Australia. Apart from Denis Compton – a notable omission, because his first duty under contract was to play football for Arsenal – and of Charles Barnett, who never saw eye to eye with Walter Hammond and declined, the MCC side was almost as strong a one as could be fielded. Most of those who had fought Australia to a halved series in the summer were there, and MCC had given some of the fluid places to such up-and-coming young men as Hugh Bartlett, who had had a wonderful season culminating in his magnificent 175 in $2\frac{3}{4}$ hours against the Players at Lord's, Norman Yardley and Paul Gibb of Cambridge and Yorkshire, and the promising Lancashire wrist-spinner, Len Wilkinson.

South Africa's strength was problematical to the extent that in seven years they had played only two Test series, one in England in 1935 when on a dusty spinners' pitch at Lord's, and thanks to an exile Greek called Xenophon Balaskas, they had won the only Test of the five that had been brought to conclusion, the other directly following at home, against Australia, wherein O'Reilly and Grimmett were too much for them. Since then Herby Wade, who had led his country to the first-ever win in England, had retired, and Jock Cameron, his vice-captain, had died of enteric fever at the

age of 31. In these circumstances the captaincy had been awarded
to Alan Melville, who had led Oxford and Sussex with credit but
had never played in a Test Match. (That this is a rare distinction
goes without saying, but a few others have captained their country
on first playing for it, notably George Mann and Tony Lewis.)

I cannot let the name of Cameron pass without, in paranthesis,
paying a brief tribute to his memory, however belated. He was,
first, a magnificent 'keeper with a quiet, almost nonchalant manner,
second perhaps in his craft only to Bertie Oldfield; he was a fear-
some bat who added a rare glow into the otherwise mild complexion
of South African batting; not least he was a man of great charm
and chivalry, an outstanding personality among the remarkably
popular South African teams of his day. As it was, Melville came
out of the series as well as could be, despite the fact that, hampered
by a fielding injury, he did not find his batting form until the
fourth Test. There was a classic elegance about Alan as a batsman
that set him quite apart. If in the hereafter I could summon a side
of my own choice purely for the pleasure of watching it, his claims
would be hard to resist.

So, too, of course would be those of his opposing captain who
could not do anything other than gracefully on the cricket field or,
for that matter, playing any other game. Watching Wally Hammond
on the deck-tennis court aboard ship one understood why he was
supreme as a slip-fielder. He played golf infrequently yet to a
handicap of two or three. His wooden club strokes through the
green seem in distant retrospect to have had the power and timing
of a Nicklaus. He was in his element at billiards – and, for that
matter, at the bridge-table. As a captain he was, by contrast,
defensive and quite lacking in flair and inspiration. He had an easy
ride in South Africa in that his side never failed to make as many
as were needed, while the bowling was always stronger and more
varied than the opposition's though similarly apt to be frustrated by
the deadening ease of the pitches. Off the field he could be good
company with those who amused him, cool and detached with those
who did not. Seeing him at close quarters for three months on this
tour I felt he was the wrong man to lead England on future tours
abroad – Australia was coming up in 1940/1 – while realizing the
difficulty in asking such a tremendous cricketer to step down. As
things turned out, of course, the selectors did not have to face the

problem until 1946/7 when in Australia one's fears were sadly confirmed.

At this remove there can be little point in saying much about the cricket in South Africa apart, perhaps, from noting certain significant contrasts as compared with today. Though Compton, and also Barnett, Maurice Leyland and Joe Hardstaff were missing, Test centurions all in the Australian series just completed, six of the England batsmen made hundreds against South Africa (Hammond, Paynter, Valentine, Ames, Gibb and Edrich), though their number did not include Hutton whose marathon 364 of the previous August had surrounded him with a transcending glamour. Think of other fine players of that immediately pre-war period who either seemed to be just coming up or who had rendered great service and were still making bags of runs, and give a thought to the difficulties of our Test selectors of the '70s: Sutcliffe, the Langridges, Dollery, Norman Oldfield, Fagg, Gimblett, Robertson, Keeton, Washbrook, O'Connor, Brookes, Fishlock, Cox, Wyatt, and the remaining two batsmen present on the tour but unable to win a Test place, Yardley and Bartlett. This is a fair assemblage of batting talent – 25 all told who played at one time or another for England, with others good enough to have done so – a company which, but for the war, obviously must have made an even bigger impact than it did. I would like to think that anything approaching their technical equivalent was available today.

In bowling the discrepancy in quality as between then and now is less marked except regarding spin, and in particular wrist-spin. In South Africa four of the five major wicket-takers, Wright, Verity, Goddard and Wilkinson, were spinners. Indeed MCC took only two quicks, Farnes and Perks, with Edrich capable of having a fling and Hammond always in the background, little though he used himself. Contrast that with the present when the first thing is to write down four or five fastish men plus, of course, Underwood and perhaps one more. No wonder so much big cricket now lacks subtlety and glamour. There can be little attraction without variety, and precious little variety without spin.

The last Test was due to be played to a finish according to the tour playing conditions if neither side led in the rubber by more than one. Hence we returned to Durban prepared for a marathon since England were one up, having had an overwhelming win on this same Kingsmead ground in the Third Test. Nearly forty years later this 'Timeless Test' is still a byword for boredom and futility, and the impression it made was so deep that in fact there has never been another since. After the war the then foremost cricket countries – influenced also by the fiasco at the Oval in 1938 when England, thanks chiefly to Hutton's prodigious vigil of 13 hours 20 minutes, won by an innings and 579 runs – decided, 'Never again.'

Personally I would like to see a match to a finish tried as an experiment once more, at least in Australia where all Tests used to be played on this basis, and where even today it should be possible to produce a pitch with sufficient pace to encourage a positive attitude on the part of both batsmen and bowlers.

The trouble at Durban in March 1939 was a pitch of such blameless ease that no bowler could make an impression against batsmen geared wholly for defence. South Africa, winning the toss for the first time, determined to bat for as long as possible and did so for 13 hours, on the assumption that England would be obliged to bat in the fourth innings – some time – on a worn pitch. As it turned out when rain brought the game to an unlamented end on the tenth afternoon the only marks on the pitch were the shallow indentations behind the stumps made by the wicket-keepers. The business part of the pitch was still flawless, the reason being that after two overnight storms the groundsman was able, according to the playing conditions, to roll at dawn. Thus he made three virtually new pitches, each of which, after the moisture had been drawn off by the scorching heat by the time the day's play started, was even slower and easier than the one before.

Students of history will be familiar with the *Wisden* version of this extraordinary game which covers three and a half pages of the 1940 volume. Written at second-hand it relates all the sixteen records – the longest game ever, in which the most runs ever were scored (1981), and so on and so on. The account is peppered with more superlatives than would have been used, I'm sure, if the writer, N.P., had had to endure it in the flesh. My abiding recollections are of the sole commentator's struggle to keep going for two hours a day without assistance, in great heat and high humidity, when the action was so turgid: the crowds, big at the start, getting smaller and smaller as the game grew (theoretically at least) to a

climax : and above all the complete indifference to the result of
the players on both sides as at the end of all the effort, with the
rain teeming down outside and the bags packed for departure by
train that evening in order to catch the mail steamer leaving from
the Cape three days later, they relaxed in one another's dressing-
rooms over copious draughts.

Happily I kept a cuttings-book of this, my first Test tour – as I
have done of all subsequent ones – and the faded pages make
fascinating reading – to me at least, since there was a great deal
of correspondence in the South African Press about the broadcasting, and feature articles about the broadcaster. The *Cape Argus*
devoted a page to 'The Voice of Cricket, the Story of the Man
with the Mike'. And all of it, or almost all, was embarrassingly
flattering. After the first two Tests in which my work 'pleased every
listener in the country' a deputation apparently waited on R. S.
Caprara, Director of the SABC, pleading for more commentaries,
which were promptly granted, in Afrikaans as well as English.

To a young man feeling his way this sort of thing from the
columnist of the *East London Dispatch* made life taste all the better.
It was pleasant, for instance, to find waiting on the *Athlone Castle*
before we sailed a letter from the Director of Publicity for Johannesburg saying that 'no more able and acceptable talks have ever been
heard than the ones you have given to South Africa'; also a cable
of congratulation from Cyril Vintcent, the chairman of selectors.
I could have had the freedom of South Africa in the spring of 1939
– but, of course, this was the South Africa of the great Imperialist,
Jan Smuts, not that of Malan, or Verwoert, or of Vorster.

One encountered the black South African only in friends' houses
where the servants, in retrospect, with their simplicity, humour and
natural good manners, seem not too unlike the West Indians one
came later to know so well; in domestic surroundings, and at wayside stations where cheerful urchins offered delicious peaches for
sale at the train windows as one relaxed in one's coupé.

But then we saw even less of the Afrikaaner, very few of whom
in those days either watched or played cricket. I suppose one
realized vaguely that this lovely country embraced not one nation
but three, or four, or five; outwardly, though, all was peaceful and
serene. Had we but known, the end of an era was not far away.

10

A Diplomatic Sidelight on Bodyline

I expect it may have been a blessing in disguise, from my point of view, that my introduction to touring abroad with MCC as a cricket-writer came on that peaceful expedition to South Africa rather than, as so nearly happened, with Douglas Jardine's side to Australia six years earlier. That I would have reacted strongly against Bodyline bowling as devised by Jardine and executed by Larwood and Voce I cannot doubt. All that I have heard and read about it, to say nothing of the thoroughly distasteful impact made on me by subsequent fast bowling in Test cricket that has overstepped the borders of intimidation, convinces me that my instinct would have been wholly hostile to this fast, short bowling on the line of the batsman's body to a field of half a dozen short-leg fielders placed to catch the protective stroke.

While that MCC team of 1932/3 was making its stormy progress round Australia the cricket public at home had the choice of only three first-hand reports on which to make their judgement. One came from Jack Hobbs who, as the most distinguished living English cricketer only recently retired from Test cricket and still playing for Surrey, and under Jardine at that, was in an unenviable position : his cables were non-committal though he condemned the bowling methods roundly on his return home. The other famous cricketer writing for the English papers was Warwick Armstrong, the old Australian captain. In his reports he was bitterly critical of Bodyline – but Armstrong's own sportsmanship was not highly regarded in this country as a result of his leadership of the 1921 Australians.

The third report was that of Bruce Harris, my colleague on the *Evening Standard*, a trained journalist but with absolutely no cricket background or experience. He alone of the three declared what English readers most wanted to hear, that the tactics of their side were all fair and above board. If I had gone to Australia in Harris's place people at home, I'm pretty sure, would have been given a different picture. They would have been asked to swallow some unwelcome medicine.

For a young man of 25, however, it would have been a terribly taxing first assignment. Could I have told the story day by day objectively, judicially, dispassionately in the midst of the prevailing tensions and uproar? Who can say? As it happened, it was not until after the war that I found myself faced with cricket controversies which had diplomatic implications beyond the game itself.

I have written fairly extensively on the subject but I return to it here since intimidation by fast bowlers is a current danger, the rights and wrongs of Bodyline are to this day not generally understood in England, and certain evidence on the subject has come my way which has not hitherto seen the light of day.

For instance, on the journalistic side Reuter's correspondent, Gilbert Mant, who was dissuaded from giving his version of the tour afterwards by his then chairman and has never done so since, recently sent me the following interesting account of his situation as the one agency correspondent with the team. He says:

My real reason for writing to you is that I recently read for the first time your admirable *Sort of a Cricket Person*, which I greatly enjoyed. In it you mention my association with the Bodyline Tour, and I thought you might like to know the background to my silence on the rights and wrongs of the question in my Reuter cables; bearing in mind that Reuter was only supposed to supply the scores and a factual account of the play.

But the Bodyline Tour was exceptional in many ways. My own appointment as the Reuter–PA representative was the result of a Reuter–PA internecine feud. The PA wanted Southerton. Reuters wanted me (I was a staff member) – and Reuters won. I think, in retrospect, it might have been better for cricket if it had been the other way round, as Southerton might have been very outspoken about Bodyline (presuming he would have disapproved of it) and would have had the authority of a well-known cricket writer to do so.

As it was, I was unknown and had also committed the cardinal crime of being an Australian, and from the moment Douglas Jardine discovered this I was suspect in his eyes. He really was a paranoiac Australian-hater. We had hardly any communication throughout the tour, though I was the best of friends with every-one else in the team.

It made my job very difficult and was all the more reason why my reports had to be scrupulously factual and non-partisan. The team were in the same boat when England–Australian relations became strained to breaking point. They had to stick together regardless of their private feelings on Bodyline. Very few of them, especially professional batsmen such as Herbert Sutcliffe, wanted Bodyline in county cricket. As a sort of cricket person myself, I was appalled at what it would do to social club cricket. But, being an Australian, I felt that my lips were sealed, so to speak, and my motives would be suspect.

The only other English correspondents on the tour were Jack Hobbs (ghosted by Jack Ingham) and Bruce Harris. Hobbs was definitely anti-Bodyline, but Jack Ingham understandably saw wonderful copy in the general uproar and the Australian 'squealing'.

Bruce Harris (who became my close friend until his death) was a tennis writer and knew nothing whatever about cricket. He became Jardine's disciple and Bodyline, therefore, was justified without any thought for the future of cricket.

So, you see, the British Press had no way of learning the deeper implications of Bodyline and the real feelings of many members of the English side. Southerton might have made all the difference.

On the way back to England, I wrote the first chapters of a book about the tour. I asked Sir Roderick Jones, then chairman of Reuters, for permission to submit it for publication. When I told him I was taking an anti-Bodyline attitude he said, 'I think it would be better if you did not go ahead with it' – so that was that. He obviously did not want Reuters to be involved in such a controversy.

Since Southerton was just about to become editor of *Wisden*, and as such wrote a judicial condemnation of the methods used in the edition of 1934, there is no reason to doubt that from first hand he would have been equally critical. His words would have carried considerable weight. But there was also a significant diplomatic exchange on the burning question as between Adelaide and London apart from the cables back and forth (there were nine in all) as between the Australian Board of Control and MCC.

It was at Adelaide in the third Test that the Australian indignation at the bowling methods reached its climax. It was here that Woodfull and Oldfield were seriously injured, here that the police were massed behind the stands ready to intervene if the crowds stormed the field and attacked the England players, from here that the Australian Board sent its cable to Lord's deploring their team's 'unsportsmanlike' behaviour.

It happened that the Governor of South Australia, Sir Alexander Hore-Ruthven (later Lord Gowrie) was home on leave at the time, but there was another Englishman at Government House, and a cricketer at that, Legh Winser, the Comptroller – now 92 and still going strong. Winser, he has told me, was approached during the match by three prominent citizens of Adelaide, the editor and manager of the *Advertiser* and the general manager of Elder, Smith, the shipping line, asking him to urge the Australian acting Governor to cable Hore-Ruthven acquainting him of the danger of the situation. In the end Winser himself sent a wire composed by these three and he has often claimed to me that it was this wire that led to the end of the controversy.

On its receipt Hore-Ruthven went to see J. H. Thomas, Secretary of State for the Dominions, in London, and when he returned to Adelaide he followed up the interview with the following letter:

21st June 1933

Dear Mr Thomas,

Since I have been back here I cannot help being rather perturbed over the result of these unfortunate cricket incidents which you and I discussed last spring, and I am afraid that they have had a serious affect on the good feeling of the two countries. We both had the opportunity of observing the very strong anti-Australian feeling which had been aroused in England by these incidents, and on my return here I find a deep sense of injustice and a genuine feeling that the true facts of the case have not been fairly represented at home. This atmosphere, I feel, at all costs, we must endeavour to remove.

The cabled reply of the MCC Committee to the Board of Control has just been published and I am afraid has caused a certain amount of disappointment. In all controversies there are two sides to the question, and I will try and put to you as well as I can the Australian point of view, which it is felt here has not been thoroughly appreciated, but I know how difficult it is to realize both sides of the case at a distance of twelve thousand miles.

The reply is criticized on the grounds that the MCC have decided that there is nothing wrong with the Leg Theory or Larwood's bowling methods. Later on they say they will carefully watch this method of bowling during the present season and invite opinions and suggestions with a view to enable them to express an opinion at a special meeting of the Imperial Cricket Conference later on.

To announce first of all that they consider the leg theory perfectly correct, and later on to say they will express an opinion at the end of the season seems to be hardly consistent. The MCC say they have reached this conclusion after hearing the views of Jardine, Warner and Palairet. Jardine's views are, of course, obvious, but what views Warner expressed we do not know – if he supported the leg theory he must have altered his view considerably since he wrote his article in the 1930 edition of *Badminton*, and which has been freely quoted in Australia, and reads as follows :

'It is, of course, nearly always possible in a one, two or three day match to prevent your opponents winning, in the event of their getting level or ahead of the clock, by instructing your bowlers to bowl a good length outside the leg stump, with six or seven fieldsmen on the on side, but for ourselves, and we believe the vast majority of cricketers, we regard such tactics as unsportsmanlike, and quite contrary to the spirit and traditions of the game, and we would scorn such a manœuvre, and would rather suffer a hundred defeats than put it into practice.'

It is realized how difficult it would be for the MCC to admit the Australian point of view without appearing to let down their own men, but if we claim to be fair-minded people surely the

Australian side of the question should also have been heard before a definite announcement was made.

I confess that until I arrived out here I was under the impression that the Australians' attitude with regard to Jardine and Larwood was not altogether warranted, but since I have been back and have had opportunities of discussing the question with sound, reasonable men, I am forced to the conclusion that the Australian case had far more justification than one would have been led to suppose at the other side of the world. When you have practically the unanimous opinion of thousands of spectators who have watched cricket and played cricket for years that the old spirit of the game was not being maintained, and you have fair-minded men of well-balanced judgement leaving the ground in disgust and refusing to return, you must seek for the reason.

I saw most of the matches in the previous tour, including the one in Adelaide when England won by 11 runs, and the atmosphere of the crowd on that occasion was all that could be desired, and the barracking was confined to a few hooligans on the mound, so there must have been some reason for such a very marked change in the behaviour of the crowd during the last Test here when murmurs of disapproval came from all parts of the ground.

The MCC accuse the Board of Control for not checking the barracking, but how can you control fifty thousand indignant people? There is only one way – remove the cause – and the trouble will cease. It has been pointed out here that leg theory and barracking are two distinct questions, one affecting the playing of the game by the players, the other the conduct of the spectators, and should be considered separately.

The leg-theory question is a technical one which only experts can decide. Barracking is a question of good manners which public opinion alone can deal with, but to mix up the two is confusing the issue and can only lead to further recrimination and ill-feeling. It is also felt that the initial mistake lay in the selection, as Captain, of a man of Jardine's temperament and reputed antipathy towards Australia which had not escaped notice in the previous tour, and that it is hardly 'cricket' on the part of the MCC to allot Australia all the blame for the trouble which subsequently arose as the result of their unfortunate selection.

If a team is not sent home to England next year and we admit that England and Australia cannot settle their cricket differences, it will not only widen the breach between the two countries, but our prestige as sportsmen will suffer all over the world. But if a team is sent, the proper atmosphere must be created beforehand, both here and in England.

The MCC have evidently decided that they cannot admit any justification for the Australian attitude without appearing disloyal to their own men, and reasonable people out here appreciate their difficulty, but the English Press are not tied down in this way, and if properly informed can give a fair presentation of the case from both angles, and if the leading newspapers can make the people realize in England that there are two sides to this question, and that the Australian point of view must in all fairness be considered, it would have a very good affect here and pave the way to a reception of the Australians if they go to England next year. The leading newspapers here are being very moderate and reasonable at the present moment. I enclose a leader from the Adelaide *Advertiser* which could not be more helpful or in better taste.

Individual players, too, have restrained from comment but the ill-timed effusions of Jardine and Larwood have added fuel to the fire, and a headline in an English paper AUSTRALIA RECEIVES WELL-DESERVED SNUB FROM THE MCC has only increased the friction which already exists.

Australians are, I know, susceptible to criticism, but they are equally susceptible to sympathy and consideration, and any indication, however slight, that there was some justification for their attitude, would go a long way to banish the feeling of injustice which now exists. That feeling rankles even to the extent of reluctance to buy English goods, which business men inform me is going on to a certain extent in this city today.

So I am sure you will agree with me that this sense of injustice must be removed and the English Press seems to be the best instrument to bring this about.

So if you could use your good offices with the leading London

editors, these unfortunate misunderstandings would disappear and
we could resume our cricket contests in the happy and friendly
spirit which has always existed in the past.

(Sd.) A. Hore-Ruthven

The Rt. Hon
The Secretary of State
for Dominion Affairs,
London.

Jimmy Thomas would have received this forthright appraisal
shortly before making his Bodyline reference in the speech at
Claridge's mentioned in the previous chapter. Whether he made
any serious effort to adjust public opinion by an approach to Fleet
Street who can say? However, in May 1933 the first Lord Hail-
sham, then Secretary of State for War, had been nominated as
President of MCC. We can therefore safely assume that Thomas,
on receiving the letter, will have communicated it, along with his
own observations, to his Cabinet colleague, who will in turn have
acquainted the MCC Committee with what must have seemed to
them disquieting criticism from an influential quarter.

Even though the MCC Committee neglected to call in evidence
either Bob Wyatt, Jardine's vice-captain, who was always dead
against Bodyline, or Gubby Allen who played throughout the
series, bowling in an orthodox manner, having refused Jardine's
plea to revert to a leg-side field, the truth during the summer seems
gradually to have filtered through to them, almost despite themselves.

David Wilson, son of C. E. M. and nephew of Rockley, recently
came across a letter of that period from his father to his uncle
quoting Lord Hawke, the Treasurer of MCC, saying that the real
problem was to prevent Bodyline recurring 'without letting down
Douglas Jardine too badly'.

It must have been difficult for those at home to make up their
minds as to the rights and wrongs of Bodyline at the time, in the
light only of the first-hand reports of Hobbs, Armstrong and Harris.
But there had been a certain amount of what one might term
'modified fast leg-theory' in English cricket the preceding summer,
by the famous Notts pair, Larwood and Voce, by Bowes for Yorkshire, and also by Farnes both in the University Match and for

Essex. Pieter van der Bijl, who got a Blue that year for Oxford, was a vast fellow not nearly nimble enough on his feet to avoid a man of Ken Farnes's pace 'digging them in', and I can hear now the bull-like bellows that echoed round Lord's as he took the ball willy-nilly on various portions of his anatomy from the waist up.

Leonard Crawley was one of the first to realize what was afoot, as may be judged from this letter published in *The Times* a few days after the Adelaide Test:

27th January, 1933

Sir,

May I trespass on your valuable space to discuss the article which appeared in your pages on January 19 with regard to the protest recently received by the MCC from the Australian Board of Control against the employment of a 'leg-theory' in cricket?

In the first place, though McDonald and Gregory did undoubtedly send down an occasional ball at the batsman's body, they cannot be said, anyway while playing for Australia, to have employed a 'leg-theory', in that such balls were exceptional and were bowled to a field with only two men on the leg-side. It is surely unfair to compare these tactics with the policy of delivering six such balls per over to a field so set as to penalize a batsman who is defending not his wicket, but his head. The last thing I wish to do is to bring a charge of malice-aforethought towards the batsman against either our captain or the bowlers he employs. But that our 'shock' bowlers bowl deliberately at the batsman's body cannot honestly be denied.

The real objection of the Australians, your correspondent alleges, is to the 'array of leg-fielders'. I submit that it is to this, in conjunction with body-line bowling, that the Australians very rightly, in my view, take exception. As long as these tactics are allowed, the batsman will be frightened into giving up his wicket, and if Bradman cannot survive them, I am satisfied that not one of the great players of the past could have fared any better.

It would obviously be impossible for even so august a body as the MCC to dictate to a captain as to how he should place his field. But a short-pitched ball is a bad ball, and one which, without the remotest chance of striking the wicket, stands a considerable chance of doing the batsman bodily harm. And it seems to me that the very least that can be done in the best interests of the game is to empower the umpire to 'no-ball' a bowler for pitching his deliveries short. But to my mind the whole question demands consideration from an entirely different angle. Your correspondent urges the point that 'Cricket is not played with a soft ball, and that a fast ball which hits a batsman on the body is bound to hurt'. Rugby football is also considered by some a fair training ground for manly and courageous virtues. And yet in the event of a player wilfully hacking, tripping, or striking another player, instead of going for the ball, the referee is required by the Laws of Rugby Football to order the offender off the field on the second offence. It seems to me that the analogy between this and the policy of deliberately bowling at a portion of the batsman's body which is not obscuring the wicket is a fairly close one; and the penalty is as well deserved in the one case as the other. In either game enough knocks are given and received in the ordinary course of events to satisfy the most bloodthirsty fire-eater among the spectators. But I would like to see some of the most eloquent supporters of the 'leg-theory' step into the arena against a bowler of Larwood's pace and face it for themselves.

Yours, etc.,

Leonard Crawley.

One result of this prescient and thoroughly damning summing-up – written, of course, by a current top-class cricketer and, incidentally, a fine player of fast bowling – was an invitation to Leonard from Sir Stanley Jackson (also on the MCC Committee) to come and see him. When Leonard did so and gave some sort of practical exposition of the problem faced by the batsman Jackson said, 'Well, if this sort of thing had happened in my day I would not have played cricket.'

It was touch and go whether or not the Australian tour of England arranged for the following year would take place. In the end the MCC Committee decided only by eight votes to five to confirm the invitation, and the Australians accepted to come, though not without misgiving. For until Jardine himself settled the matter shortly before their arrival by opting to report the Australian tour rather than play against them there was no certainty he would not be chosen. What the effect of that might have been in Australia

Hore-Ruthven pointed out in a letter to Plum Warner on 5 February 1934, of which the following is part:

> The Jardine question is very important and from what I can see from the signs out here, the only thing which could disturb the harmony players and public are all anxious to maintain would be to put Jardine in charge again. The whole atmosphere will be altered if he is made captain. The players will go on the field with a feeling of irritation and suspicion, and it will play into the hands of the extreme element here who wanted to demand guarantees that Jardine would not be captain and that body-line bowling would not be allowed, and they will say at once that 'Gentlemen's Agreements' are no good to them, and in future we must have the written guarantees. And, moreover, the sensational section of the Australian Press will make the most of it and start the controversy all over again.
>
> So if you want the game to be played in the proper spirit and the whole controversy buried once and for all, keep Jardine out of the picture on any plea you can find. I know the difficulties of not appearing to let him down, but the question is so vital, not only from the point of view of cricket, but of the friendly feeling between the two countries, that some excuse must be found for leaving him out. As once a sore is opened again it is going to be very difficult to heal, and all the soothing syrup we have administered of late will be wasted.
>
> You may think that I am exaggerating the facts that Jardine's captaincy would give rise to, but it has been my business to make a careful study of Australian mentality for the last six years and I have no doubt as to the repercussions this would cause on men's minds out here, and these are not only my personal opinions but are shared by many who are far better judges than I. So I think it best to speak one's mind openly, and I hope you will forgive me for being so frank.

I don't suppose for a moment that the Governor of South Australia was overstating the case, for the accusation that the Australians were squealing had added insult to injury with a vengeance. Here are some verses published in England at the time which, as one remembers it, illustrated pretty well popular feeling in what Australians of those days generally referred to as 'the old country':

> Indignant daughter of the South,
> We always have admired your pluck;
> But now you're rather out of luck
> Why not preserve a firmer mouth?
>
> Where is that tough Australian grin?
> When, Digger, did you learn to faint?
> Can you not take without complaint
> A dose of your own medicine?
>
> Finish this futile brawl today!
> We won't believe the paradox,
> A whining Digger funking knocks;
> Come on! One up, and two to play!

Reading this sort of stuff almost, though not quite, gave me some sympathy with the outlook of the writer of one of the most hate-filled letters I've ever had. It was written after reading *SOCP* by a citizen of Bourke, New South Wales, whose antipathy to the Crown and all things British apparently stemmed from the events of this tour of 1932/3.

So much for the intimidation inherent in Bodyline. It is a subject, needless to say, that has a sharp relevance now. The law may have been tightened to prevent a modern Larwood bowling persistently short and fast on the line of the body with a crescent of six short-legs and a long-leg – only four or five short-legs and two or three long-legs if the batsman was a good hooker! But the fast bouncer bowled to excess is likewise certain to provoke ill-feeling and is physically perhaps even more dangerous in that the victim does not know when it is coming. Woodfull's Australians at least were sure they need not concern themselves with the off-side since there were only two fielders there, a sort of fly-slip most of the way back to the fence to cover the snick and a man close in front to prevent the stolen single.

I will not here remount my hobby-horse, though it has been out to grass for a while. But it is interesting that in the Hore-Ruthven–

Warner correspondence Plum suggested drawing a line across the pitch, any ball short of which should be penalized. Fast bowlers come and go in cycles. For a while in the late '60s there wasn't a fast bowler in the world remotely comparable in speed to Lillee, Thomson, Roberts, Holding and Daniel. There was no call then for any legislation. But if extreme speed persists, and umpires remain as reluctant to adjudicate on the intent to frighten as they always have been, that horizontal line may yet come, repugnant though its introduction would be.

I I

Aspects of Oxford

I lived briefly in Oxford before the war, in Holywell, and for six years afterwards at Pusey House. It might be more accurate to say I was based at Pusey House, because though I had no other home I spent little time there out of the University term. For the rest of those years, 1946 to 1952, I was mostly on the business of the *Daily Telegraph* either at home or abroad, or playing cricket or golf, or putting up, in London, at the Bath Club or in Rye at the Dormy House. I was never an undergraduate. Hence the title of this chapter.

There are those who love England more than the English; some (possibly including myself) who have never had children are fonder of them than those who have. There can be an inherent attraction in what one has missed. By the same token I who was never 'up' had a deeper affection for Oxford, I'm sure, than many who with various degrees of benefit and pleasure, and emerging with various degrees or none, had been through the system. For the best part of half a century I never drove in over Magdalen Bridge without a thrill of anticipation, or left without a pang.

The lure of the Parks in early summer and the annual shaping of successive University XIs; reporting the sterner battles at Iffley Road in winter; much keen if not too serious golf at Frilford Heath and Huntercombe; the easy companionship of Vincent's; glimpses of college life from several angles; the high table at Christ Church and more modest Senior Common Rooms; havens of hospitality and fellowship, butteries, pubs and lodging-houses; the civilized Christian quiet of Pusey House and the peace of one's own rooms therein; the bells, and the spires, and the mellow beauty of halls and quadrangles; pervading all, the company of friends : the sum of these things made for me the magic of Oxford.

It was my job which took me there first, to watch the University play rugger, and my first recollection is of staying in Wadham after a game as guest of a childhood friend, Kenneth Hood, a Cheltonian, and the pair of us getting, I regret to say, deplorably drunk. I became Rugby football correspondent of the *Evening Standard* in 1927, so the occasion might well have been the visit to Iffley Road of the Australian Waratahs on whom, incidentally, the University inflicted their first defeat.

With the publication of Evelyn Waugh's *Diaries*, and other recent memoirs of the '20s and '30s, it must almost seem to younger generations that Oxford in those days was awash with drink, tempting to excess a horde of potential alcoholics. This was far from the truth. The aesthetes of Waugh's day led lives as far removed from that of the average undergraduate as those of the rich and noisy members of the 'Bullingdon'. Yet in those carefree days when liquor was cheap the undergraduate who seldom frequented his college buttery or a favourite pub for a pint or two of beer was probably the exception. And there were certainly many more 'parties', both in college and out, both spontaneous and prearranged.

One regular port of call of which I usually seemed to know the inmates was 'The Old Parsonage' at the near end of the Banbury road, a Trinity lodging run by a venerable landlord, much beloved and also much put upon, so short-sighted that he never had an idea who was on his premises at any given time. After some exceptional hilarity had led to trouble the President of Trinity referred to the house, so it was reported, as 'a focus for hospitality' – an understatement if ever there was one. (Strange how such a phrase sticks in the mind after so long!) They were sporting types who inhabited 'The Old Parsonage', and if ever a roll-call could be made I suspect that their war record would be found to be spectacular, their casualties likewise.

Why, I wonder, did I develop a distinct partiality for the dark blue rather than the light, since I soon had friends at Cambridge and came to know it scarcely less well? Probably the preference derived first from following the fortunes of two Cranleigh contemporaries, H. P. Jacob who captained Oxford at Twickenham in 1925 and M. A. McCanlis who did so at Lord's in 1928. Maurice indeed was a double Blue for cricket and rugger, and both he and Jacob played rugger for England. Between them they made eight appearances against Cambridge, most of which I contrived to see. But my fancy may also have derived from a natural sympathy for the under-dog, since the '20s was a golden period in Cambridge sport. On the football field it was in several instances easier to get an international cap than a Blue.

Two wholesale defeats running at Twickenham against Cambridge sides of much brilliance seemed to tie in with allegations of Oxford decadence. In parenthesis stronger evidence on this score seemed to be forthcoming when the Oxford Union decided after an historic debate that they would refuse to fight for King and Country. That, however, was in 1933, by which time Oxford were giving as good as they got at Lord's and Twickenham if not, emphatically, between Putney and Mortlake.

I happened to be dining in the 'George', a convivial restaurant then and for many years after, presided over by Mr Ehrssam, when the result of the debate came through. It was greeted as something of a joke by our sporting company, who had little respect for Union pretensions : if I can trust my memory at such a distance I think – no, I'm sure – that at the mature age of 26 my reaction was of consternation. We know now that this piece of undergraduate nonsense helped to persuade Hitler that England, let alone Oxford, was decadent and ripe for plucking.

The debate wherein the Union 'under the inspiration of a Mr Joad passed their ever-shameful resolution' is referred to by Winston Churchill in Volume I of *The Second World War*. He continues :

It was easy to laugh off such an episode in England, but in Germany, in Russia and in Japan the idea of a decadent, degenerate Britain took deep root and swayed many calculations. Little did the foolish boys who passed the resolution dream that they were destined quite soon to conquer or fall gloriously in the ensuing war, and prove themselves the finest generation ever bred in Britain. Less excuse can be found for their elders, who had no chance of self-redemption in action.

Churchill also remarks that Lord Lloyd, who was on friendly terms with Mussolini, 'noted how he had been struck by the Joad resolution'. At this time C. E. M. Joad was an atheistic pacifist. Later he recanted on both counts. He will be remembered as a member of the popular original BBC Brains Trust, and towards the end of his life was converted to Christianity and received into the Church of England.

To me the headquarters of the OURFC at Iffley Road spells not decadence but courage and stamina and every masculine virtue – heroism indeed, especially in the battles between adolescents and the more mature and physically stronger visitors from the Commonwealth such as the All Blacks and Springboks which, with the annual 'Stanley's Match', were the red-letter days.

I can see now the steam rising from the sweating packs on an autumn afternoon of driving rain and mud when the 1935/6 All Blacks came. Oxford, with three-quarters of the game gone, were only a point behind at 5–4. Micky Walford in the centre makes a sudden break from his own half, and feeds the blond figure outside. Down the right touch-line, straight towards us in the pavilion, flaxen hair streaming, streaks Alex Obolensky with his unique flash of speed. Amid the high-pitched squawks of the boys of Summer Fields and the Dragon School clustered behind the goal he rounds Gilbert, the great full-back, and touches down beneath the bar. John Brett kicks the goal, the 'Varsity lead 9–5, and visions arise of the first defeat ever administered to these mighty New Zealanders on English soil.

Again Obolensky crosses, but the touch-judge decides he has put a boot-stud on the line. The All Black forwards make a last tremendous effort, and from a maul in the corner Sadler, the scrum-half, wriggles over on the blind side. All rests on the kick from the touch-line with the heavy, greasy ball. The odds are long against him on such a day, but Gilbert lands the goal, and a few minutes later Oxford are making a lane for their conquerors and applauding them in : 10–9 the score and if ever honours are easy this is the day.

A couple of months later at Twickenham England with their Russian prince on the wing beat the All Blacks for the one and only time in this country, thanks chiefly to 'Obo' who scored two tries including one of the great ones of history, wrong-footing the entire defence as he cut inwards from the right in a swift, slanting run that finished half-way between the goal and the left corner-flag. There was never a nicer man than Alex, who, flying a Hurricane that crashed on landing, became the first of oh ! how many distinguished Rugby footballers killed in the war. Of the Oxford XV of 1937 only eight survived.

The late Ross McWhirter in the *Centenary History of the OURFC* says that Obolensky captured the public imagination more than any Oxford player since Ronny Poulton, and he records also that before playing a match in London Alex used to lunch off a dozen oysters at the Sports Club. Walford, by the way, was an outstanding Oxford sportsman, in the last decade of peace second only to Owen-Smith. At rugger, hockey and cricket he played more than 150 times for the University -- which must be a record. As a Sherborne master later he made thousands of runs for Somerset in the holidays. He had many international caps at hockey and might easily have had one for rugger.

Apart from such bright particular stars as these what glamour used to surround the University sportsmen of the inter-war years – and, for that matter, for a decade or so afterwards! Oxford used to arrive at Twickenham in a fleet of Rolls-Royces, decked with dark blue ribbon as though for a wedding, and they came with the sea air in their lungs from the luxury of the Grand Hotel, Eastbourne, their headquarters for the final training period. (A touch of showmanship this which strongly suggests 'Uncle' Stanley.)

Pampered? By modern comparison, yes; but in return they maintained high standards both of performance and sportsmanship. The *History* quotes Dr Edward Nicholson, who hooked for four years for Oxford and five times also for England, as writing of the University Match : 'It was quite the fastest, most paralysingly exhausting, and invariably the cleanest game of the season.' Denys Swayne (also a Dr) is even more explicit regarding his two appearances : 'Both games were . . . played in a, now unknown, spirit of genuine good fellowship and I cannot remember a single incident of unpleasantness.'

Now unknown! From what little I see the stricture is blatantly evident today when the sort of men who comprised the old University teams are rare indeed. The ethos is quite different. The British sporting world generally – not only the football scene – used to be very much the better for the example of the Blues, both dark and light, who in general were admired not only for their prowess but for being the men they were.

This should not be read as derogatory by the University sportsmen of the '70s who are, like the rest of us, victims of their environments, brought up under a much-changed social order. They get up to Oxford and Cambridge today despite their games ability, and in consequence University sport, far from leading the field, struggles to hold its own. The optimists say there are some signs of a change of heart. They think the University disturbances of the '60s have awakened college authorities to a revision of their selection methods, that character may again begin to count for something, as well as A levels. Pray Heaven they are right.

I cannot pass by the name of Ross McWhirter with such a casual mention. He was foully murdered, it will be recalled, before Christmas 1975, when Self-Help, the organization which he and his twin brother, Norris, founded, was in the act of setting up a newspaper designed to function despite the Trade Unions if extreme elements at a time of crisis sought to compound confusion by shutting down Fleet Street. He died for freedom as surely as those of the Oxford generation senior to his died in the war.

Ross's most massive memorial is, of course, *The Guinness Book of Records*, started by the twins, which has sold over twenty-five million copies in thirteen languages. He was a man of many parts whose qualities I came to know well from our long association watching football together all over the place from Murrayfield to Paris. But the *Centenary History of the OURFC (1869–1969)* was a challenge after his own heart wherein he combined with Sir Andrew Noble to produce one of the classics of sport.

When the book was being written 743 men had represented Oxford at Rugby football. There are biographies of all 743 within its dark blue covers, those of almost all the survivors of that number gleaned from personal correspondence with Sir Andrew. The latter was refused permission to send a printed notice by his son-in-law Kenneth Spence, captain in 1952, chairman of the Centenary Committee. Accordingly he wrote or himself typed 1500 letters. Not a bad effort from a distinguished diplomat who at the crown of his career was Her Majesty's envoy at, successively, Helsinki, Warsaw, Mexico and The Hague. 'People makes games what they are,' I wrote when reviewing this remarkable book for the *Sunday Telegraph*,

and the qualities of courage and self-discipline necessary to win a rugger Blue are eloquently portrayed here both in the epic struggles themselves and, no less, in the subsequently distinguished careers of most of those who have worn the dark blue jersey.

There have been bishops and Cabinet ministers, ambassadors, judges, and penal reformers, headmasters, colonial governors, experts in the arts, captains of commerce aplenty.

Trade and industry, the teaching profession and the Law account for more than half the total. The Church, the Civil Service and Medicine follow, in that priority. The whole saga of endeavour is a striking refutation of Kipling's tedious gibe at 'muddied oafs'.

It is time to take our leave of Iffley Road and the strong whiff of embrocation and tea and rock-buns warmed by the cheerful fire in the pavilion grate, pausing only to note that though numerically Oxford is smaller than Cambridge, and in most sporting contests there is a slender balance of wins in favour of Cambridge, in this, the manliest of games, Oxford's total of victories has never been headed. It is a singular fact that eleven times in the early days – and again last December – Cambridge drew level, or retained parity. Oxford so far have always gone ahead again – which gives a special flavour to the match in 1977. Of the 95 meetings since 1872 (war years excluded) each claims 41 victories, and there have been 13 draws.

Let us now change seasons and turn into the University Parks in the middle of which the OUCC since 1881 has held its precious ten acres by a Decree of Convocation which we may pray is never countermanded. It is a ground on which cricket is played rather than a cricket ground since there are no permanent seats other than in the pavilion, and only a circular rope divides the field from the meadowland surrounding it. Within the rope are deck-chairs and beyond it, facing the pavilion at the northern end, is a deep row of trees of almost every variety from the poplar to the copper beech. It is the trees which in spring leaf make the glory of the Parks and justify its claim to be the loveliest ground in the world on which first-class cricket is played.

Since no money could be collected in the Parks (a regulation since to some extent modified) the Australians used to be played on the Christ Church ground, and my first recollection of cricket at Oxford is of the visit of the first of Woodfull's two teams in 1930. Don Bradman, who had taken England by storm, arrived on 28 May, needing 78 runs to reach his thousand in May, a golden milestone reached hitherto only by a select company of four, W.G., Tom Hayward, Walter Hammond and Charlie Hallows of Lancashire. When Australia declared with 406 on the board the University had dismissed only two of them but one of those wickets was Bradman's – LBW to Garland-Wells for 32. Seeing that over his career the Don made a hundred every third time he went to the crease it is passing strange that in six innings against Oxford and Cambridge he made only one, at Fenner's. Going on from Oxford to Southampton, by the way, in 1930 he just reached his thousand on 31 May before rain ended play for the day.

Considering the far greater esteem in which University teams were held between the wars and for a while afterwards compared with the present it is worth noting that their performances against the Australians were usually modest to a degree. The decline in status is a matter far more of social attitudes than cricket prowess. So far as most varieties of amateur sport are concerned a wide general interest has dwindled to indifference. More's the pity.

The best showing by an undergraduate against the Australians in my experience was Derek (F. C.) de Saram's hundred on the Christ Church ground in 1934, a lovely innings by a graceful and talented cricketer. Derek came from Ceylon. He could easily have had a lawn-tennis Blue but joined the cricketers when he decided that with the lawn-tennis authorities his colour seemed to be unacceptable. The young are normally more open-minded – civilized indeed – than their elders in matters of race. This is the only instance of its kind that ever came to my notice as far as the Universities were concerned – and it happened more than forty years ago! On the other side of the slate one can think of several coloured sportsmen who were quite exceptionally popular – Kumar Shri Duleepsinhji (shortened at Cambridge to 'Smith'), Jahangir Khan and his son Majid, 'Buck' Divecha, 'Monkey' Cameron, the Pataudis, R. K. Pitamber, Baig and Goonesena, to name a few.

Many of my early memories of the Parks centre on Raymond Robertson-Glasgow who in his *Morning Post* days used to find his way there as often as he decently could. Before school term began one would see also in the nets or the Long Room Harry Altham and

Frank Gilligan, eldest of the Gilligan trinity, who had been invited up to help sort out the new material, and to be on hand for advice, by the captain of the year. At least two other very good cricketers, 'Hooky' (D. V.) Hill of Worcestershire and J. C. Masterman, saw a lot of cricket, on and off, despite their busy preoccupations; nor must I forget Geoffrey Bolton, who in his retirement wrote the history of the OUCC, and who claimed in his book to have seen a part of most of the matches in the Parks during his 47 years of teaching at Summer Fields. There was usually a supply of informed opinion, in and around the pavilion, of which almost every captain had the good sense to make use.

The captains, in those days of cheap newsprint and much longer reports, might find value, too, in the comments of Crusoe and others – almost all of them constructive and kindly-intentioned. I could scarcely calculate how many thousand words I have written in my time on cricket and football at Oxford and Cambridge.

I can date my first certain remembrance of the Parks as the match against the Indian tourists of 1932 for a thoroughly flippant reason. On the last afternoon around tea-time Crusoe and I were changing for a net and to our great amusement found ourselves overhearing, in the next compartment of the changing-room, an excited Indian argument as to whether they should go for a win or play out time. This was punctuated by a deep and oft-repeated refrain from one of the batsmen : 'EYE play my hook-stroke – we win de match.' In the event they scrambled the runs – thanks to the hook-stroke.

I expect the final details would have been duly noted down by some undergraduate friend to whom Crusoe, when he was tired of recording the dull prosaic facts of a game, would have entrusted a flimsy pad which he called his 'Washing Book'. The Parks, as might be imagined, were Crusoe's spiritual home beyond all other. He was reminded of the old Greek poet's lines about 'the plane whispering to the elm in the beautiful season of spring'. In cricket terms he called them 'a refuge for the connoisseur'.

One year, 1933, Oxford seemed well equipped all round apart from a lack of opening bowling, so 'Nippy' Hone, the captain (now Sir Brian, a distinguished Australian educationist) had the bright thought of parading a selection of strongly-built Authentic cricketers who could bat and field well, and trying them out as bowlers in view of Crusoe and the rest of the cognoscenti.

From the inspection was selected Richard Tindall of Winchester, who duly buckled down to the job and in the next two summers took 50 wickets for the University including five in an innings against the Australians. In view of his subsequent high reputation as a coach it is interesting that, though Alf Gover had not long won his place in the Surrey side, Richard went off to him for some coaching which Alf was kind enough to give on a day when the county had no fixture. The Blues of those days certainly did not lack help and encouragement – while this perhaps is a suitable moment to note the great friendliness which then existed generally between amateur and pro.

Since R. G. Tindall was one of the lost generation and, incidentally, an original Arab and a great friend to me a short sentimental tribute may perhaps remind old and young alike of how in this as in all wars it is the best who are the most likely to go. Richard was one of a gay Trinity company which included Gerald Micklem, whose lifetime of work for golf is a byword; Alan Young, recently retired second master at Bradfield and a good games-playing all-rounder; 'Jimmy' (E. H.) Moss, an admirable Malvern golfer and cricketer; Alan Holmes, an Etonian scholar and cricketer, and John Darwall-Smith, footballer and cricketer, headmaster of Lockers Park, who died recently. Of these Moss and Holmes were also killed, as were ten others of the immediately pre-war Oxford cricket sides.

Richard got Blues for cricket and soccer and nearly had one for golf. A good second in history enabled him to go as a master to Eton where in a few years he made a lasting mark. A serious underlying purpose was masked by abundant humour and a vast enjoyment of life. He was said to have appeared for Early School still wearing the white tie in which he had returned from a night in London only in the nick of time. He was killed in North Africa, and so was spared the decision whether to take a house at Eton, or to enter the lists for one of the major headmasterships which could surely have been his.

If I attempted to sketch some of the Oxford sportsmen of my writing time I could quickly run out of space. There is, however, one, a contemporary of Tindall's, whom I cannot pass by, not only because he was a marvellously gifted sportsman but because he epitomized without compare the amateur spirit at its best and most attractive.

When 'Tuppy' (H. G.) Owen-Smith went up in Michaelmas 1930 he had already as a 20-year-old made a gallant hundred in a Test Match for South Africa at Headingley. So a cricket Blue was assured, and he made his mark at Lord's in all his three years, especially in the first when Oxford, after being catastrophically beaten the previous year, won a highly dramatic victory after fielding out on the first day to a Cambridge score of 385. This was the match when Alan Ratcliffe, having been dropped by Cambridge, came in at the last minute and broke the existing record with an innings of 201. Pataudi, 'the Noob', said: 'They *threw* the runs at him; I shall beat it,' and promptly made 238 not out, taking his cue from Tuppy who, with him, scored 78 in an hour and a half. Then Tuppy with sharp wrist-spin and E. M. Wellings with off-breaks spun Cambridge out and 'at long last Oxford could take down their harps from the trees by the waters of Babylon' (Bolton's *History*!).

I can see Tuppy now skipping yards down the pitch and again and again smacking Arthur Hazlerigg on the full past extra-cover into the old A & B stand beside the pavilion. He showed his footwork, too, in the ring, where he boxed three years against Cambridge as a welterweight, and also, especially, on the football field where an uncanny sense of position as well as wonderful hands made him one of the finest full-backs I ever saw. In 1933, a great year when seventeen present or future internationals played for the two sides at Twickenham, Tuppy seemed at times to be taking on Cambridge single-handed. The following year he won the first of his ten international caps, and in 1937 he led England to the Championship and Triple Crown. No other South African has captained England on the football field, though, of course, Tony Greig has led England at cricket.

He was of only average height and physique but wiry, strong, well balanced, with the fastest reflexes and the heart of a lion. In appearance and approach he was casual to a degree. Anyone's bat would do for him, and he might easily go to the crease without bothering to put on a box. He was essentially the man for the big occasion – which was no doubt why he once somehow in a club match contrived to allow me to make a hundred off him.

Apart from war service in the South African Army Medical Corps Tuppy has spent his life doctoring in the Cape since qualifying at St Mary's. Of all the great sportsmen among the Rhodes Scholars none surely ranks higher than he. South Africa's answer to C. B. Fry? Certainly, but what a complete contrast in physique, mentality, and temperament!

Almost anything would have been acceptable when first-class cricket returned to the Parks in 1946, but, thanks largely to the presence for the first two years of a truly great cricketer in Martin Donnelly of New Zealand, who attracted record crowds to the Parks, the University began with a rare flourish. The counties naturally needed time to recover, while returning servicemen augmented the normal source of supply. Even so Oxford's record over the five years 1946–50 makes remarkable reading:

Won	Lost	Drawn
22	14	26

All but five of the victories were gained over counties, including two 'straight' (i.e. without declarations) in successive years against the full Yorkshire side.

In 1949 Oxford inflicted on the New Zealanders their only defeat of the tour, a game I remember because for the only time in all but fifty years I reported a day's play of which I had seen extraordinarily little. The fact was I had been bidden to lunch at *The Times* by the proprietor, J. J. Astor, and after a brief wrestle with my conscience, accepted. What lay behind the invitation? 'Beau' Vincent, their cricket correspondent, was coming up to retirement age and though I was happy enough at the *Telegraph* no one is the worse in Fleet Street for an alternative offer. So I went to London from Oxford by train, reckoning to be back and in the Parks soon after tea. I was, of course, civilly entertained at Printing House Square, but when Astor started talking about the Cricket Writers' Club, of which I was chairman, I surmised that this was no more than a courtesy invitation in return for the Club's to him when we had entertained the New Zealanders just previously.

Hustling up to the Parks I discovered with a mixture of pleasure and dismay that on this second day, on a horribly spiteful pitch, some twenty wickets had already fallen, and the New Zealanders were fighting for their lives. The *Telegraph* cutting of my report at this distance reads none too badly, so I conclude that I must have had a competent fellow keeping *my* washing-book.

During my time at Pusey House I was naturally fairly close to the successive cricket captains who were, in order, D. H. Macindoe (1946), M. P. Donnelly, H. A. Pawson, C. B. Van Ryneveld, D. B. Carr, M. B. Hofmeyr and P. D. S. Blake (1952). Certain ideas for strengthening the OUCC took root in my mind, and I fear I risked the charge of not minding my own business by giving them a brisk airing. It seemed ridiculous, for instance, that for the purposes of Test profit allocation Oxford and Cambridge should rank with the least of the Minor Counties and receive only a derisory percentage. I stirred friends at Lord's to the extent of getting the Universities' share each up to half that of a first-class county. (Today they get a flat £3500 each plus a Benson & Hedges share, on which, in the most economical way, and with modest help from subscriptions and gates, they just manage to survive.)

Then when the good years suddenly dried up it seemed highly desirable that there should be a resident professional coach to advise the captain and bring the best out of the talent available. Charlie Walters, Tottenham Hotspur footballer and Oxfordshire cricketer, had long been the net bowler and a very good one, but he scarcely pretended to teach the arts of batting.

In the autumn of 1949 we seemed to have found the ideal man in Stan Squires of Surrey, a fine player, a splendid person and a very funny one whose whimsical humour would have been much to the undergraduates' taste. He had himself been coached by Aubrey Faulkner at his School of Cricket, so his credentials were impeccable. A pub was to be made available in Oxford by Abingdon Breweries to keep him occupied in the winter – he was then a licensee at Kingston Hill. All was settled over a day's golf at Frilford and dinner at Vincent's afterwards with Donald Carr, the captain. Then within a couple of months, at the age of 40, Stan died of a rare disease of the blood.

Though several professionals have since rendered good service in the Parks for limited periods, and Arthur Milton last year gave admirable help, no real full-time substitute for what was envisaged in Squires's case has emerged. Nor so far as I know are there modern equivalents to the Altham critical fraternity of times past.

A lot has always depended on the personality of the captain. Nowadays even more depends, since the number of potential Blues coming up is smaller, and the best must be brought out of everyone. Several notably good captains – M. J. K. Smith, for instance, A. C. Smith and R. M. C. Gilliat – have laid in the Parks the foundations which have led on to success in the wider cricket world on coming down. There have also been some terribly depressing years when Oxford cricket in the hands of poor players seemed to have lost almost everything, including enthusiasm and the will to learn. Thank goodness, things at the moment seem somewhat on the mend.

The standard of much of the play in the 1976 University Match was quite encouraging – provided one could forget one's irritation at the effrontery of men on both sides wearing peculiar caps rather than the dark and light blue which has been the proud uniform of their vastly more illustrious predecessors for a century and more. One becomes more tolerant of many things, I find, when one reaches the sere and yellow, but not the flaunting of convention for no discernible reason, knowing that the doing so will give offence.

After which little burst of spleen we might change games again and make our way out of Oxford down past the station up Cumnor Hill, and away to Frilford Heath where both just before the war and for several years after I spent happy hours innumerable. Compared with the official University course at Southfields, which is built on clay and used to be glutinous to a degree in wet weather, Frilford is beautifully dry, sandy, gorse-, bracken- and heather-covered. (Henry Longhurst used to swear he once lost a shoe just sucked into the Southfield ooze while playing there for The Society; but I believe the drainage is now much improved.)

Frilford was the first golf club I ever joined and in 1937/8 I played there a lot of golf far beyond my station with K. B. Scott, Tom Harvey, present captain of the R and A, John Lawrie, who became the much-loved 'stuttering doctor', Dickie Twining, Roger Kimpton and Peter Foster, all of them Blues, as well as various dons rather more adjacent in skill to my 12 handicap. Ken Scott, whom I once saw defeat Cyril Tolley in the Putter, might have been a real Walker Cup high flyer if he had survived the war.

The club secretary used often to join us, Dick Wickham, a highly amusing character with a somewhat dyspeptic exterior which was inclined to awe the membership. What alarmed them more was Dick's form at the poker table. He was Winchester founder's kin, with light blue eyes set in a complexion matching the red of the Old Wykehamist tie he often wore. As an item of poker equipment those unblinking blue eyes were much too formidable for the honest citizens of nearby Abingdon, and when some of them were thought to be staying away from the club for fear of being drawn in it was said that the directors warned poor Dick off the card-room.

But I recall one Wickham triumph of a very different order the telling of which at this distance can scarcely hurt anyone. There was among the women members a Lady Bountiful highly esteemed and very much at the centre of club affairs. She was inclined to win stroke competitions with great regularity, so that horrible rumours began to be whispered that – well, there might just possibly be certain arithmetical inexactitudes in her card.

The secretary was asked to address himself to the matter, which he duly did. The next competition day the suspect went out as usual with her regular lady companion, unaware that Dick was on her track. Literally. He assured us on his honour, fixing us with those blue eyes, that he had positioned himself comfortably in the bracken armed with a periscope to keep the lady under the keenest watch. Alas, when at the end of the round the secretary compared the scores he had noted for various holes with those written down and signed by the companion (who, by the way, was a very poor player fully occupied in scratching along in sixes and sevens or worse) he found serious discrepancies.

What then to do? Confront the culprit and cause a certain furore and resignation? To do nothing would be patently unfair to the rest of the lady golfers of Frilford Heath. But those expecting a dramatic climax must, I fear, be disappointed. The secretary, having pondered the matter, then simply posted a notice on the board. In future, it stated, in order to speed up play, there would be two handicap divisions and members of the one accordingly were not to play in competitions with those of the other. Thus the lady was separated from her companion – who, we may charitably suppose, may in all innocence just have put down what her mistress told her. Whether or not the latter suspected she had been rumbled, she took out no more cards while retaining her membership.

Few, I expect, will dispute the moral of this cautionary tale – whether in sport or the sterner affairs of life. If it can decently be done it is usually best to avoid a row.

The great J. H. Taylor laid out Frilford's original 18 holes to which were added behind the clubhouse as it then was a shortish and absolutely charming nine. Another J. H. – J. H. Turner, the long-serving and popular club professional – designed those, the perfect short course for those with an hour or so to spare after tea.

A few years ago I returned to Frilford after a long absence to play, for the one and only time in my life, in a Pro-Am, and found two 18-hole courses, our favourite little nine now incorporated into the lesser one. For me this was a debit item on the account, but indubitably it is to the good that an area where there are few courses of much account now has 36 holes in fine golfing country of the heath type with a more than adequate clubhouse in addition.

The Thomas Cook Pro-Am was more than I bargained for since I found myself, with two others, partnered with Peter Oosterhuis, the chief attraction. Those acquainted with my swing will wonder that I had the nerve to tee up with a crowd of many hundreds lining the fairway at the first hole and indeed following us faithfully all the way for upwards of four hours in what was for me the protracted and unfamiliar ritual of a four-ball. To start with, the crowd were altogether too close on the leg-side for my peace of mind. However, after one out of the heel had skimmed their heads they swiftly heeded my field-placing, those at mid-on moving appreciably wider.

The best are often the nicest to play with at any game, and our man was no exception though he had a troublesome back and could do no better than a 73. On handicap we amateurs were able to improve this by quite a few strokes but not sufficiently to look like winning. As we brought up the tail-end of the field a crowd in thousands surrounded the 18th green on to which, shaking in every limb, I somehow deposited a 6-iron and with the putt even rimmed the hole for a birdie three. Wonderful on this evidence what the mechanics of fear can achieve!

Huntercombe, a course of great charm beside the Oxford–Henley road, used to be the scene of a match between the Arabs and the Oxford second team or Divots until we removed our golfing activities to Sandwich. It was owned for many years up to his death by

Lord Nuffield, the great car manufacturer who as William Morris had started life running a bicycle shop in Oxford. Nuffield came to own it – as was commonly said, and I believe accurately – in this way. He was himself a member, but, when his wife wanted to join, her nomination was turned down. How any committee thought they could reasonably refuse the wife of a member baffles belief. One can only suppose that a ladies' committee was concerned, but as it all happened 40-odd years ago it might be difficult to verify the details. Anyhow, shortly afterwards little Nuffield returned home one day and told his wife it would in future be quite in order for her to play: he had bought the place, lock, stock and barrel.

One Sunday after lunch I was driving off against the Divots, with his lordship and a few friends in rather hilarious form round the tee. When I remarked on this to someone they said: 'What's he laughing at? Your swing, of course.' It's said to be quite a simple matter nowadays getting one's method 'shot' on video-tape, played back in slow motion, and stopped at appropriate moments. No doubt it might be very helpful to some, but somehow I can't quite face it. (Let me interpolate here, at the plea of my wife, who has suffered enough from it in all conscience, that my swing does owe some of its peculiarity to the fact that an attack of polio when a POW has left me with a withered left shoulder. I was lucky, of course, to get away so lightly. And I can't help laughing at the remark of a boy caddy who after my initial stroke said, 'Here, I've carried for you before!')

Most of these sporting delights would have been out of my reach had I not had permanent lodging inside the somewhat stern modern Gothic building lurking behind the trees half-way up St Giles on the south side, known as Pusey House. I tried to express in *SOCP* something of my gratitude to Canon Frederic Hood, the Principal, who devoted thirty of the best years of his life to the pastoral care of undergraduates and others at Pusey. He took me in when I was recuperating from three and a half years as a POW of the Japanese, and there I was allowed to stay until the wish to give shelter to my invalid mother caused me to move to St John's Wood in 1952.

It was at Pusey, with its staff of four priests and an annually changing selection of resident undergraduates, that I was able to strengthen my shaky hold of the fundamentals of Christian belief and to convince myself of the essential place of the Church of England within 'the one holy catholic and apostolic Church', belief in which we proclaim in the Creed.

There will certainly be readers of this book to whom either the subject of religion, sad to say, is anathema, or who, understandably enough, prefer that I should stick to things I allegedly know something about – of which, they might well suppose, religion is not one. So I will confine myself briefly – and no doubt in somewhat naïve lay terms – to one theme which has fascinated me since the beginning of my years at Oxford, and those who shy away may pick up these peripatetic memoirs a page or two farther on. My theme is reunion and the urgent and obvious need for Christians to resolve their differences and so make a common front against the rival philosophies of capitalism rampant on one hand and international communism on the other.

During my time at Pusey House the various branches of Christianity were segregated to an extraordinary degree. True, we had some personal contact with the Revd Nathaniel Micklem, principal of the nonconformist Mansfield College, on one side of us but almost none with the Dominican fathers of Blackfriars on the other. Little white-haired Dr Micklem was a distinguished Protestant theologian and a man of wide culture and sympathies. He was a welcome guest in the dining-room but hardly in the chapel. As to our Roman Catholic neighbours a high defensive barrier divided us. We saw nothing of one another : indeed I am surprised to notice from the photograph taken in the quadrangle of Pusey after the Diamond Jubilee lunch in 1947 that Fr Gervase Mathew, the distinguished antiquarian and historian, had graced the occasion from next door.

Beside Freddy Hood in the middle of the group was on one side Lord Halifax, our chairman of Governors, and on the other the Archbishop of Thyatara, who was probably the only other non-Anglican present. Long before the present quite different ecumenical climate, by the way, Anglicans were on amiable terms with the Orthodox Churches of the East whose doctrinal position, as I understand it, is that the Western Church has been in error since the Great Schism of 1054. Thus Canterbury is in no different a situation from Rome, from whom it split at the Reformation.

But the barriers were within the Church of England as well as outside. At Pusey House, which exists to further the principles enunciated by Pusey, Keble, and the other great Tractarian revivalists, one learned how the Anglo-Catholics of the nineteenth century had had to suffer persecution and ostracism from within the Anglican communion. There were desperate people called 'Kensitites' who disrupted services because they disapproved of vestments and ritual. One heard how a mob recruited from Plymouth docks had descended on a little church in the Cornish fishing village of St Anthony-in-Roseland, tied up the parish priest who over the years had beautified it into quite a renowned sanctuary of peace and prayer, and then proceeded to break it up, piece by piece, in front of his eyes. There were other wanton desecrations of this kind, if not perhaps so spectacularly awful. Anglo-Catholicism to certain rabid Protestants meant an aping of the ways of Rome, and brought out the deepest anti-Papal prejudices.

Personally I find worship made easier in a setting of beauty and dignity. If one believes that God is present on the altar in the Blessed Sacrament surely only the best is acceptable in reverence of ritual, in music, and in the externals of service? Yet these things are matters of individual taste and preference. Many are happy only with the simplest expression of worship. What has always seemed particularly odious to me is a denial to other people of the liberty to worship in the way that suits them best.

However, such internecine militancy seems happily in the past as far as Anglicans are concerned, and indeed the attitudes of Christians towards one another have been remarkably softened since Pope John spread out his arms and smiled at the world and conveyed that unforgettable picture of a universal Father-in-God.

The Second Vatican Council, which he called, by ordaining the saying of Mass in the vernacular, and by stripping Roman Catholic devotions in certain respects, has occasioned much controversy and divisions which one can indeed trust may become dissolved in time. The changes and modifications have, I suppose – at a cost – simplified the Mass, and thereby surely made it less of an incomprehensible mystery to many non-Roman Christians. This circumstance may be seen in the context of the ecumenical spirit of the '70s, of the greater fraternization, and a new willingness among the churches to work together in social and charitable fields.

The findings of the Anglican–Roman Catholic International

Conference while indicating that there are hurdles still to be negotiated – of which the validity of Anglican orders may not be the least difficult – give hope to fairly basic Christians such as myself that inter-Communion, as a step preparatory to organic unity, may at least be much less remote than the most optimistic could have hoped quarter of a century ago.

On the reverse side of the ledger, so to speak, must be the move in some parts of the Anglican communion towards the ordination of women. They have their own ministry of service, heaven knows, both inside and outside the religious orders. To give countenance to the idea of admitting women to the priesthood for the first time after all but two thousand years, in the knowledge that the idea is anathema both to Roman Catholics and the Orthodox Churches at the very moment when at least a degree of reunion has become substantially nearer than at any time since the Reformation, would seem to be lunacy: after which heartfelt diversion let us return to post-war Oxford.

With several generations foregathering after military service the post-war period was naturally a vintage time both within the games world and beyond. At Vincent's, apart from such distinguished Blues as I have already mentioned, were to be found the great athletes, Roger Bannister and Chris Chataway, and rugger players such as J. O. Newton-Thompson and M. B. Hofmeyer of South Africa, and Jika (H. B.) Travers of Australia. All these three played football for England, and incidentally were also cricket Blues. Brian Boobbyer had similar credentials. John Kendall-Carpenter was also a tremendous forward of that period. Of the team he led to victory at Twickenham in 1950 six were internationals and three more became so. The previous year when Oxford went to Twickenham unbeaten there were eleven present or future internationals in residence. On the soccer field Oxford contributed more than a half-share to the combined University side, Pegasus, that twice won the FA Amateur Cup. It was very much a time for all-rounders – that Pegasus side included the cricket captains, Pawson and Carr. University golf was not perhaps so strong, but there was at least one very high-class golfer in John Kitchin who played for England while an undergraduate.

As one who has been a grateful guest so regularly – has indeed enjoyed the hospitality of most of this post-war roll-call of talent and of many others besides – it would ill-befit me not to say a word or two about Vincent's. To start with, who was Vincent? The answer is prosaic: he was the publisher and stationer in the High Street who rented to the club its first rooms on its foundation in 1863. It has a maximum of 150 members – it used only to be 100 – and although the best games-players are likely to be members it has never been a Bluetocracy.

The founder, W. B. Woodgate, ordained that members should be 'selected for all-round qualities; social, physical and intellectual'. Certain Blues thought not to fulfil these criteria have been kept waiting – some for ever. The fact that no one can be elected until his third term – it used always to be his second year – makes for a certain maturity. In all the years in which I knew the club well there were always members whose games-playing was an almost incidental part of their University life. It was never then hearty – in the sense perhaps that in its palmy days the larger and broadly similar Hawks Club of Cambridge might have been so described, at any rate by Oxford men.

Every President since 1863 is portrayed in the smoking-room, mounted in chronological order in large multiple frames, and the list includes, of course, many of the household names in British and Commonwealth sport. But each head-and-shoulders is of the same modest size. Almost the only ostentatious note – and that a mild enough one – is that the pewter tankard out of which one drinks one's beer will probably be inscribed with the name and year of one of these magnificos.

It was characteristic of Vincent's that for many years, almost alone among sporting clubs, there was no tie. When after the first war they decided to have one the dark blue tie with silver crowns was chosen, which is the prototype of the countless others with crests or emblems instead of stripes. Along with the reddy-brown and yellow of the Hawks it is the most widely-known sporting tie in the world.

It says much for the regard in which old members hold Vincent's that when a large-scale appeal for funds was recently made a thousand or so of them subscribed £70,000. An average contribution of £70 a head illustrates, incidentally, that the virtues that qualified them for Vincent's in youth seem to have served these generous men well in life since.

There was until comparatively recently another club – and to this apparently I was eligible for membership – called the Carlton which had a wonderfully easy atmosphere and desirable premises looking down the Broad from the corner of George Street. Named after *the* Carlton Club it was distinctly though not too aggressively Tory with a good many members who have since come to political distinction. Edward (now Lord) Boyle, also a regular attender at the Pusey House High Mass, has been at the time of writing perhaps the most successful, though he has now abandoned Westminster for the Vice-chancellorship of the University of Leeds. Edward claims to have scored more runs for Eton than any other boy, the disarming explanation being that his eyesight was too poor to allow him to become a cricketer, and he therefore coveted and acquired at an early age the post of scorer to the XI. He was always such a devoted follower of Sussex at Hove that I cannot think his loyalties have been seduced by residence in Yorkshire. Nothing is accepted up there anyway, short of a birth qualification – though you can catch them by asking where Lord Hawke was born (answer Lincolnshire), and, for that matter, Geoffrey Keighley (answer Nice).

Richard Hornby was another all-rounder of this post-war time more interested then in winning a soccer Blue than in politics which he entered after a short while teaching history at Eton. He was one of the young Turks of Macmillan's last administration, a contemporary in government with Sir Peter Kirk, who went on to play a prominent part in the Council of Europe before leading the British Common Market delegation.

Peter, who lived a while at Pusey House, inherited something of the oratorical gifts of his father, the famous Kenneth, Bishop of Oxford, one of the most gifted and beguiling speakers I ever heard. It was no surprise to anyone when he attained the presidency of the Union, the traditional milestone on the way to Westminster. He was in the House from the age of 27 until his recent tragically sudden death, from sheer overwork, at 50.

I must beware of sustaining this social diary note much further, but it is a pleasure to record how stimulating, after the long years of war, I found the companionship of these and many other Oxford men of this period despite the gap of a decade or two in our ages. In a way one was reliving some of the lost years, bound by a variety of common interests, a love of games, war service, and in some cases the Church and things of the spirit.

A friend of many of us and a man who had a serious influence (though no one could be less serious) on every age and walk of life in Oxford, town and gown alike, was Colin Stephenson, who soon after the war became vicar of St Mary Magdalen's, the church that stands like a beleaguered island amid the swirl of Oxford's traffic opposite the junction of St Giles and Beaumont Street with the needle of the Martyrs' Memorial almost on its doorstep.

Colin went to Cranleigh soon after I left and was an early product of the long and distinguished headmastership of David Loveday. A naval chaplain in the war, he suffered the loss of a leg – and almost his life – when, walking alone in the Ceylonese jungle, he fell down an overgrown, disused well. After many months of suffering, endured with that infectious gaiety which was his most persistent characteristic, he came to revive a church with a long Anglo-Catholic tradition which under an old priest had lost most of its flock. Vulgarly speaking, the competition among Oxford's many churches – plus the Cathedral and the college chapels – was remarkably keen. Colin, however, very swiftly made his mark, and by the attraction of his personality, and a certain knack of showmanship, let it be confessed, gathered almost as wide a cross-section of men and women, boys and girls, as can ever have assembled, week by week, indeed day by day, under the Anglican fold.

If a young man wished to experience the exercise of the Catholic religion in all its mystery and liturgical beauty he had the choice of Pusey House on one side of the road, St Mary Magdalen's on the other. And despite all the counter-attractions both were apt to be full. After ten strenuous Oxford years Colin moved to a cure fully as exacting though in a more peaceful setting as Administrator of the Shrine of Our Lady of Walsingham.

It is an extraordinary characteristic of the Church of England that one part of the church may be quite ignorant of what is happening elsewhere within it. Thus it will be news to many that to the Shrine at Walsingham, from March to November in a ceaseless flow, come parties of pilgrims from hundreds of Anglican parishes all over England. On the Whit bank holiday there is a National Pilgrimage to which thousands gather on the spot to which came on foot the early kings of England. There are retreats and conferences, so that one way and another the hospice is rarely out of use. The revival of the Shrine in the '30s was the work chiefly of Alfred Hope-Patten. Colin Stephenson succeeded him, and the Shrine prospered, and its adherents multiplied, as his church had done.

Ten years as Administrator so taxed his strength that he moved upstairs as it were to the less exacting Mastership of the College of Guardians of the Shrine, and it was not long after his change of post that while at Oxford, 'doing duty' while his successor as vicar was on holiday, he died suddenly of a heart attack in his old home in Beaumont Street. He was only 58, and the day was the Feast of the Assumption. At his Requiem Mass his old headmaster, then Bishop of Dorchester (whose churchmanship was some way removed from Colin's), told how when he had once arrived at St Mary Magdalen's to preach the sermon at the end of the service he found in the vestry a decanter of sherry and a note : 'Take two glasses to get rid of the incense.' The Bishop did not avail himself but afterwards their laughter 'echoed merrily in this House of God'.

Three sermons were preached at different services after his death. As it happens I saw the text of them all, and each mentioned his conviction that worship was not meant to be exclusively solemn. Ann and I were married at All Saints', Margaret Street, by Colin, and he was coming down to Sandwich to stay and preach at the parish church in just a few weeks' time.

There were also other older Oxford friends such as Tom Parker, a Pusey House librarian and later chaplain, and don of Univ., a distinguished theologian who in lighter moments kept up to date as an authority on Bradshaw's Railway Guide. His knowledge of time-tables and the history of every line is formidable; scarcely less surprisingly he is an authority on the City livery companies, especially that of the Butchers where I dined during his Mastership. Is it not some of the best minds that are the farthest ranging? Tom Parker had, and I expect still has, a Pickwickian look, as of a jovial friar. I always understood his ecclesiastical stance was somewhat extreme for preferment in those days, but he was a marvellously sympathetic pastor to the young.

John Masterman and Gathorne Girdlestone I have already written about, but 'Hooky' Hill fits in nicely here. He was Colonel D. V. Hill, Royal Artillery, but it is as Hooky that the name will strike a chord with those who knew him before the war as Officer Commanding the OUOTC and after as Steward of Christ Church.

There are some lucky men – not very many – who without in the least seeking it achieve an almost universal popularity. 'He never had an enemy' could surely be said of Hooky from his days as a gunner subaltern when he emerged as an Army fast bowler. While doing a Territorial adjutancy at Worcester he was recruited by Worcestershire, and over two summers at the end of the '20s he often shared the new ball with the famous in-swinger, Fred Root. He would have done so more frequently but for some tiresome MP who asked a question in Parliament requiring to know how an officer in the armed forces was enabled to spend the summer playing cricket.

The other side of the coin came uppermost when Hooky was captured at Singapore, and I have a very distinct recollection of him sharing a tattered tent in the rainy season, at an evil camp beside the Burma–Siam railway called 'Kanu', with another Lieu-tenant-Colonel RA called 'Macky' Moore. My party were in transit on the River Kwai heading farther north and as we left at dawn there was the rare diversion of seeing a captured animal of the cat tribe, probably a cheetah, whom the Japs had snared into a pit and were teasing into a fury.

The rice (there was little else) blew out some people including these two colonels, and as we flogged on I rather envied their lot. Relatively speaking (strictly) they seemed rather comfortable. Later in captivity, however, when I found myself with them in what passed for a hospital camp I wouldn't have been in their shoes (or clogs). They were known by now as 'the hernia twins', and ultimately 'Weary' Dunlop (now the famous Melbourne surgeon, Sir Edward) was obliged to perform two of his renowned operations without much if anything in the way of anaesthetic.

They survived, as did many far worse cases involving arm and leg amputations, thanks to the devoted skill of doctors, Australian and British, working with the crudest instruments and scarcely any drugs.

Hooky next turned up in my life when soon after the war he was appointed Steward of Christ Church. I recall calling in to J. C. Masterman's rooms to take him off for a round of golf and finding him at work assessing literally hundreds of applications for the position, most of them from retired servicemen. Hooky must have won from a very distinguished field a job for which he was ideally suited. Managing the domestic affairs of a great college was a specially taxing job in days of every sort of shortage and with a long back-log of work necessarily left undone during the long war. His tact and good nature made him particularly popular in the Senior Common Room, as I had plenty of opportunity to judge as his guest. Dining at the High Table in the hall of Christ Church among that distinguished company, and listening to the talk over the port and dessert in the Senior Common Room afterwards of such men as Robert, now Lord, Blake (quite a good cricketer, by the way), Hugh Trevor-Roper and 'The Prof', Lord Cherwell, made some memorable evenings. Cherwell, the great scientist, would seem the last man to be identified with sport. But in younger days he had been a very good lawn-tennis player, and it was in that capacity he was invited to play at Charlton near Oxford, the home of Lord Birkenhead. Another guest was Winston Churchill, and from that day sprang the friendship that was to have such great wartime consequences.

One night at Christ Church I brought off a minor sort of coup which I hope was not rated an abuse of hospitality. I had been asked to try and find a place at Oxford for a relation of some South African friends, and the credentials of the young man had already been rejected by two or three colleges. His academic qualifications were no more than average but he was a promising games-player and had the highest recommendations as to character. Sitting next to Dean Lowe I said how sad it was that Colleges seemed nowadays to judge candidates for entry solely on examination results. In his strong Canadian tones the dean rose as I had hoped and said that Christ Church was not bound in any way. They chose exactly whom they pleased and would I let them have the relevant papers. The young man was duly admitted, got a respectable degree as well as a rugger Blue, captained the college cricket side and was president of the Junior Common Room. So Christ Church got a good bargain in Christopher Saunders who is now a king-pin in the sugar world of Natal. Perhaps this illustration of all-round merit makes an appropriate end to another chapter which has brought out many examples thereof. But the subject, of course, is almost endless.

12

A Northern Journey

These recent chapters have breathed, some of them, rather an academic ring, so what fresher antidote than a pilgrimage to the North, and what more blissful start to it than a run from Oxford in the blossom-time through the vale of Evesham to Worcester.

I was once upbraided by one of three sports editors under whose charge I worked for referring to some cricketers from Notts and Derbyshire as 'northerners'. He declared that a straight line drawn from the Mersey to the Wash leaves Nottingham a little to the southward and Derby distinctly more. When I pointed out that another line extending from the Humber to the Mersey excluded Sheffield from the North and only fractionally let in Manchester we agreed to let the matter drop.

Whether there be a precise demarcation I don't know. The fact is, though, that in cricket terms there is such an over-weighting – in terms of quantity not quality, let it be added – that one tends to think of Surrey, Middlesex, Kent, Sussex, Essex, Hampshire, Gloucestershire, Somerset and (begging their proud pardon) Glamorgan as being irrefutably southern; the midland group centres on Worcestershire, Leicestershire, Northants and Warwickshire; then up above we have the great counties of the Roses with their neighbours to the southward, Derby and Notts.

But in any case this is no Baedeker tour but rather for my young Australian's benefit a taste on the palate of the particular flavour of the cricket one encounters as one journeys north. Many would say that it needs some of the northern brand of cricketer to give the necessary leaven of toughness to English cricket. I am a bit suspicious of generalizations of this kind, thinking easily of great cricketers from the South who were as stuffed full of stout-hearted effort from the start of the day to the end as any Lancashireman or Tyke: equally a few of the latter whose effort was not most conspicuous when their side were going badly. No, we have our Paynters and Leylands, our Stathams, our Bedsers and Edriches –

our Hirsts and Richardsons and as many more if we turn back the pages far enough – and they are just Englishmen, at their most indomitable and tireless, rather than representatives of their own particular county. It used to be said, of course, that a strong Yorkshire meant a strong England, and there was often truth in that since the most powerful county was probably providing the biggest nucleus.

The County Championship has been contested 94 times excluding the wars, if the generally-acknowledged starting date of 1873 is accepted, and of these 94 titles Yorkshire have won 29 times. Proceeding south (and excluding years without an outright winner) we find Lancashire with 8 wins, Notts 6, Derbyshire 2, Worcestershire 3, Leicestershire 1, Warwickshire 3, Middlesex 6, Surrey 17, Kent 5, Hampshire 2, Gloucestershire 2, Glamorgan 2. Of the four who have never brought home the title Essex and Somerset have reached as high as third while Northants were runners-up three times and Sussex actually six.

After which historical preamble let us guide our friend clockwise and north-westwards, from Oxford up to Worcester, not eschewing, if we're feeling rich, the gastronomical delights of the 'Lygon Arms' at Broadway en route. Perched beyond and above the meadows through which flows the Severn, almost up to the boundary's edge, Worcester Cathedral holds the eye without too consciously dominating the scene. The ground today with certain useful amenities donated by the Supporters' Club is just what a county ground ought to be, and that naturally has to include the field itself. In old Fred Hunt's day at close of play when Don Bradman had come in from making his regular double hundred (236, 206, 258 and 107 were his scores in the Australians' opening games at Worcester) they used to bring out the bowls and the jacks, so smooth was the outfield. This perfection is said to derive from the fertilizing it gets when the river floods in winter – a local parson is said, varyingly, either to have swum across the ground or to have caught a salmon from the pavilion steps. But let's give the groundsman the credit. Hunt was a good 'un, and so, too, is Gordon Prosser, who has twice recently won the top award for his craft offered by Watney's.

Talking of Watney's – or at any rate about beer – there used to be a tent whither at the season's habitual start at Worcester by the touring side certain scribes used to foregather of a May morning

as if drawn by a magnet : 'Beau' Vincent, of *The Times*, genial,
avuncular if a bit chesty after the river-damps of winter; Bill Bowes,
benign if a shade preoccupied maybe about his next edition; Denys
Rowbotham, full of some subtle theory most reasonably expressed;
Basil Easterbrook, a Kemsley and later Thomson man, rich in
esoteric and often entertaining information; Charlie Bray, of the
Herald, a good Essex bat in his day, and cruelly christened the
'Ranji of Leyton'; his most unusually abstemious partner-in-crime
and assiduous news-collector Crawford White; Alex Bannister,
equally forbearing and equally zealous; Archie Ledbrooke, the best
of mimics and the historian of Lancashire cricket, who died so
tragically with Manchester United at Munich; young John Woodcock who soon qualified for 'the club' and comfortably held his own
in it; all these and more but above all Crusoe, whose laugh and
wit and unique sense of the ridiculous made beer-tent, dressing-
room, club or pub a warmer and more delectable place for his
presence.

The essence of Crusoe, I fear, escapes my pen. Though in company he sparkled, a deep private melancholy which Elizabeth, his
devoted wife, regularly underwent and best understood was seldom
far beneath a jesting exterior. There was never a party that was
not the happier for his presence. In an appreciation in the *Cricketer*
after his death Sandy Singleton, who had been an old friend of his
since undergraduate days, said that a solemn schoolmaster once
preposterously proposed that Crusoe be banned from Vincent's
during term-time as a provoker of undue hilarity. The motion found
no support. For Crusoe made no enemies except priggishness and
pomposity. To Sandy when Crusoe entered the Parks, where under
some captains a certain over-earnestness was inclined to develop,
'it was as if the sun had broken through'.

His style of cricket-writing was as idiosyncratic as the rest of him.
Much of his work, happily, is still in circulation, but not his day-to-
day *Morning Post* accounts, from which Ray Robinson culled this
characteristic opening to a Test report :

Wall opened the bowling for Australia and appeared to be making
the ball rise. I use the word 'appeared' because the architect who
designed this press box had a poor idea of angles. From the seat
occupied by your correspondent, four fieldsmen, one batsman and

one umpire were on view – a quorum perhaps but hardly satisfying to the eager critic.

How often has one suffered – how seldom composed a grievance a
quarter as effective or amusing!

In earlier days, joining us in a glass in the beer tent might be
'Barmy' Gilbert (H. A.), a boon pal of Crusoe who did most things
with the ball and had days of triumph rather earlier in his career
than my own recollection of him on the field.

Gilbert Ashton with a wave and a laugh might shepherd his
Abberley boys across our bows to the more decorous lawns of the
Members' Enclosure; or Reg Perks appear, not inapt in reminiscence, especially if he had just effected a shrewd car exchange at his
premises over the bridge. In the cricket sense Worcester was a half-
way place, savouring more of soft West Country airs than the rigours
of the North.

Edgbaston, the next stop, was cosmopolis by contrast, ample,
spruce, affluent, with every amenity that the comfort-loving midland
patron could hope for. It was not always so. In the days of Freddy
Calthorpe and Bob Wyatt and the everlasting R. V. Ryder as secretary there was little enough in the bank. But Edgar Hiley and his
Warwickshire Pool, and the imaginative use made of the money
during Leslie Deakins's long and fruitful secretaryship, have brought
about a transformation quite extraordinary.

I can sidestep leftwards just far enough to say that I've at least
once played cricket in Wales, at Marchwiel by Llangollen where the
Free Foresters after a week-end of merriment unconfined were
thwarted, if I do not do my kind host, Jimmy McAlpine, an
injustice by some slight lack of clarification regarding the tea
interval. This was the first of what is still a popular two-day match
– a survival, and not the only one, of two-day country-house
cricket, than which there is none better.

But we are within hail of Chesterfield where bitter, swirling winds
did not dissuade the locals from their first sight of Don Bradman :
nor did he disappoint them. Catch Chesterfield with its crooked
spire on a day of warm summer and there are few better fields
for a day's drowsy watching.

Not that it's somnolent as a rule when Derbyshire and Yorkshire
clash in the border country. They do so at Chesterfield, but no

more, alas, at Bramall Lane. As all the world knows, Bramall Lane now means Sheffield United Football Club, and no longer the strange unlovely compromise whereby the pavilion, perched on top of the road called Cherry(!), gave on to bleachers, some covered, some not, to either side of the field down as far as the playing square. Beyond this the stands and the rougher texture of the soil proclaimed the predominance of the other game from September to May.

Grimy, unlovely though it was, there was a warmth and a wit about cricket at Bramall Lane that set it apart. The pitch was as good as any (after the first hour perhaps) and in its day it had been good enough for a Test against Australia – in fact just one in the classic 1902 series. It reads like a wonderful match, though Australia won easily in the end despite the smoke-stacks which made the light 'appalling'. This at least cannot have been the match from which derived the libel that the stacks were always stoked up when it was t'others' turn to bat. The local brewery were the culprits, but no doubt it was Yorkshire's adversaries on whom they worked their fell designs.

With his perfection of economy Jim Kilburn wrote:

> From its pavilion and stands there was not a tree to be seen, and both sight and sound reflect encircling industry. The clatter of passing tram-cars and the scream of a saw-mill and factory hooters make a background of noise to the cricket.

Yes, but it was at Sheffield that cricket gained its first toe-hold in Yorkshire, and its crowds were often the biggest in the county. Abbeydale Park is a pleasant ground on which I have enjoyed batting, and the Yorkshire Club are enabled as I write to play some week-day games there. But Sheffield Collegiate have their own uses for it, and it will be a loss to the game if some well-worn ground cannot be adapted to suit the grinders and ensure the visitors a fiery welcome somewhere nearby in the South Riding.

But let us continue our circumnavigation left into Lancashire, coming first to Aigburth, a ground which houses a club of long and proud associations, the Liverpool CC. I hold many recollections of Aigburth but the sharpest is of a feline, sinuous, sallow bowler with a long, light-treading run delivering a ball of explosive speed that knocked the stumps all ways. Bradman b McDonald 9. The date was 11 May 1930, and for the protagonists, E. A. McDonald and D. G. Bradman, it was their one and only meeting on the cricket field. McDonald was a great fast bowler, at his peak some would rate him as high as any, and it was only to be expected by those who knew him well that this expatriate Australian who in the '20s had brought four Championships to Lancashire, would pull out something special for his young fellow-countryman who was monopolizing all the headlines.

Of all the great feats achieved by overseas players in English cricket McDonald's record for Lancashire can stand comparison with any. Remember he was 32 when he arrived at Old Trafford and that in those eight summers he took more than a thousand wickets. He endured to nearly 40 on a diet wherein beer was said to play a considerable part. Latterly Lancashire used to put him to grass as it were with friends on a farm just before the return Roses' match, and he would return refreshed to bowl his damnedest for Lancashire in the crucial Championship games of August.

It was a curious game wherein Peter Eckersley, later to vacate the Lancashire captaincy, first to take a seat in the Commons and then to give his life in the Fleet Air Arm, made top score for his side in both innings, and the Australians did not emerge without anxiety. It was Bradman's first appearance in Lancashire where, as it happens, his record is more modest than anywhere. Though he made two second-innings hundreds against Lancashire the best of his eight first innings there was 38. In no other corner of Australia or England (excepting Northants) was his ratio of failure so high – by his own standards. Of the nine Test centres where he played, only Old Trafford is missing from the marvellous roll of 29 hundreds.

The Liverpool club itself was highly selective as to quality, and used to run their own southern tours as well as taking the leading part in the Liverpool and District Competition in which I was lucky enough to be able to play a good deal in the summer of 1941 while the 18th Division, scattered over Lancashire, was waiting to be sent abroad. In 1939 Liverpool boasted three recent University bowlers of distinction all well known to me, John Brocklebank, Alan Barlow and A. R. Legard, a Winchester and Oxford scientist of much erudition who was therefore (presumably) known as 'Loopy'. Thus I gravitated to Aigburth and on the Friday evening before the first match took a net before being hastened back to our quarters by the air-raid sirens. This heralded the first of the four consecutive raids on the Liverpool docks. When we turned up next day for the game the field was spattered with shrapnel and there was a small hole in the face of the pavilion made by an ack-ack shell which by a remote chance had killed an ARP warden inside.

The order of the time being to take what relaxation we could, the game took place, Swanton, sent in first with Eric Greenhalgh of Lancashire, impetuous as ever running himself out for 60-odd on the third run. Our opponents were Bootle, whose opening bowler was one of the first black West Indians I had ever played against. Our captain was J. R. Barnes, a whimsical man of great cricket knowledge who had played in the triumphant Lancashire sides of that most delightful of men, Leonard Green. (It's a good quiz question: who led his county for three years and won three championships? Only Stuart Surridge with five in five beats this.)

Our after-match drinks were rudely curtailed by the sirens, pre-saging the second and the worst of the raids, of which we, not being required to assist, got a ghastly grandstand view from our head-quarters, the golf and country club at Childwall. On the Monday of this first week-end of May our brigade trundled out east to the Pennines for a long divisional exercise. Also moving on foot or bicycle seemed to be half the population of the city intent on avoid-ing a fourth night of horror. One could not avoid the feeling that Liverpool had had about as much as it could take. The essential services – gas, electricity and water – were scarce or non-existent. The casualties were very heavy. One shuddered at what we might see when we were due back in the middle of the week; but merci-fully and mysteriously Goering had decreed after four nights that the attacks should be directed elsewhere.

The cricket in the Liverpool and District (each side being allowed one pro) was wonderfully keen and good, and did much to convince me that the strong southern antipathy to leagues was a snobbish rubbish. Huyton (Sir Harold Wilson's constituency), Neston, Formby, were other of our opponents, and I think it was at South-port where the laugh was very much on me. Some business con-nected with a court-martial prevented my arriving until around 3.30, and I hustled in, struggling with a cricket bag of pre-war size, urged on by sympathetic spectators near the gate.

'Eh oop, laad, tha's late, tha knows.'

'Liverpool will have missed thee.'

'Let me carry tha' bag.'

The score on the board was 10 for no wicket, with Liverpool in the field, and I concluded I'd missed surprisingly little. Not so – we had already been bowled out (one short!) for 15! I never missed my innings either before or since, apart from declarations – but at least, unlike Ian Peebles in his youth at the Cape, I was not reported in the Press as 'Absent Bathing'.

I never got the impression that the twin centres of Lancashire cricket, Manchester and Liverpool, were unduly devoted to one another, the power being at Old Trafford and the great men in the shipping and cotton worlds of Liverpool no doubt supposing that they could run things much better. Personally I was fond of nearly all of them in both camps and came to know the Lancashire cricketers better than most, since it became established for me to collect a side of formidable personality and lustre to play Didsbury and District on that smoothest and greenest of suburban grounds on the Sunday of the Old Trafford Test in aid of the beneficiary of the year. Big crowds came in all weathers and thus were gathered sums which in those days were rather startling. I proudly receive the annual fixture-card which proclaims me a life member of Didsbury.

The facilities for 'the media' have usually been worse at Old Trafford than most places. For years, broadcasting from a little green box perched at the top of the terrace in front of Trafford Park station, one had the feeling that a strong gust of wind might deposit one in the street below. The Press box was an uncomfortable eyrie at the other end, generally dirty. But the Lancashire Committee at close of play provided a warmth of welcome to players and writers that almost disarmed criticism. Occasionally, identity on such occasions is apt to become somewhat blurred, and there was the meeting between a senior and respected colleague of mine who (like others, is it being said?) was inclined to lay down the law without regard to any economy of words.

Launching forth one day, he found an oldish chap who made him a polite audience, and sometimes chipped in with an apt observation. At length the sage moved on, and as he did so said:

'That seemed a pretty knowledgeable sort of chap: any idea who he is?'

'Oh, didn't you know? I'm so sorry. It's Ernest Tyldesley . . .'

The selection of distinguished professionals to county committees has long been a commonplace – and in the nature of things they must one day command the scene unless, which Heaven forbid, they are elbowed out by business men; but I have an idea that Ernest was, very properly, almost the first of his kind.

As might be expected, cricket societies proliferate in the cricket-loving industrial North. There is a tie I often wear because it is of a particularly agreeable dark blue, discreetly dashed with red roses and golden wheat-sheaves, and it reminds me of Arthur Wrigley, who invited me to go up and talk to them, the Lancashire and Cheshire Cricket Society, of which he was the moving spirit, in the Old Trafford pavilion.

He was the first of the genus Broadcast Scorer, now promoted to 'statistician', and soon maybe in line for some further titular dignity. Lancashire answered the BBC's plea for a scorer for Howard Marshall at the Old Trafford Test of 1934 by providing a young man said to be good at his sums, young Wrigley from the ground staff. There must have been premonition somewhere since England totted up their then record score in England, 627 for nine, to which Australia, set on their way with Gubby Allen's opening over of thirteen balls, riposted with 491. Altogether Arthur had plenty to keep him busy while Howard had no need to rely on some sort of improvised messenger system as had been the case in the previous Test at Lord's where he had been graciously allowed to recount Hedley Verity's fifteen wickets in the Test from a window over the Tavern at square-leg. Thereafter, until his premature death, Arthur was our regular BBC scorer, and a pleasanter, less obtrusive fellow to work with would be hard to find. He was a leg-spinner who used to come and bowl in the Didsbury matches.

It would need a far sharper psychologist than me to try and identify, let alone explain, for the benefit of my faithful Australian friend, the contrasting characteristics that one is inclined to encounter on either side of the Pennines. There is an asperity of manner sometimes encountered in Yorkshire that is rare to the westward. May it have something to do with the Gulf Stream? At all events it could be said to me perhaps, as to another ruddy southerner bold enough to air his views at a Roses' Match : 'An' what's it to do with thee?' Something of the warmth behind the bluntness of speech I must try to explain to my companion – and this is a combination not unknown in the Antipodes, after all – as we make the long trek north-east over moor and fell, avoiding the smoke-stacks where we can though taking in, of course, the soaring wonder of York, to the most northerly of the game's great outposts at Scarborough.

The fame of the Scarborough Festival – where, refreshed by the North Sea breezes at the summer's end, the greatest used to give of their best on the field because it would have been altogether foreign to their nature to play the game in any other way – must lie largely in the past, though it is still kept a popular attraction by the Fenner Trophy, while Yorkshire happily also continue to use their splendid, salubrious ground, so full of history, for other occasions. The old conception of Festival cricket with no reward beyond the satisfaction of a fight well fought weakened, by the way, long before the onset of the one-day competitions which are nowadays blamed for almost everything.

We Arabs on our Northern Tour used to play Scarborough, and be allowed to dine in the 'Cricketers' Room' at the Grand, having had, I'm glad to say, none the worse of the exchanges on the field, before moving on to be tested by Sir William Worsley's XI on the best of all country-house grounds at Hovingham, and finishing with two days against the Yorkshire Gentlemen at Escrick. Life for some of the wandering clubs is much more difficult in these days of almost exclusive league cricket, but it seems that the YGs, like others among the best of their venerable contemporaries, still flourish.

Writing of Hovingham reminds me it was for many our final sight of Maurice Leyland, who used generally to umpire. The last time, when Parkinson's Disease had taken firm control, Maurice was obliged to stuff one hand permanently into the pocket of his white coat to keep it steady. Now it could be said of several that they exactly expressed the spirit of Yorkshire cricket – A. A. Thomson, who saw his fellow-Tykes as truly as any man, described George Hirst as 'almost the Creator's original sketch for the Yorkshireman', while Hedley Verity, of course, comes simultaneously to mind – but did anyone epitomize all that was best in Yorkshire cricket better than Maurice?

When England were playing their annual Test at Headingley we generally all stayed at Harrogate, a watering-place (not deficient in

stronger cordials and congenial bars in which to drink them)
remembered also for sumptuous hotels with ear-trumpeted old
ladies, the long two-hundred-acre Stray that gives the place an air
of space and elegance, a vast cathedral-like church called 'St Wil-
frid's – they should change the 'i' to an 'e' for Yorkshire's sake –
and a pleasant, trim cricket field with a single stand, on which
Maurice Leyland learned to play, and which has for many years
inhabited one Championship match, if not more. Spiritually it is a
thousand miles from the gaunt battle-grounds of Headingley and
Park Avenue down the road.

Yet Harrogate is the setting for one of my best-remembered
Yorkshire matches. It was in 1962, the last of the season, and the
situation was that Yorkshire needed to win to gain the Championship, while if they failed to do so Worcestershire would have the
title for the first time in their history: all the ingredients of drama
then, and the little field filled to bursting. Furthermore no TV
coverage had been arranged, and for the second day the BBC, in
response to many complaints, sent up a single film unit (no doubt
all that was spare) and asked me to double my *Telegraph* work and
do, without benefit of a monitor, what amounted to a permanent
sound commentary since the high spots were being recorded for the
evening programme.

Bryan Cowgill, then head of TV sport, came up to hold my hand,
and we both thought the technique such a good substitute for the
full treatment that it deserved a trial the following year. (Perhaps
in these days of economic stringency it may happen yet.) However,
first came anti-climax because on the second day, with the board
showing Glamorgan 65 and 13 for none, Yorkshire 101, a light
drizzle held up everything. Another big crowd sat on with true
northern phlegm, remarking what a luvly morning it had been at
Cleethorpes, and little less attractive apparently at Redcar. In the
end nothing could be done, and so on the third morning 10,000
came in for the kill.

The pitch, well prepared but damp, helped spin, wherein Yorkshire in Don Wilson and Ray Illingworth had the edge. Ken Taylor,
having made 67 out of the 101, was bowled first ball second innings
when Yorkshire had eventually to go in to make 66 to win. It didn't
sound much, but with more dark clouds building up excitement was
intense enough before, around tea-time, young John Hampshire

brought Yorkshire to victory by seven wickets. It was then that the other Wilson, Vic, the Malton farmer, was serenaded at the end of his retirement season, having become, at the third attempt, the first Yorkshire professional ever to win the title. To which it should be added that until 1960 the amateurs had always been in charge since 1883 when Tom Emmett had handed over to Lord Hawke. The amateurs had won 22 titles since 1873 when the Championship is generally held to have started in earnest. After Wilson's victory Close won four times in eight seasons before being removed from the job, and taking a new lease of life with Somerset. Yorkshire have not taken the title since.

However, let me not run into contentious areas, and just record in relation to that great occasion at Harrogate that Philip Sharpe took his 71st and final catch of the season, thus topping the Yorkshire record of John Tunnicliffe. In cricket history only Walter Hammond (78), M. J. Stewart (77) and P. M. Walker (73) have swallowed more – and maybe none of them ever caught 71 on the off-side. Philip has no exceptional reach or height (like a Woolley, a Hammond or a Gregory). Granted an exceptional speed of eye, he has exemplified, as of course Bobby Simpson, the great Australian did, the virtues always impressed on slippers, but so hard to pursue : 'Never anticipate, never snatch.' Let it coom to you! Easier said than done.

I came upon the Test scene in 1930, and so Headingley for me spells the Bradman epics and all the glamour of a Test series in England. It means, first and foremost, his innings in 1948, wherein, faced with a fifth-day target that was away beyond the imagination of the normal cricket intelligence concentrated round the ground, he decided that the game might be as easy to win as to draw – and duly won it. History has no parallel to the Don's achievements for Australia at Headingley – six innings, once not out, 963 runs, 334 the highest of four hundreds, average 192.60. He has often maintained that if he could have his choice of batting conditions he would plump for England rather than Australia, and I imagine that the memories of Headingley, starting with that stupendous day, 11 July 1930, when he returned at the close of play, apparently as fresh as when he had started, with 309 runs on the board against his name, must have helped decide the matter in his mind. The boundary seems to – and I believe does to the extent of at least a small drop – fall away from the Test pitch to all points of the compass, and Bradman stroked it hither and thither apparently according to his whim. Others naturally have played notably dominant innings here – the names of Eric Rowan and John Edrich come to mind. But Bradman at Headingley was something apart. It was as though the greatest batsman was determined to exercise his will on the supreme English county.

The *Daily Telegraph* – need it be said? – is very properly respected among sportsmen for its restrained, balanced presentation of games, cricket surely not least. Yet there was a time shortly after the William Berry (Camrose) take-over from the Lawsons when they were still searching for the right sporting formula. After Philip Trevor, their trusty cricket and rugger man, died in 1933, they were for a while in a difficulty, and for the 1934 Australian Test entrusted the report to a sports journalist of the old school chiefly connected with boxing: Ben Bennison by name. On the second morning he opened, and with much indignation circulated round the Press box – it even got as far as a tyro like me – a wire from the paper critical of his first day's report, and concluding with seven words heavy with insult: 'For future treatment suggest see today's *Express*.' I can see now old Bennison's face purple with fury. In effect he was being advised to take as his model a man with a peculiarly abrasive style and a diabolical facility for creating trouble, whose name was anathema in the more responsible circles – Trevor Wignall. He had a frog-like countenance, and was said to be the highest-paid sporting man in Fleet Street: not that that was saying a great deal in the '30s.

However, cricket in the *DT* was soon in safe hands – after Philip Trevor came Howard Marshall and then for brief periods just before the war the famous names of Warner, Robertson-Glasgow and Jardine. The *Express* for their part used Wignall as an explosive columnist, and turned over their cricket-writing to an enthusiast for the game with a nice turn of wit who was also a dramatic critic, William Pollock.

Headingley is accorded a Test a year, rather than its senior, Old Trafford, simply because the support is larger and more constant and despite perennial trouble with the pitches, which in ideal conditions can be easier than almost any but have a history that can only be described as mixed.

It is a curious paradox that the largest and in cricket terms most thickly populated English county is alone in not owning its own ground. Headingley belongs to the Leeds Cricket & Football Club – Rugby League. However, the County Club now at least have their own premises (square of the pitch) which comprise offices and changing-rooms.

The last of the great Yorkshire centres we must look in at is Park Avenue, Bradford, the smallest rectangular stadium with the short straight hit where Arthur Wood with cruel banter remarked to Hedley Verity that he had Jock Cameron in two minds: he didn't know whether to go for fours or sixes – the answer, you will remember, being 30 in the over, three of each.

I recall two extraordinary games at Bradford, one indeed simply a freak of nature. In mid-May 1948 Yorkshire had a heaven-sent chance of beating the Australians (lacking Bradman) on a pudding, having had the luck to win the toss and bat before the top was knocked off the pitch. While they were over-cautious when the going was good at the climax the spinners erred in line and length, and thanks to an 18-year-old prodigy named Neil Harvey the Australians somehow pulled through by four wickets. (The scores were Yorkshire 71 and 89, Australians 101 and 63 for six.) In the crisis I stood and watched at the football stand end with Emmott Robinson, and the old man was distressed beyond bearing. Long-hops we saw, and full pitches: it were sinful. Even an animated conversation on the wool trade or the stock market, I can't recall which, petered to a halt at this profligate throwing away of a golden chance.

The other match was the Test Trial of 1950, included more as an inspection of the candidates for Australia than for the West Indies series just due to begin – badly though, as it turned out, we were worsted in that. Bradford after rain can be (or at least then could) almost the most spiteful pitch in England, and I recall asking the great Yorkshire panjandrum of the day at the start of the summer, a month or so before the match, whether the pitch would be covered.

'No, no,' said he, 'they must take it as it comes.' And take it they did. Laker for the England team captured eight for 2 on the pitch of his dreams, a lot of aspiring young talent in the Rest team was whisked out twice for nothing at all, and by lunch on the second day the young had been duly defeated and the farce mercifully ended. The scores that were in the book bore singularly little relation to what was going soon to be needed at Melbourne, Sydney and Adelaide. A chance of adjudging method on a true surface and of imbuing self-confidence was foolishly lost, and – irony of ironies – when F. R. Brown's MCC side was chosen a couple of months later Laker was not among those named to go to Australia!

It may have been at Bradford, though I incline slightly more to Bramall Lane, that in a game between Yorkshire and Middlesex things got altogether too heated on the field, and as a result Middlesex threatened to cancel fixtures. The Yorkshire captains of the '20s were an amiable lot, and in moments of stress it was common knowledge that some of the less inhibited characters in their charge grew, shall we say, over-enthusiastic.

Middlesex, as I say, took offence on this occasion but when provoked some of them were no angels, clad in white samite, mystic, wonderful. There were faults on both sides, for sure. During the winter following, a meeting of some sort was called at Lord's to discuss the matter, Yorkshire naming as their representative none other than Rockley Wilson. Living at Winchester he had no doubt less far to travel, but I expect the Yorkshire committee may well have thought that Middlesex were singularly unlikely to put anything over on him. Nor did they. At the meeting Middlesex proposed that to cool the atmosphere the fixtures arranged between them for the following summer should be cancelled. (In those days counties played a varying number of matches, the title being decided by percentages.)

'All right,' said Rockley at this, 'but just remember; if you drop us for one year, we'll drop you for fifty.'

Whereat all talk of cancellation ceased, and no doubt those concerned made a special effort next season to keep on their best behaviour. 'Ah,' I can imagine the young thinking at this, 'so they weren't all so perfect in the old days as we're led to think!' To which I might add, of course they weren't. Cricket is a red-blooded game which has excited high passions since Hambledon and before. *Sometimes* these have spilled over. In general, though, if one can trust one's judgement on such a matter, the cricketers during most of my time were guilty of fewer lapses from self-discipline than those of today. I am very far from indicting the moderns *en masse*, especially when one thinks of the abject deterioration of manners in other popular sports. But I wish more of them would appreciate that a game can be none the less relentless for being civilly fought.

But let us leave Yorkshire on a cordial note, and to descend into Nottinghamshire. If we are allergic to motorways or prefer the direct route, the road leads through Barnsley and Rotherham, between which stands the mining village of Wombwell. Roy Kilner, that admirable cricketer, was born and died here. As a place Wombwell is unremarkable, no candidate for a scenic beauty tour. Yet its Cricket Society, started in 1951 by Leslie Taylor and Jack Sokell, who still function as president and secretary respectively, is known throughout the world of English cricket as a focus of no ordinary intensity. The list of notabilities whom Jack Sokell has persuaded to come from all over England to speak there (and who have accordingly enjoyed the warm hospitality of Dr and Mrs Taylor) now numbers over a thousand and contains almost 'everybody'. Often they pay the society the undeniable compliment of coming a second time. They – or, rather, I can say 'we', being a patron of the society with a silver goblet 'for services to cricket' to show for it – enthuse the young with coaching prizes and scholarships and even give encouragement to a hard-working and much-maligned fraternity by naming a 'Cricket Writer of the Year'.

What the Wombwellites enjoy at their weekly winter meetings at the Horse Shoe is an evening of reminiscence, frank and with a touch of humour, from someone of distinction in the game who is prepared to match with equal freedom the answers to their questions. I should have to try to procure for my Australian an invitation to Wombwell.

There are few grounds in England so rich in history as Trent Bridge, and I can say that I knew Notts in the days of their power since they were a team of rare skill and individuality until the middle of the '30s, and in my young days their visits south were significant happenings in the summer cycle, especially the traditional visit to the Oval at August bank holiday. But as a force in the game Notts suffered in close succession two malign blows, one self-inflicted, one a matter of economics, and they can be counted still among 'the big six' only in the sense that they remain among the six counties who from the dawn of the Championship have more victories to their credit than defeats.

The first misfortune, of course, was their leading part in the

Bodyline drama, and their persistence in it after it had been generally condemned. The second could not be helped: it was simply
that the chief source of supply dried up as the miners' lot was transformed. In their essay on Notts in *The World of Cricket* written in
the mid-'60s G. N. B. Huskinson and the Rev. Arnold Doxey say:
'Since the war only one ex-miner (F. W. Stocks) has been capped by
Notts, whereas between the wars the team rarely took the field with
less than six.' Harold Larwood headed a notable company which
hailed from Nuncargate. Bill Voce *walked* from Hucknall (Byron's
burial-place) hoping for a trial at Trent Bridge. The colliery towns
and villages had traditionally been the nurseries of Notts' cricketers,
and when this source dried up Notts – until the general importations
from overseas – have struggled to find talent.

It so happens that my first memory of Trent Bridge is of the first
Test of 1934 – the first, in fact, between England and Australia
since the Bodyline tour. With Jardine in the Press-box, Larwood
having, no doubt through a ghost, fanned the flames once more in
an article in which he virtually excommunicated himself, and Voce
not being considered, the air was heavy with tension, and the
Australian victory on the last evening was received with a pointed
lack of acclaim. Bob Wyatt had broken a thumb, and the England
captaincy was taken over by Cyril Walters though he was junior to
most in the side – a decision no doubt hard for the young reader to
credit. One cannot exactly defend it except to say that whereas
Walters was leading Worcestershire at the time no one else in the
side had had any captaincy experience.

The selectors (Jackson, Perrin and Higson) were said to have
offered the England captaincy for this match to Pat Hendren, who
both in age and experience was by far the senior man. But Pat, at
45 still well worth his place but obviously coming towards the end
of the road, did not relish a fresh responsibility of this magnitude,
and who could blame him?

In fact the captain who came near to calling down the sarcasm
of the critics on this occasion was Bill Woodfull. Always a cautious
fellow, he carried on the Australian second innings on the fourth
morning for an hour and a half, leaving England 380 to win in less
than five hours on a pitch which was dusting. He won, after an
afternoon of the utmost suspense, by 238 runs – but with ten minutes
only to spare. This was the only series in which I saw Grimmett

and O'Reilly operating together, and this is the match in which I always recall them, spinning away, tireless, ingenious, remorselessly accurate, everlasting. O'Reilly, as it happened, had eleven wickets to Grimmett's eight, and here is their aggregate analysis:

Overs	Maidens	Runs	Wickets
184.1	92	249	19

If some may be thinking, 'And they call our batting slow nowadays!' they have the support of *Wisden*, who thought that England 'played into the hands' of Grimmett and O'Reilly 'by failing to realize that bolder methods were more likely to achieve the draw'. But is English Test history not studded with examples of caution failing where more initiative might have either won or saved the day?

No doubt George Gunn, 55 but not long retired, would have been there, philosophizing in the way that Neville Cardus has immortalized to the effect that 'batsmen have always taken too much notice of the way field's set or state of the pitch. What's more, they take too much notice of the bowling.' Allow what you will for the exaggeration in this sort of dry observation, it still retains a healthy element of truth.

It was only a few days later that there occurred the game which really brought the Bodyline business to a climax in that as a result of it Lancashire suspended fixtures with Notts. When other counties later threatened to do the same the Notts Club had no option but to apologize, and also to sack Arthur Carr, the captain with whose connivance (to say the least) Larwood and Voce on some occasions had in 1934 reverted to the methods used in Australia which before the season began all the county captains had agreed they would not countenance.

According to Ledbrooke (whose Lancashire history, granted his limitation as to space, is surely a model of what such a book should be) a dressing-room row preceded the start, after which Larwood bowled like the wind, and Lancashire found themselves dismissed for 119. Notts replied with 266, and the game looked to be lost and won. But now Lancashire began the fight back, and as they did so the Notts' fast bowlers bowled shorter and shorter. Lancashire were pummelled black and blue, but they stood up to it all. Ernest Tyldesley made a magnificent hundred, Frank Watson 63, Lionel

Lister 86, while Peter Eckersley (40) and George Duckworth (26) took out their bats in a tail-end stand that ended with Eckersley's declaration at 394 for seven. Ledbrooke called this 'one of the most glorious passages in the county's history'.

Then justice! There was a bit of rain, the Lancashire spinners got to work, and the tenth Notts wicket fell to the third LBW appeal in what must have been the last over, bringing a highly astonishing victory by 101 runs. Lancashire threw the stumps in the air in their jubilation, Ernest Tyldesley of all men is said to have hurled the ball into the crowd, and on their return to Old Trafford the bruises of certain batsmen were photographed as evidence on committee orders.

But what a magnificent cricketer was Harold Larwood, and what a tragedy he fell into such evil hands! On the first morning of this fateful game his analysis at one point was six for 1 – it was 'the most brilliant exhibition of speed bowling ever seen'. The following morning, going in at No. 10, he made 80 including six sixes in three-quarters of an hour.

Larwood has long been domiciled in Australia, while Bill Voce has since done great service for England and Notts as a bowler and for Notts also as a coach. All acrimony at Trent Bridge is a thing of the distant past, and one today can enjoy with serenity a pavilion and a field steeped in history: an inn, too, for that matter, for was it not William Clarke's marriage in 1838 to the landlady of the Trent Bridge Inn overlooking the river that set everything in train? While Mrs Clarke managed the pub (still known as the TBI), her husband made a cricket ground out of the adjoining meadow, so perfected his art as to become the best bowler of his day, and announced that the men of Notts would play all and sundry. With success his ambitions grew even greater: he founded his own touring All-England XI and so spread the gospel of cricket far and wide to pastures new.

Clarke was the original cricket impresario, paving the way, if you like, for W.G. and the endemic rivalry between North and South and the growth of the county system. When old Clarke got to work at Trent Bridge, our Australian may be reminding himself, Melbourne was no more than a village, his native Adelaide a mere gleam in the eye of its creator, Colonel Light.

The last time duty took me to Trent Bridge was in 1973 when

against New Zealand Tony Greig underlined his full potential to the most grudging of the critics by making his first Test hundred in England *in two hours and a half*. It took me back (so listeners were informed that evening and *Daily Telegraph* readers next day) to the prime of Ted Dexter. But I recall the game now also for a sadder reason. The new electronic scoreboard was in use, having replaced the vast Australian type, which was the only one of its kind ever built in England. Frank Gregory, the Notts President, was at pains to show me that this new board was just the first stage in a building plan round the eastern side designed to make the Trent Bridge ground safe for cricket for ever. There is no need to repeat the details here – the broad principle being that the Club itself was to have a 50% share in the project, and also that it was about to lease the land due to be developed, not to sell it. Thus there would be a continuing interest and control. Within a few years Frank became such a recognized expert in the best utilization of cricket-club-owned property that he was made chairman of the TCCB Development Committee, and as such visited every major ground in the country.

The melancholy part of this story is that last year Gregory met sudden death when on holiday. A fellow-guest on a yacht fell overboard. He dived to the rescue, which was successful; but he succumbed to a heart-attack. Frank had just given up the Notts presidency after an eventful five-year spell, and the TCCB were hopeful of making greater use of his powers. Others, of course, were and are deeply involved in his Trent Bridge scheme, but I do not disparage their part, I think, when I say he was the initiator – a pioneer in the tradition of Clarke himself.

Continuing our erratic, vaguely clockwise path we leave Nottingham for Leicester encountering there, if we are lucky, not only Mike Turner, whose title is secretary-manager and under whose hand things have changed so greatly for the better both on the field and off, but also E. E. Snow, the club's honorary librarian and archivist. The latter, one of a distinguished brotherhood comprising also C. P. and P. A., will tell you that because, as in the areas of Sheffield and Nottingham, piece-work was general and men worked accordingly in their own time, cricket flourished in Leicestershire as early as anywhere outside the Weald and London itself.

This is no doubt true, but in view of recent happenings one can say now what it would have been too hurtful to suggest hitherto that Leicestershire have often been a drag on the Championship. Over spans of decades and more the figures speak for themselves. Yet the year before their centenary in 1973 the county won their first trophy, the Benson and Hedges, and that was the first of four titles in four years, all gained under Ray Illingworth, the culmination being the Championship in 1975. As with their Northamptonshire neighbours, current holders of the Gillette, the cupboard is no longer bare, and the game is the healthier for it.

Leicestershire under the most experienced captain in the game are an able side; yet others with greater talent have achieved a good deal less, and I believe that counties may more and more tend to entrust the running of their affairs to a relatively small executive with a youngish man brought up in the game at the tiller. My instinct tells me that Leicestershire's rise in the cricket world which obviously owes most to the present secretary-manager and captain had its genesis in the arrival in 1950 from Worcestershire of Charlie Palmer, who acted as both secretary and captain over seven difficult years and now casts a benign eye on the scene as chairman of the club.

When I first knew Leicestershire cricket they played on the Aylestone Road ground in the shadow of the generating station. There in 1930 Don Bradman was proceeding blithely to follow his opening double-hundred at Worcester with another and had only 15 more to get when rain – or maybe it *was* sleet with a touch of snow – ended the proceedings. After the war the club had no more than a toe-hold from the education authority on the run-down Grace Road ground, which is now theirs and as pleasant a place to play and watch as could be hoped for in the heart of an industrial city.

I spoke of the Snows. Many in the cricket world will know that Philip is the father of Fiji cricket – he was for many years a civil servant there – fewer possibly that the famous novelist, Charles (Lord Snow of Leicester) when he was a don at Christ's in the '30s used to contribute the Cambridge notes to the *Cricketer* and was a very passable player. Very punctiliously did he gather his material at Fenner's, as I well remember.

It is via Cambridge surely that we may bring this peregrination to an end, with a look at as perfect a field for cricket as any seen before, and a word no doubt with Cyril Coote who has been so

much more to many generations of undergraduates than a groundsman, and for upwards of forty years just about the best in the
business at that. Cyril, despite a 'game leg', permanently stiff at the
knee-joint, made a lot of runs for Cambridgeshire, including at
Fenner's an innings of 150. I like the idea of its creator thinking as
he prepares his pitch, 'this one's a beauty', then hopping off his
motor-roller and making the most of it.

Ted Dexter's batting generation was not the only one that profited
from Cyril chucking balls at them by the hundred from half-way up
the net. Cyril has seen a famous company of great cricketers come
and go, and is succinct and realistic about them all. He is clear
that the best of the batsmen was Peter May, and has no doubt
that Majid Khan, son of that admirable Cambridge all-rounder
of the '30s, Jahangir, has been the best University captain of his
time. (Welsh readers may be specially interested in this assessment!)

The story is told of a lovely innings being played in his last year
by Majid, to the evident pleasure of a cluster of senior dons in the
pavilion. 'You'd better make the most of it, you know,' said Cyril
Coote to them. 'It'll be the last of its kind you'll see here unless
some of you gentlemen change your admissions policies.' Happily,
at Cambridge as well as Oxford, there have been some recent signs
that at some colleges a shift of emphasis is discernible in favour of
the choice of men with interests other than the purely academic.
Nothing revolutionary, you understand, but the trend may grow.

It is a shock for those visiting Fenner's after an absence of years
to find a crescent of flats where used to be the old pavilion that
housed the cricketers and the athletes for all but a century. However, its functional successor on the far side of the field makes up
in comfort what it lacks in grace, and the great tradition of
Cambridge cricket is exposed in the new Long Room for all to see
in the names of every team to have played against Oxford, depicted
in gold on long green wall panels, since the first University Match
150 years ago.

If I mention Cyril Coote as a stalwart Fenner's figure I cannot
ignore J. G. W. Davies, who has done a vast deal for Cambridge
cricket since his oft-recalled feat of bowling Bradman for a duck.
Through a busy life, first as head of the University Appointments
Board, until lately as a director of the Bank of England and now as
Treasurer of MCC, Jack in his office of honorary treasurer of the

CUCC has kept a shrewd hold on the purse-strings with one hand and, as it were, the wolf from the door with the other. It cannot be disadvantageous to the two Universities that in one of the chief seats of power at Lord's is someone with a unique knowledge and experience of the problems of University cricket – which, though much of the power and the glory have gone, may still have an important part to play in the English cricket scene.

13
The 'Cricketer' Story

One evening in 1920 after a day's play at Lord's I was chatting with Plum, whom I had known since my brother Tip's Oxford days in the late 1890s. I knew that it was his last season in first class cricket and I suggested to him that in order to preserve the best interests of the game someone like he (*sic*) should start a paper devoted to cricket.

Plum loved the idea. It was decided to form a company to run the paper. Plum thought of the name. It was accepted without question and the paper under his editorship appeared for the first time on Saturday, 30th April, 1921.

So, according to G. N. Foster, when Michael Melford in editing *Pick of the 'Cricketer'* sought to discover the genesis of the magazine, it happened : and, of course, it has been going uninterruptedly ever since. Strangely enough Plum in his *Long Innings* goes into no detail on the matter beyond saying that in 1921 he 'undertook the editorship of the *Cricketer* as well as becoming cricket correspondent of the *Morning Post*' – a position he retained for thirteen years. But Geoff, youngest of the seven Fosters, was a games zealot of the first order and also a man of ideas in the sporting world, as well as a gifted all-rounder. Knowing him well later, as I did, I can hear him saying in the Middlesex dressing-room, 'I know, Plum, what you must do. Your life is in cricket – you must start a cricket paper.'

There could have been, of course, no better name at the masthead. Here was the man who had taken the first MCC side to Australia (in 1903/4) and retrieved the Ashes, and gone again in 1911/12 and done so a second time – a feat, incidentally, given to no Englishman to repeat since, and, in reverse, only one Australian, Billy Woodfull. Now his own first-class career had ended in the most dramatic, story-book way with a Middlesex victory against all the odds over Surrey at Lord's, and Plum, their captain, waving his Harlequin cap, carried from the field on the shoulders of the crowd.

Plum was a batsman only a little short of the highest class who, despite persistently frail health, made nearly 30,000 runs. But his chief fame, naturally, was as a leader, and his devotion to the game and adherence to its best interests had always come across to make him a highly popular figure with the crowd.

When the summer of 1921 opened he had more than quarter of a century of first-class cricket behind him, the war years included, and as it turned out he continued to serve the game in more capacities than anyone either before or since for more than quarter of a century more. He had written several books already, and several more were to come. He was to combine serving almost uninterruptedly on the MCC Committee and acting as chairman of selectors with day-to-day editing and reporting. In the remaining years of the '20s he played a good deal of lesser cricket, and extended his experience of the game overseas until at the end the list included, besides Australia and South Africa, the only other Test countries of his day, his native West Indies, New Zealand, Canada, USA, South America, Portugal, Holland and Denmark. Strangely, since it was the ultimate symbol of imperial power, and one which must have made a strong romantic appeal to him, the only country of cricket significance he never visited was India. When the second war came, and the MCC Secretary, Colonel R. S. Rait Kerr, was recalled to the colours, who would step into the breach but Plum?

He was 66 when he was appointed deputy assistant secretary, and so he remained throughout the war, not content with just keeping things ticking over but, despite all hazards and difficulties, organizing regular programmes of one-day matches, and in 1945 the vastly successful Victory series. Finally – if all too late – the crowning honour of the Presidency was bestowed on him by his predecessor, the Duke of Edinburgh, in 1950, in his 77th year. Such in brief was the career in cricket of the man who on page one of the first issue of the *Cricketer* in 1921 under the heading 'An Editorial Foreword' declared his policy :

> The popularity of, and interest in, cricket, not only here, but in every part of the world where Englishmen are gathered together, was never greater than at the present time. Cricket, indeed, as Tom Brown has told us in the best of all school stories,

is an institution and the *habeas corpus* of every boy of British birth, for it is a typically British game.

The Editor believes that there is room for such a paper as the *Cricketer*, which will endeavour to criticize justly and to comment fairly and accurately not only on first-class cricket, which, after all, is but a small part of our national game, but on Club, Services, and School cricket as well. The very essence of cricket is camaraderie and good sportsmanship, and the contributors to the *Cricketer* will strive to write in such a spirit, hoping thereby to spread an even greater love of cricket than exists at present, and, at the same time, to educate the general public in the finer points of the game.

Unexceptionable ambitions, and, as might have been expected, in such august hands the *Cricketer* maintained them unswervingly. The editor went on to announce his intention of covering the game 'in our Overseas Dominions', and then proceeded to introduce his chief contributors. Apart from himself it was a strong list that came out of the hat: Maclaren, Jessop, D. J. Knight, Altham, G. N. Foster, F. B. (Freddy) Wilson, and a leading cartoonist of the day, Charles Graves, whose page-one effort showed a cherubic Plum taking guard, with the *Cricketer* superimposed on his Harlequin cap, and the caption, 'A Youngster with a Future'. Maclaren was not only one of the greatest England batsmen but a tremendous pundit. No name was surrounded with greater lustre than that of Jessop. Donald Knight was a current England player and the master-in-charge of cricket at Westminster. Altham was in the thick of public-school cricket, and it was to this that he devoted his early articles. Freddy Wilson, free-lance contributor to *The Times* on every conceivable game, supplied some of the lighter touches, and they cannot have come amiss to younger readers, especially those whose interest had been wooed by a long essay forbiddingly entitled:

FOR THE SCHOOLBOY

BY A. C. MACLAREN

HOW TO BECOME AN INTERNATIONAL BATSMAN

The old maestro certainly did not write down to his public. Today it reads somewhat indigestibly – possibly because there were only three paragraphs to the page!

There is very much an old-world air about the early issues, and according to the custom of the day it was surnames only for the pros and 'Mr' invariably for the amateurs. Plum was, above all, a man of great courtesy, and one finds a good deal of polite circumlocution. He is inclined to 'venture to suggest', and enquire, 'if I may be allowed to say so'. Yet he does 'say so' in his reports of the Test Matches of 1921 with a good deal of critical emphasis at times. Above the editor's Notes and Comments are printed the most hackneyed line in all the verse of Newbolt (in his prime in 1921): 'Play up, play up, and play the game.'

Though the leagues of Lancashire and Yorkshire were given previews in the first issue their doings were not regularly covered, and it's hard to think the *Cricketer* made a great impact in the North among practising cricketers, though it certainly at once did in the South, for club scores were a feature from the start. All county and University scores were given in full, and the public schools were generously catered for. The Minor Counties had a fair showing too. There was a good deal of reminiscence – too much by present computation – but I for one lapped it all up, and indeed can scarcely remember the time when I was not a reader.

The *Cricketer* sold for 6d, as it continued to do for twenty years, and by the end of June 1921 things were apparently going pretty well.

We regret (*sic*) to announce that practically all copies of the first two numbers of the *Cricketer* have now been disposed of . . . The management are prepared to consider applications for copies of the first two issues from persons who desire to become annual subscribers; but in such cases a charge will be made for the first two numbers of 2s 6d each in addition to the annual subscription of 14/- . . .

In the Special Jubilee Issue, published in the spring of 1971, we printed several letters from original subscribers, and I have little doubt that these words will be read by at least a few who bought or were given the magazine from its inception. One of our 1971 letters came from a man who did great work for cricket in the USA, J. I. Marder. He was indeed for many years our regular correspondent in addition to being President of the USA Cricket Association.

John Marder died last year, and the recollection in his letter of his 'conversion' struck a nostalgic note which has perhaps a message for the players of today. His father had bought him the first issue (which he still possessed), and he read of Armstrong and his team who 'appeared to him like supermen'.

A few weeks later at Trent Bridge I spoke to Jack Gregory. He stopped near the pavilion door and I shyly congratulated him on his bowling. Gregory sat down with me and demonstrated his bowling grip – this from a man who had just humbled England by taking six wickets for 58. The love of cricket was planted in me that day by a first-class cricketer who was humble enough to chat about the game to an obscure 12-year-old.

No doubt some who read this will recall a moment when the seed was first planted in them, and those who have appreciated Marder's crusading work for American cricket may care to know that his devotion had its origin in the kindness of one of the greatest and personally most attractive of Australian cricketers.

The second year of the magazine was notable for the first of Harry Altham's articles on the history of the game. They were welcomed by the editor who had encouraged Harry to tackle the job. Plum described the task as monumental, 'but his knowledge is so great and his pen so facile that we are certain he will charm all our readers'. There were 91 articles in all, and the year following their ending, in 1926, they were put together as *A History of Cricket* and published by Allen and Unwin.

For all his conservatism the editor was not above dabbling in other subjects occasionally. Suddenly one comes upon an article on the prospects of growing oranges in South Africa, while F. J. Sellicks, one of the old school of ultra-respectable sporting journalists who gave the editor a good deal of technical help in the office in the early years, wrote long screeds on Rugby football when the paper appeared monthly in the winter. In 1924 the Olympic Games are previewed, but there is a stranger entry than that. On 3 May of that year *at Lord's* there took place a mixed stoolball match between teams captained by W. W. Grantham and E. T. Campbell respectively. Grantham's team had two other men and eight ladies, Campbell's only one other man. None of the men made much impact, and Campbell's XI won. The *Cricketer* gives the full score but, infuriatingly, not a line of comment.

One of the distractions (and attractions) of authorship is that one so frequently finds oneself wandering down odd bypaths such as this. Thus I can now say, though I confess I could not have done so previously, that the scoring at stoolball is the same as in cricket, that the pitch is 16 yards long, that only under-arm full-pitches are allowed, that the 'stool' which has to be hit is elevated on a stick, that the striking implement looks more like a frying-pan than a cricket bat, and that the game is said to be increasingly popular in Sussex, which indeed has its own county stoolball association.

It needs only to be acquainted with the researches of Harry Altham and others to know that stoolball is one of the possible progenitors of cricket. Plum will have known from Lord Harris and F. S. Ashley-Cooper's *Lord's and the MCC* that all manner of esoteric sporting pursuits had been practised on the sacred turf in times past – pigeon-shooting and 'frequent hopping-matches', for instance – and as many others forbidden; but never apparently stoolball. Yet on 3 May the editor pointedly took himself off to the Oval to see Surrey's opening match against Glamorgan. Perhaps it was the thought of ladies at Lord's that he couldn't quite take, though, goodness knows, he was a gallant among ladies' men who later opened the columns of the *Cricketer* to women's cricket. One wonders how it came that the bare score appeared – perhaps Frank Sellicks slipped it in at the last moment. At all events, by the evidence of the *Cricketer* of 10 May 1924 the women cricketers of England and Australia who stepped out of Lord's pavilion on 4 August 1975 were not the first to disport there with bat and ball, by half a century.

Such flippancies aside, the most significant incident in the story of the *Cricketer* had occurred early in 1923 when a keen young club cricketer called Arthur Langford met Plum Warner and suggested to him that he might supply him with Notes on club cricket. The editor agreed, and so began an association that ended only with Arthur's retirement in 1968. He told the story of his work for the *Cricketer* with characteristic modesty and understatement on his giving up the editorship in the autumn of 1966. There was apparently something of a financial crisis in 1928 as a result of which Sellicks's services and also those of an advertisement manager who had certainly brought remarkably little grist to the mill were dispensed with. 'In effect,' wrote Arthur Langford, 'the staff was reduced to Sir Pelham, a secretary, an office boy and myself.'

A. W. T. Langford, though not so designated, was the assistant-editor, responsible for all the mechanics of the job and, incidentally, getting the advertising. By now fresh names were appearing as contributors: Frank Mitchell, Aubrey Faulkner, R. C. Robertson-Glasgow – whose first writing was published in the magazine – Sir Home Gordon, 'Country Vicar', and, most important of all, F. S. Ashley-Cooper.

It is not the least of the curiosities surrounding cricket that it has attracted as passionate devotees educated men whom nature never intended to be cricketers, and who in most cases never aspired to be, but whose total involvement in the game almost precluded every other interest. Ashley-Cooper's name must head the list of all such. He seems rarely to have watched cricket, though for one season he served as secretary of Notts. Arthur Langford says that though he wrote nearly all the Notes and Comments (which was really the most important feature in the paper as well as much the longest), he only once saw him in the *Cricketer*'s office. He was weakly, short-sighted, 'almost albino' according to Home Gordon, and followed no profession, yet his researches into cricket, especially its remoter past, produced according to *Wisden* '103 books and pamphlets on the game dealing with cricket in England, Australia, South Africa, New Zealand, India and other places, besides a very large amount of matter including 40,000 biographical and obituary notices, every production from his pen, moreover, being characterized by phenomenal accuracy, to secure which he spared neither time nor trouble'.

Wisden as well as the *Cricketer* had every reason to be grateful to Ashley-Cooper, for he was for more than thirty years responsible both for their Births and Deaths, which at his own death ran to all but a hundred pages, and for the Cricket Records section which from two pages when he took it over he expanded to sixty. There was a kindred spirit employed in the Reading Room of the British Museum named H. T. Waghorn; together they researched there unceasingly – in the case of Ashley-Cooper largely among newspapers and magazines printed before 1830! The Nyrens and the Mitfords, the Pycrofts and the Haygarths, the Waghorns and the Ashley-Coopers – they are a wonderful company of dedicated men, and, though he died before his 55th birthday, for the scope and accuracy of his work Ashley-Cooper surely stands alone. It is thanks to them, and to their modern successors, of course, that cricket is such a marvellously documented game.

So far as the magazine was concerned Ashley-Cooper's accuracy was reflected during his time throughout the paper, and the general note of urbanity struck at the start was maintained. But, as I have said, Plum was a great one for decorum, and came down sharply enough on any departure from good manners. For instance, the account of a great dinner at the Savoy celebrating the centenary of the University Match is critical not only of the speeches but of their reception.

There was a good deal of chattering during the speeches, and though, admittedly, it was a festive event, when a man like Lord Harris, who has done so much for cricket all the world over, is speaking, one expects, and especially from University men, that deference and attention which are his due.

The great Harris apparently 'was not at his best', and no one seemed to get beyond 1875. The University Match which had just taken place was scarcely referred to, and none of the young was invited to speak. Ten years later when the 150th Anniversary of the founding of MCC was celebrated, also at the Savoy – the first dinner I remember attending as a Member – Plum was equally critical of the speeches, and in *Lord's*, published almost ten years later, came down hard on Gubby Allen.

'A Country Vicar' was well launched on his memories in the mid-'20s, and he continued for more than twenty years, writing in every issue, a remarkable record of stamina and imagination if nothing else. It was agreeable nostalgic stuff, with touches of humour and gentle irony, and extremely popular with the limited public for which the paper catered. But my suspicious mind suggests that part of the charm for Plum of this ceaseless cascade of words was that they were either cheap or even written 'for love'. The country vicar's real name was Randolph Llewellyn Hodgson. He had a living at South Baddesley near Lymington, Hampshire, and, according to Langford, he heard 'Angela', who became his wife and was very much part of the reminiscent story, reciting at one of Clara Butt's

Four faces of cricket : **9.** Jack Hobbs, greatest of all professional batsmen ;
10. Plum Warner, whose life was the game ; **11.** R. C. Robertson-Glasgow, humorous
essayist, author, reporter, and bowler for Oxford and Somerset ; **12.** F. S. Ashley-Cooper
(1877–1932) despite ill-health from birth perhaps its most profound and prolific
historian and researcher. The biggest contributor to the *Cricketer* in its first decade,
he wrote 103 cricket books and pamphlets including *Lord's and The MCC*
(in collaboration with Lord Harris).

13. Bishen Bedi : of India and
Northamptonshire, the finest
exponent in the world today of the
neglected arts of flight and spin.
Does not Tony Greig seem to be a
little slow in backing-up?

14. Rôles Reversed : Colin Cowdrey
presents Peter May to the Queen at
the Lord's Test of 1961 against
Australia. Peter had been ill, and
Colin, his regular vice-captain, had
deputized in his absence.
Cowdrey's last Test was in 1975 at
Melbourne, aged 42 ; but May,
England's finest post-war batsman,
bowed out of Test cricket at 31,
following this series.

concerts and fell for her at first sight.

If I remember Frank Mitchell aright Plum would not have been so lucky with him – and in any case he was a professional journalist. Mitchell had an unusual career in sport. He was a Yorkshireman, a bull of a fellow who won Blues at Cambridge for cricket, Rugby football and athletics, made a lot of runs for his county at the turn of the century, having as an undergraduate captained England on the football field. He went to South Africa with Lord Hawke's team of 1898/9 and played in what posthumously became Test Matches, was subsequently secretary to Sir Abe Bailey, the mining millionaire, fought in the Boer War, and brought two South African sides to England, the second for the ill-fated Triangular Tournament of 1912. He was a strong character, and at times a prickly one, as comes out in his life story as related by him in 'My Innings', which ran through the issues of 1935, and which was only ended by his death that winter. He also wrote regular topical comment as 'Second Slip'. Plum obviously had a soft spot for him, and in his obituary notice said he was what John Nyren would have called 'a good face-to-face man'.

Mitchell when captain of Cambridge was at the centre of a storm which seems to have blown up with a curiously rapid violence when in the University Match of 1896 he ordered one of his bowlers to give away extras in order to ensure that Oxford could not follow-on, which was then obligatory. Stanley Jackson had ordered C. M. Wells to do the same thing three years before without it causing much fuss. Now the pavilion was in uproar, and a comical sight it must have been as Cambridge on coming off the field were loudly abused by MCC's distinguished membership of the day, all in morning dress, as was then and for long after the fashion at the University Match. They will have included, incidentally, W.G. himself, decked out in full fig, who came to see W. G. Grace junior go in first for Cambridge and to his father's great mortification collect a pair, bowled each time. Cambridge were said to be upset by the demonstration and lost six wickets for 61, and, though Cambridge recovered, Oxford made 330 for four in the fourth innings to win a great victory. Mitchell's plan therefore misfired, but the majority on reflection decided that it was the law that was the ass, and it was promptly changed to make following-on the option of the fielding side.

So long as cricket pursued a reasonably tranquil path Plum's equivocal position as editor on one hand and selector and administrator on the other merely meant that as regards matters in which Plum was officially concerned the comment was provided by Mitchell under his pseudonym of Second Slip. A flavour of mutual admiration sometimes grated a little, as when Second Slip commended the editor (then in his upper fifties) on an innings at Lord's which had won the day for MCC against Holland, and Plum added an editorial note saying no, no, the writer was too kind! Inevitably the *Cricketer* was regarded as the voice of the Establishment, but this did not automatically condemn it, as it would among so many today.

When the position became an embarrassment both to Warner and Mitchell, and a frustration to the more perceptive reader, was during the explosion of feelings engendered by Bodyline. In the issue of September 1932 Second Slip gave Bill Bowes a rare roasting for bowling short at Surrey (and in particular Hobbs) in a championship match at the Oval. This was a modified form of what came to be called Bodyline by a bowler substantially slower than Larwood and less awkward to play when bowling short than Voce. 'Bowes should alter his tactics. He bowled with five men on the on side, and sent down several very short-pitched balls which repeatedly bounced head-high and more. That is *not bowling*; indeed it is *not cricket*, and if all the fast bowlers were to adopt his methods there would be trouble and plenty of it . . .' He concludes : 'Bowes is not doing justice to himself, to his ability, or to the game of cricket by such methods.' Not much doubt where Second Slip stood! George Macaulay by contrast got off pretty lightly for bowling two fast high full-pitches – the word 'beamer' was not then in use – in the same innings against Jardine, who played a wearisome innings of 35 in 2½ hours.

So one turns to the first issue published after the tour in Australia, the Spring Annual of 1933, and to Second Slip's leading article, written no doubt while Plum was sailing home, promisingly entitled: 'Leg Theory: What is to be done?' Poor Mitchell! He began his piece, believe it or not, with the best part of a column applauding the royal interest in cricket on the strength of the King's congratulatory telegram to the team on the regaining of the Ashes. Readers were reminded of Prince Albert's patronage, and how Edward VII had once played for IZ at Sandringham!

When Mitchell eventually got down to the happenings of the tour it seemed that the captain 'has been inexorable but right: no one can point to anything done by our team which has not been in accordance with the best cricket'.

The article ended by referring scathingly to experiments in certain additional protection for the batsmen, and decided that, this being the age of disarmament, such devices should be forbidden. Assuming the Spring Annual got as far as Sydney the comments of someone like Jack Fingleton, as both cricketer and journalist, would have been interesting to hear.

By the next issue of 6 May the team's eight-month tour was over and those 'who have represented us so nobly' were being welcomed home. Furthermore, 'with the various controversies which have raged and may yet be open for discussion we do not propose to deal'. Plum, now back in the saddle, his tour managership over, clearly could not allow anything to be said on the central issue while MCC enquiries were pending, though he discussed at length the individual form of the MCC team and their opponents.

When, late in June, MCC sent back to Australia their considered summing-up of the upsets of the tour, having heard their selected evidence, and the *Cricketer* leader dwelt thereon, the accent had changed rather to a determination to keep a careful look-out, and to obtain the views of captains and others: but there was also a good deal of tut-tutting about Australian barracking and the failure of their authorities to do anything about it which tended to overlook the justification for it all. In his heart of hearts Plum, if not Frank Mitchell, having seen Larwood and Voce regularly at work with the whole leg-trap paraphernalia, must have been pretty sure that if the situation had been reversed English crowds would not have sat silent while their own men were being so dangerously assailed.

Indeed we read that spectators at the University match were far from pleased when Kenneth Farnes bowled fast leg-theory persistently against Oxford. This unexpected happening on such an occasion elicited rather less condemnation than the terrible crime of some of the Blues turning out at Lord's with hip-pockets! Altogether there was some fairly barmy stuff from the pen of Second Slip in 1933, and when Constantine and Martindale bowled unadulterated Bodyline on an extremely mild pitch in the Old Trafford

Test, and Jardine countered it by making a hundred, the fact and its significance were very much underplayed. 'None of the England batsmen appeared intimidated, none complained, but they were all liable to be out in the leg direction.' It's hard to believe that neither Mitchell nor Plum knew that after Hammond had 'sustained a horrible blow on his face' he simply had a crack and got out, and on returning to the dressing-room announced that if the game was coming to this he had no wish to play it. As might be said nowadays, the row with Australia had blown the *Cricketer* temporarily off course.

On the lighter side E. W. Swanton (the *Evening Standard* cricket correspondent) made his first appearances in the 1932/3 Annual and in the Spring Annual of 1933, though not, naturally, on the issues of the moment. 'Cricket at Eastbourne: Pleasures of the Saffrons' gave a picture of the season's cricket there and asked the question:

> Who can wish for a more lovely sight than the Saffrons as you enter from the Town Gate, the white pavilion, bordered with geraniums, framed in the background of the great hill, tall elms on one side, Larkin's Field, golden with buttercups, on the other?

My second article attempted to have a look at some cricketers of the future, and concluded that the old brigade were so firmly at the top that there seemed no great rush of youngsters to supplant them. I thought we had not seen the best yet of Cyril Walters, who had not then played for England though he was due to top the averages against Australia a year hence: but at 27 he was hardly a discovery. Nor exactly were Reg Perks or Jim Sims, though their England days were some way ahead. The one prophetic remark that bears repetition was my final one:

> I will, in conclusion, make one extremely long shot. Kent have a sixteen-year-old googly bowler called Wright. I have not seen him in the open, but on matting under cover he can be almost unplayable. There are more unlikely things than that he should be the 'discovery' of 1933.

I had understated his age by a couple of years, but he had played only one first-class match at this point and failed to take a wicket. Doug's development was more gradual than I had envisaged, Kent being wisely content to bring him along gradually in the shadow of Tich Freeman. But by 1938 he was playing for England, plainly a man of the highest possibilities, and though the war took away six of his prime years he finished with 34 Test caps and more than two thousand wickets. Like Ian Peebles and Freddie Brown he had learned the wrist-spinning art at the Faulkner School of Cricket: how marvellous if a new race of spinners – of this and every sort – can be shaped and encouraged at the MCC Indoor School!

Little Sir Home Gordon was coming into the picture in the '30s and had an exchange of correspondence with Neville Cardus from which he did not emerge too badly. 'That Socrates of cricket', as Home described Cardus, had been saying more or less that the age of greatness was past. Home Gordon replied:

At the dinner at the Hotel Metropole last August, given by the Jam Sahib of Nawanagar to the Australians and Sussex, Mr Archie Maclaren jeremiahed in the same strain. I volunteered to reply and was cheered to the echo for saying there is nothing so depressing to the cricketers of today as being run down because of players who, to them, are only traditional. Having seen cricket ever since the first Test in 1880 I declared it as good as ever it was. Fielding and wicket-keeping are on a higher standard than pre-war: Duleep follows Ranji, Bradman succeeds Trumper, probably Verity will replace Rhodes, and McCabe fill the shoes of Macartney.

Cheered to the echo he was, with the Sussex players, I expect, exchanging many a knowing wink. For, though Home Gordon may well have *seen* more cricket than any man before or since, even that kindliest of men, Arthur Langford, in his 1966 valedictory piece, said that,

'although he mixed with all the great players, English and over-seas, covering a period of more than fifty years, he knew very little about the game, mainly I suppose because ill-health prevented him from taking an active part in cricket'.

When Mitchell died Home really came into his own, leading

each issue with his article 'In the Pavilion', over his own name.
Poor Arthur had to sub him and

he was a rare problem. His copy was extremely difficult to read,
and he left no room for corrections, which made things extremely
awkward as he was alarmingly inaccurate . . . Apart from
inaccuracies he often had an odd way of expressing himself, and
I remember that on one occasion instead of saying that Sussex
had lost seven matches he wrote that they had suffered seven
discomfitures. On another occasion when Sir Pelham remon-
strated with him, he replied : 'My dear Plum, Neville Cardus has
his style, I have mine.'

What a worker Arthur Langford must have been in those days,
much greater even though his effort was due to become! Apart
from much of the ordering of articles, he subbed the paper, and
saw it to press at the printers besides contributing two or three or
four pages of Club Notes, which must have necessitated a vast
amount of telephoning and correspondence. Oh, yes, and he was
advertisement manager in addition.

When war came Plum went to his duty at Lord's, the office was
moved complete to the Langfords' house at Surbiton, and despite
all the difficulties, somehow or other, the *Cricketer*, albeit in smaller
format, continued to appear. Meg Langford began her devoted task
of working up the subscriptions department, and Arthur was
enabled to go on editing 'virtually on an honorary basis', as he said,
thanks to his being offered a temporary job at the BBC. A. C. L.
Bennett, who made many thousands of runs for the BBC both
before the war and after, arranged this, and E. L. Roberts, the
well-known statistician and a frequent contributor, nobly braved
the Blitz and all the hazards of wartime travel to see the magazine
to bed, week by week in summer, and handling the two annuals
out of season, the printers being now – of all places – in Bermond-
sey. There must surely be a place in cricket's Valhalla for E. L.
Roberts, who was rewarded, according to Arthur, with 'a mere
pittance'.

The Langfords wrote to '100 or so enthusiastic supporters of
cricket, asking them to make a donation so that we could carry
on. In return they would receive copies as published.' I cannot
remember being one of the chosen hundred, but am glad to think

that I contributed a short series of articles in 1941 while waiting to go overseas. Unlike another POW, Terence Prittie, I did not attempt to send back anything from captivity. The Germans allowed not only his article on cricket as played in the moat of the Polish castle which was being used as a POW camp but even sketches of the moat. The Jap reaction to anything of the kind I scarcely care to contemplate.

After the war Plum, now in his seventies, confined his activities to receiving visits from Arthur, who continued to carry on from Surbiton, and to run the paper, both editorial and business side, in double harness with his wife. For a while the post-war boom kept finances buoyant, but in the later '50s times grew harder while Arthur was growing no younger. (He was four years older than the century.) The average age of the directors (Plum, Buns Cartwright, Gerald Crutchley and Arthur himself) must have been nearer 70 than 60, and in 1960 the Dickens Press, thinking they saw an opening for a livelier magazine, started *Playfair Cricket Monthly*, with Gordon Ross as editor.

Plum about now donated his shares to his younger son, John, who rallied several of his friends in 'the media' to help Arthur and him run the paper: he also roped in John Haslewood, a solicitor by training and a director of Watney's. I have a last letter from Plum dated February 1962 saying how glad he was that I was prepared 'to take an interest in the *Cricketer*, which we are reorganizing', and adding some flattering things about the value my influence might have. From this time several of us put a lot of work into the paper, which remained under Arthur's editorship, and with John Warner for a while directing the business side.

But we all had our own jobs to do, and there was really nothing in the till. Nor can a magazine be successfully run by an editorial board. The best that can be said is that the ship was kept precariously afloat for three years or so until Hutchinson (whose chairman, R. A. A. Holt, and vice-chairman, Noel Holland, had both been cricketers) in 1965 obtained a controlling interest. This arrangement saved the *Cricketer*, and assured the future of the Langfords – which had always been the twin objects of all concerned. The magazine's peregrinations were, however, far from over. Hutchinson, of course, are distinguished publishers of books, not magazines, and in 1970 B. G. Brocklehurst, a director of Mercury House, on

behalf of the latter effected an essentially amicable transfer. Thus
Ben Brocklehurst, of Somerset, took on the managing directorship
from 'Bimby' Holt, of Sussex, my position remaining (which it does
still) as editorial director.

Finally when Mercury House after eighteen months or so showed
a disposition to close down the magazine Ben Brocklehurst took the
courageous step of acquiring it from them, and severing his Mercury
House connection, thus putting his business future at obvious risk.

Happily the picture now is one of steady prosperity, with the
print order touching 40,000, and the seemingly ever-increasing
costs of production balanced by revenue from promotional sources,
as well as from the big increase in sales and advertising revenue.
The circulation was not much more than 10,000 when Hutchinson
came in, and around 15,000 at the time of the Brocklehurst acquisition. In 1973 the present owner acquired *Playfair Cricket Monthly*,
which, concentrating on the first-class game, had enjoyed a reputation that ensured, with minor changes of editorial emphasis, an
amiable blending of the two readerships. A further result of this
merger was the welcome addition of Gordon Ross to the Board
and his editorship of a new periodical of record, the *Cricketer
Quarterly*.

My own connection with the magazine I look back on with the
knowledge of mistakes made, crises narrowly surmounted, and
satisfaction that the work and responsibility are now in the safest
possible hands. It was a narrow squeak at one time, but the fact is
that the game has had the benefit of an independent periodical for
57 years. We can look forward with assurance to a Diamond Jubilee
in 1981, and many a *Cricketer* anniversary thereafter. That cricket
needs a responsible paper scarcely needs emphasis. If this can be
illustrated by one fact it is that, although contributors' rates were
so low as to be almost nominal (they are now more realistic) I
believe that I only ever encountered one refusal: he was a famous
England cricketer who a few months later sent me an article off
his own bat. John Arlott, who has surely spoken and written more
words about cricket than any man these last thirty years, never
declined, and his copy was never late. The same could be said of
John Woodcock, *The Times* cricket correspondent who for many
years has covered the Test scene for us. David Frith, the present
editor, an Anglo-Australian and an author of distinction aside from

his work for the magazine, tells me much the same state of affairs obtains today.

Soon after we joined the Hutchinson stable A. S. R. Winlaw came up with the idea of a knock-out competition for Old Boy sides to be played on a limited-overs basis on Sundays. His enthusiasm won over the directors and hence the *Cricketer* Cup, for which there were 16 invited entrants in the first few years, the number being soon doubled to the present figure of 32. In 1967 the first finalists were Repton and Radley, each led, as it happened, by men who had captained England, Donald Carr and Ted Dexter respectively. Repton won the day, and Ted contributed not only 80 not out for Radley but a suitably generous and light-hearted account of the game to the September issue.

The sun shone, and a good crowd came to the Guards' ground at Burton Court, and Patrick Eagar took some memorable pictures including one showing Mme Pol Roger giving the Cup, with Lord Nugent, a past president representing MCC, at her elbow. The photograph reminds me of the most improbable slip made by Tim Nugent which occasioned some merriment. Mme Pol Roger's famous firm had given us a generous sponsorship : hence her presence. His lordship, having said all the right things about the competition and the match just lost and won, concluded, '. . . and now I have great pleasure in introducing to you Mme Bollinger, who will present the Cup.' The lady rose to the occasion splendidly. She said that Mme Bollinger was a friend of hers whose wine she sometimes much enjoyed. However, on this occasion she hoped the winning captain would accept a case of Pol Roger. It turned out that Tim Nugent happened also to be a friend of the head of the rival firm, and could offer no other explanation of his tongue leading him astray.

It so happens that we have never been off the champagne standard, for Moët et Chandon stepped in in 1971, and apart from prodigal hospitality on the day actually charter an aircraft to take the winning team and wives or girl-friends to Rheims for a memorable annual autumn day at the Château de Saran. The cricket is strenuous enough in the *Cricketer* Cup, but it is a nice point whether this part of the prize does not make greater calls on the winners' stamina than the final.

In answer perhaps to the unspoken question, I might add, as

chairman of the competition since its inception, that the choice of schools to be invited (necessarily an arbitrary business) was gone into by a thoroughly conscientious committee which spent several hours weighing up all available evidence. Only one school declined, but there is a queue waiting the chance to come in, and it is a recurring regret to have to say that we feel we cannot go back on the undertaking we made to several of the leading wandering clubs that we would not institute another round and so make further inroads on their fixture-lists.

Tonbridge have the best record in the Cup, having appeared in half the ten finals and won three of them. Winchester and Malvern have won twice each, Repton, Rugby and Brighton once. Charterhouse, Harrow, Radley, Stowe, Dulwich, and Blundells have reached Burton Court and lost. Most of the other twenty schools involved have had several successes : only one, and they not by any means the least keen, have yet to score a victory. After the first final Dexter wrote that 'perhaps the best feature of the new competition was that first-class cricketers rubbed shoulders with week-end clubmen. It was not always obvious exactly who was who, but the mingling was healthy and enjoyable.' Though county cricket is nowadays almost a closed shop this is still to some extent true, and I hope it remains so. As I have written elsewhere, in my playing days it was one of the joys to meet high-class, even great cricketers in club matches, and it was to the clear benefit of all parties. In a more general way I'm sure it's true that this competition has given that extra inducement to good cricketers to keep playing, and to play a bit more, and maybe with rather more effort than might have been the case otherwise.

I have written at some length about the *Cricketer* Cup partly at least because it triggered off an almost universal desire among southern club cricketers to try some form or other of the competitive cricket which had always existed in the North and Midlands, but which had hitherto been taboo with them. In 1967, so far as I am aware, there was no other knock-out or league cricket of any substance in the South. The following year we established by means of a questionnaire in the magazine that a club competition on national lines would be popular. More than three hundred clubs applied. They were cut down regretfully but carefully to 256, and in September 1969, at Edgbaston, Ronny Aird, as President of

MCC, was presenting the cup donated by Derrick Robins to Hampstead, the first winners of the *Cricketer* National Club Knock-out, more often shortened to the NCKO, until now under the aegis of the NCA it has been re-titled the Club Cricket Championship.

As soon as Ben Brocklehurst came into the picture he got working on a national competition for villages and persuaded Michael Henderson, managing director of John Haig, to sponsor it. Hence the Haig National Village Championship which attracts an annual entry of more than 800 and is run from the magazine's office.

Of greater importance perhaps so far as the future of cricket is concerned is the vast competition for schools of all kinds which now goes by the somewhat unwieldy name of the Lord's Taverners *Cricketer* Colts Trophy. Last year at the Oval I had the pleasure of presenting the cup to the captain of Stamford – whose most illustrious product is M. J. K. Smith – the conquerors of Bournemouth Grammar School in the final of a competition for which more than a thousand schools of all sorts had entered. It doesn't need me or anyone else to underline the value of every variety of school, independent, grammar, 'direct grant' and comprehensive, meeting in rivalry, and although Radley won two years running before this 1976 final it was encouraging that some of the schools of less reputation, and often inferior facilities, got through to the later rounds. The last sixteen were an ideal 'mix' of types. It should be added that the Colts Trophy is run in alliance with the English Schools Cricket Association, and that, so great is the entry, each competition is run over two years. The boys are under 15 when they start and under 16 if they make sufficient progress the following year. Thus there are always two competitions running concurrently. The idea is to get boys keenly involved in the game before they become too heavily burdened with studying for their O and A levels.

These projects are probably more interesting to be concerned with than to read about, so I will merely add that there are also the London Schools *Cricketer* Trophy and a competition for company and municipal authority teams which is called, simply, the *Cricketer* Trophy. The nomenclature is perhaps all a bit muddling, but there is certainly nothing uncertain about the organization. It was reckoned that last year over 20,000 cricketers competed in the various affairs run from the *Cricketer* office.

All this effort is undertaken in harmony with the National Cricket

Association, the body founded ten years ago which now has Freddie Brown as its chairman, and is charged with the daunting job of ministering to the interests of every cricketer in the United Kingdom outside the first-class game. The NCA has done a particularly good job in setting up and administering the national coaching scheme, in teaching the teachers, as it were, who emerge, according to quality, with either the Advanced or the Coaching Award Certificate.

With regular and generous help from the Wrigley Foundation and the Lord's Taverners the NCA are giving aid to clubs and schools in such directions as coaching courses, provision of films and other visual aids, grants for artificial pitches, and on a wider front the sponsorship of representative teams both from and to this country. Without shouting about it, Wrigley's by the time these words are read will have contributed around £100,000 through the NCA, while the Lord's Taverners' injection into the game since a group of men prominent in the entertainment world and the arts started operations in 1950, and were lucky and clever enough to secure the permanent patronage and interest of Prince Philip, must be nearing the half-million-pound mark. We (I speak as Taverner No. 326) are an extrovert lot now grown to a membership just over a thousand, with the common bond of a love of cricket and the desire to encourage it. Balls, lunches, dinners, golf as well as cricket matches, race meetings, boxing nights – all are grist to the Taverners' mill, and most if not all of these activities seem to go with a rare gusto. So far as the Taverners are concerned that seems to be the *mot juste*.

But I have diverted long enough from the story of the *Cricketer* and I must conclude by saying a little about some of the editorial activities of the last decade or so. In the spring of 1966 we conducted a poll of readers on various aspects of county cricket, saying we did not wish to add to the 'hypochondria from which some administrators are suffering (as witnessed by the succession of changes imposed these last few years by the Advisory County Committee)', and just thought it might be helpful to discover the general view as expressed by a cross-section of the game's close supporters.

Were they as interested in county cricket as they used to be? *Yes*, to the tune of 69%. Did they want more one-day games on the Gillette pattern? *No*, by 37%, against 63. Fewer three-day matches? A ratio of three to two voted in favour. Four-day Championship matches? 24% for, 76 against.

Did they approve the 65-overs restriction to the first innings then just introduced? No – 85% against. Had there been too many changes in the laws and regulations? An even more resounding *Yes* – from 90%. As to first-class Sunday cricket – 70% approved it. The idea of sport on TV keeping them away from watching cricket was comprehensively rejected by 85%, a figure the validity of which was doubted by Doug Insole, chairman of the selectors, whom we invited to comment on the findings.

Yet though they thought there had been too much tinkering with the laws, 65% believed the bowler's run-up should be restricted. I was specially pleased about this, having long held the view (as I still do) that a maximum of 22 yards would not deprive any young bowler who had been brought up to it to exert the maximum pace of which he was capable: and how it would help the modern abysmal over rate! If we were to ask the question again today I dare say the proportion in favour of restriction would be considerably more than two-thirds.

We had Irving Rosenwater on our staff by now – he whose mastery of so many areas of cricket knowledge is such that he has been known to be barred from quizzes. John Reason was assistant-editor, and added a good professional punch to the make-up and content. Patrick Eagar was our Special Photographer, as he still is, and surely the best in the business.

It was a pleasure, as well as of profit to the magazine, that we gave their first start on coming down from Cambridge both to Patrick and to Christopher Martin-Jenkins, who spent several years with us before moving on to the BBC. He is now their cricket correspondent, and is said to be, in private, a brilliant mimic of some of his elders in the game. Somehow I cannot persuade him to perform.

When we revived the Spring and Winter Annuals in 1967 the list of contributors brings a nostalgic pang ten years later: Menzies, Bradman, Cardus, Dexter, Walter Robins, Cowdrey, Arlott, Subba Row, Richard Hutton, Parks, Bannister, Stewart, Silk and Peter Pollock were among them. There was also a lively piece full of diligent research on a tolerably gloomy subject entitled 'A Pilgrimage to Cricketers' Graves' from the pen of our present editor, David

Frith, then a 30-year-old offering his first contribution to the magazine.

Don Bradman's piece, 'Salute to Frank Woolley', in commemoration of his 80th birthday, did full justice to its subject, as may be imagined, Don had seen only two days of first-class cricket before he was first chosen for New South Wales; this was in the Fifth Test at Sydney in 1921. Frank made a 'glorious' 53, and 'the way he nonchalantly lifted the ball over the bowler's head was something I had never seen before'. (It's something we rarely see today, one might add, but we could – if only our moderns would pick the bat up straight and *swing it*.) Next time they met, Don fielded out, and saw his slow bowling aspirations dented for ever, while Frank made 219 in four hours for MCC *v* New South Wales in 1929/30. 'One of the most majestic and classical innings I have seen,' was the Don's considered judgement.

Talking of swinging the bat, Lord Cobham weighed in strongly with an article we entitled 'Coaching Broadside : Where English cricket has gone wrong'. In brief, he condemned the cult of the left elbow and the forward defensive push as the prime precept for the young, and repeated Charles Fry's great commandment : play back or drive. Introducing the author's name to younger readers I recalled that as captain of Worcestershire he once made 48 in 35 minutes, the highest innings of the match, on a bad wicket against Yorkshire, the champions, so enabling his side to win by 11 runs. Also, aged 51 as Governor-General of New Zealand, he hit 44 in 21 minutes against MCC at Auckland.

The article got us wide publicity, among others from two such contentious and widely-read characters as E. M. Wellings and J. L. Manning, both on this occasion offering support. There have been two *Cricketer* anthologies or 'picks' edited by Michael Melford : reading through these old numbers, full of good stuff, reminded me it's high time there was another, wherein Charles Cobham's article should find a place.

The Jubilee Issue in the spring of 1971 was obviously the occasion for special celebration, and I naturally assembled a strong writing team for it before leaving for Australia the previous November. Each man had a decade to explore and to express its special flavour, Aidan Crawley accepting the '20s, Ian Peebles the

'30s, Bill Bowes the '40s, John Warr the '50s, and Tony Lewis the '60s – much here could be republished with interest. Many other aspects of the game over the half-century were written about by men with special knowledge.

The star feature, however, was a selection of 'The Greatest of our Time', by four eminent judges – Gubby Allen, Les Ames, Jack Fingleton and Bill O'Reilly. Each had to choose his best twenty players, 1921 to 1971, and since someone had to exercise a casting vote I, as editor, took it upon myself. But my part was limited to omitting one of seven, for all four selectors chose nine of the twenty, and three agreed about five more. Two voted for seven, from whom, with the utmost reluctance, I relegated Jim Laker, on the grounds of his record abroad. Here was the outcome, with the individual choices :

The Chosen 20	G. O. Allen	L. E. G. Ames	J. H. Fingleton	W. J. O'Reilly
Sir Donald Bradman	I	I	I	I
D. C. S. Compton	I	I	I	I
W. R. Hammond	I	I	I	I
G. A. Headley	I	I	I	I
Sir J. B. Hobbs	I	I	I	I
Sir Leonard Hutton	I	I	I	I
R. R. Lindwall	I	I	I	I
G. St A. Sobers	I	I	I	I
M. W. Tate	I	I	I	I
A. V. Bedser	I	–	I	I
C. V. Grimmett	I	–	I	I
H. Larwood	I	–	I	I
S. J. McCabe	I	–	I	I
W. J. O'Reilly	I	I	I	–
W. H. Ponsford	–	–	I	I
T. G. Evans	I	–	I	–
C. G. Macartney	–	–	I	I
P. B. H. May	I	I	–	–
K. R. Miller	–	I	I	–
Sir Frank Worrell	–	I	–	I

The Runners-up	G. O. Allen	L. E. G. Ames	J. H. Fingleton	W. J. O'Reilly
J. C. Laker	I	I	–	–
K. S. Duleepsinhji	–	I	–	–
A. P. Freeman	–	I	–	–
R. N. Harvey	–	–	I	–
A. L. Hassett	–	–	–	I
M. Leyland	–	–	–	I
A. A. Mailey	–	–	–	I
R. G. Pollock	–	–	I.	–
W. Rhodes	I	–	–	–
B. A. Richards	–	–	–	I
B. Statham	I	–	–	–
H. Sutcliffe	–	I	–	–
F. S. Trueman	–	I	–	–
E. de C. Weekes	I	–	–	–
F. E. Woolley	–	I	–	–

Two of the four selectors, Ames and Fingleton, thought it necessary to explain at length why they had plumped for George Headley, only to find he was one of the unanimous nine. Their reasonings and regrets made good reading, as did the letters from readers on the subject. This made me realize how foolish I had been not to offer a prize for the first correct solution. Some were almost apoplectic over the omission of Frank Woolley; others such as Learie Constantine had their champions. The Jubilee cover showed the twenty heads and shoulders in a gold surround.

One was always striving to find someone to provide the lighter touch, which in the old days of course was in the inspired pen of Crusoe. But there have been others with much more than the occasional spark of humour and wit. Henry Grierson, founder of the Forty Club, contributed 'Ramblings of a Rabbit', much in the laconic style of his after-dinner speeches; Ronald Postill on the village scene could be very funny; and now we have H. F. Ellis, the celebrated *Punch* writer for so long, giving us his reflections on the current scene as seen and heard by courtesy of the BBC from his Somerset cottage.

If Crusoe can be said to have a successor it is Alan Gibson, whose *Times* reports gladden my summer and very many others'. Having

TV 1949–1976

15. *Above,* when cricket on BBC TV restarted after the war (there had been small beginnings before) it was at first confined to Lord's and The Oval, where this picture was taken in 1949. One kept one eye on the play, another on the monitor, a third on the score-board, while listening simultaneously for advice and directions from the producer.

16. *Below,* another reversal of function : for a programme commemorating the centenary of Test cricket Tony Greig asked the questions, and I reminisced about great moments and attempted to impress certain warnings for the future, as elaborated in the last chapter.

Young Bloods
at Melbourne, 1977

17. *Above*, Derek Randall, of Notts
hooks Dennis Lillee during his
scintillating 174 which all but led
England to an 'impossible' victory.

18. *Below*, David Hookes, a
21-year-old left-hander from South
Australia, playing in his first Test,
earned the warmest praise from,
among others, Sir Donald Bradman
and Jack Fingleton. Another Neil
Harvey? Readers may know by no

paid due tribute to a masterful innings by Geoffrey Boycott he had this to say – we reprinted it with permission – about Yorkshire's running between wickets in contrast to the methods of Holmes and Sutcliffe:

The present method is for both batsmen to shout simultaneously, pause, then shout again. If, as happens about once an over, this has not cleared the situation up, it is considered wise to keep shouting. This is especially the policy of Boycott, whose progress down the pitch is often one long ululation.

It was to this sound of revelry that Sharpe departed eight short of his hundred. Boycott thereafter gave his voice rather less work and his bat rather more, surging in noble waves towards his second hundred, which he reached at ten past six.

On only 45 occasions, I estimate, did Boycott give Essex the slightest hope. Just before lunch he played and missed at Boyce; at 84 he popped a ball which had checked just short of cover; there was one appeal for LBW that may not have been too far away, and on 42 occasions he might have been run out.

Great stuff this to enliven one's breakfast, and enjoyed by no one surely more than the victim.

We were guilty once of what can only be termed a major gaffe in that we published the obituary of a notability very much alive, the Hampshire cricketer and England rugger player H. L. V. Day. R. L. Arrowsmith has done the *Cricketer* the most valuable service over many years going through the death notices and advising us, with biographical details, of men whose departure might otherwise have been missed. Harold Day lived in the locality of Harrow and that was precisely where, according to the *Telegraph* and *The Times*, a certain Harold L. V. Day had passed on. Bob Arrowsmith accordingly sent us an obituary which was printed. Day on relinquishing a regular Army commission had done a fair amount of sporting journalism, but he was a gruff fellow I didn't know well, and I rang him up with some misgivings to apologize.

However, he was very civil about it, agreed readily to give us an article as positive proof that he was still in the land of the living, and sent us a very good one of his days with Hampshire under Lionel Tennyson. About four years later I was lunching as a guest at White's and in the bar with his host, prior also to lunching was Day. We had a good laugh about it, and I heard how his wife had been rather chuffed about the whole thing. 'She received such nice letters of sympathy – didn't seem to realize I had so many friends.'

One has heard of people endeavouring to be shown the notices that newspapers keep ready in type – 'in the box' is the somewhat ghoulish phrase. I have even known of men suggesting their own obituarist. It's a thought for all of us, I suppose, that when our time comes, and friends perhaps sit down to compose civil tributes of one sort or another, we are undergoing a somewhat thorough interrogation elsewhere.

I returned that afternoon to Sandwich, and was given a message asking me to ring the *Daily Telegraph*. They wanted me to write an obituary of H. L. V. Day, who had had a heart attack and died on a station platform. Well, he had certainly enjoyed his last few hours on earth : but was our meeting not one of the stranger coincidences?

There are a hundred more names I might have mentioned, and countless articles. But how can one give more than a sketchy picture in a single chapter of a magazine that has been going more than half a century? Looking back, I suppose there have been three phases in the life of the *Cricketer* : the first was the solid, decorous Establishment period from 1921 to the outset of the war; then came the cottage industry phase from 1939 until Hutchinson saved the sinking ship in 1965; finally the rise to present prosperity under the direction of Ben Brocklehurst.

I happen to think that the magazine has never given a better service to cricket and cricketers than it is doing at present; but in the nature of things I cannot pretend to be an independent witness. I can only add that I do not begrudge a minute of the time spent which perhaps could have been more gainfully, or more amusingly, employed. And I'm sure that all concerned would echo the same sentiments. What should never be forgotten is that but for Arthur Langford, and not only him but his wife who survives him, the *Cricketer* would be no more than a dim, nostalgic memory to the middle-aged and the elderly.

14

The Post-War Breed

The heroes whose images stand out most clearly in my mind are those of my youth. Possibly that is so with many or even most people. I can believe that if the young – or even the middle-aged – have got as far into the book as this they may well have done so despite the feeling that they've had more than they want of the distant past. Too much Frank Woolley! Too many schoolmasters long dead! I gladly bear the soft impeachment except in so far as it may suggest that I have little personal admiration for the cricketers of today and yesterday. For this is not the case.

It is true that, in common with most of my generation which in most cases was able to admire the best cricketers as much for the men they were as for the way they played, I abominate what is sharp or churlish or unduly mercenary in the attitude of some of the foremost figures towards the game that has given them their livelihood and their fame. Alan Ross in his review of my last book said I was inclined to make too little allowance for the stresses inseparable nowadays from cricket at the top. It was easy to sit in judgement, he implied, from the fringe of the arena. If his is a fair criticism, as it may well be, I would plead only that my concern is for the bad example that departure from the old accepted standards gives to the young and to inferior cricketers everywhere. The TV camera sees all, and the popular idols are imitated down to the smallest gesture.

The professional golfers undoubtedly appreciate this: it almost seems that the more tremendously well they play the more impeccably they behave. They give the impression of golf as a thoroughly civilized and chivalrous game – which, incidentally, is more than can be said of all of us with long handicaps.

It could not truthfully be claimed in general for the cricketers of the '70s that the better they have played the better they have comported themselves. In one or two cases the converse is true – and I am not thinking only of England. But too much can be made

227

of this, I dare say, and we may be thankful that in a world where good manners are at a discount there is still much for hoary old reactionaries to respect and admire.

So let me rectify the balance in the minds of those who think it needs doing by casting an appraising eye on some of the post-war generation of England players, starting with some of the men of the moment and working back – well, at least no farther than the war.

It is said of every generation that it lacks the personalities of the past; but are we entirely deficient so long as Tony Greig and Alan Knott, for instance, enliven the England XI? I first got to know Tony when we chose him for the Duke of Norfolk's tour to the West Indies in the spring of 1970 though, like everyone else, I had sat up and taken notice when, in his very first innings for Sussex three years earlier at the age of 20, he had made 156 in less than four hours against a Lancashire attack including Brian Statham and Ken Higgs.

In the West Indies he showed more than a glimpse of great all-round potential : above all that he had a big heart in that enormous frame. I suppose subconsciously one had an initial prejudice against a native of South Africa who had had his schooling there, playing for England, though he had qualified by a five-year residential qualification. (The rule now stipulates ten years.) But these reservations disappeared, at least as far as I was concerned, as soon as I knew his background – that his father was a pure Scot who after a notable flying career in action which brought him the DSO was sent in 1943 to Eastern Province to command an RAF Training School there. After the war he stayed on to farm and married a South African girl.

In the West Indies Tony revelled in the heat and hard wickets, and he seemed such an obvious prospect for the 1970/71 MCC tour of Australia that midway through that summer for the one and only time in my life I wrote a letter about a player to the chairman of selectors. Alec Bedser, it so happened, had not been lucky when he had seen him play – as, of course, can easily happen. (You can even find people who claim that Bradman never made runs when *they* watched him.)

Greig in fact was thereupon chosen – I don't claim, of course, that this was more than a coincidence – for England against the Rest of the World at Trent Bridge, and did well. Four days before the next Test at Headingley he dislocated a finger horribly, but was passed fit, bowled indifferently, missed a couple of catches, was dropped, and passed over for Australia. That it was a poor decision was soon obvious enough.

To be sure, Tony has shaken my confidence at times since he became a famous figure. Over-keenness – to use a less pejorative phrase than has once or twice sprung to mind – has been his bugbear. Tactically his judgement has seemed highly peculiar on occasions, even granting the manifest superiority of England's opponents, and the strain of leading his troops in one uphill battle after another. In one interview in the hundred and one to which he has subjected himself on TV he used a phrase about making the West Indians grovel which he will regret for ever and a day. Since he was appointed to the Test captaincy his Sussex performances have been curiously moderate.

But, take him all in all, we were lucky that England's fortunes rested on so broad a back. He has courage and strength, both moral and physical, right out of the ordinary. Not least he is a 'great communicator', as the phrase is, with crowds, with individuals of all ages, and, not least, 'the media'. Unlike too many of his contemporaries he can laugh at himself.

Alan Knott is an extraordinarily little man, for ever apparently staving off ills, some maybe real, more perhaps imaginary. With his exercises and his attitudes he might seem to be waging a losing battle against ill-health. Yet he never misses a match, at 31 has already exceeded all Test wicket-keeping records, and before he has finished will probably put an impossible distance between him and the rest. Add to his wicket-keeping activity the fact that since he started twelve years ago he has made around 13,000 runs, and it can be questioned whether any cricketer has ever contributed more concentrated exertion over such a period. Off the field he smiles and chats his way engagingly round the cricket world, and, if it is not tempting providence to say so, he seems (from a distance anyway) to be conquering the over-keenness that made him, in contrast with his great predecessor, Godfrey Evans, and, for that matter, most of the best in his trade, a compulsive appealer.

Exactly how does he rate as a 'keeper? The only qualification one can make may be more a matter of present fashion than his personal preference. The fact is, though, that he always stands back to anything of medium-pace and above, and so gives the batsman freedom from the fear of being stumped. Evans stumped 46 men in 91 Tests. In 89 Tests Knott's figure is only 19. Otherwise he can scarcely be faulted. I happen to think that Evans is the finest Test wicket-keeper I ever saw. Yet, taking county cricket also into consideration, year in and year out, he never matched Knott in consistency of performance.

The same can be said of Alan's almost exact Kent and England contemporary, Derek Underwood. Except that the latter has been left out by England occasionally – usually to the detriment of their chances – the careers of these two have from boyhood followed parallel courses. Even Derek has suffered from the present fetish for making slow – perhaps I should say the slower – bowling a mainly defensive weapon. How many hours must he have spent with fingers itching, watching immeasurably inferior bowlers plugging away 'seam up'? They are beyond counting. But, whether on the field or off, he is in command of his feelings. Of not many Test cricketers, constantly under the spotlight, could one say that over a span of fifteen years he has never put a foot wrong: but if this one has I never heard of it.

Having written this, however, I think of Dennis Amiss and Basil D'Oliveira, both of whom qualify without hesitation for a similar encomium with the difference only that in their different ways they have been more stringently tested. No one ever exemplified the Kipling tag about triumph and disaster more exactly than Dennis: as for D'Oliveira, when so many around him were losing their heads and saying ill-judged things over the months and years of the two cancelled tours, his comments, whether on press or radio or TV, seemed to combine the wisdom of an elder statesman with the charity of a monk. I never saw or heard from him a word or a sentiment out of place.

Basil must have realized all too deeply that he represented his race in the eyes of millions, and that the opinions – yes, and the prejudices – of many would be swayed by their estimate of his behaviour under great emotional strain. Using this method of assessment he must have achieved more than much of the well-intentioned effort of Race Relations Boards. This was similarly true surely of the great West Indians, Sir Frank Worrell and Sir Gary Sobers. From modest home beginnings they were brought up under the twin influences of strong family ties and the fellowship of the cricket field – both traditionally strong elements in Barbadian life. In both cases supreme skill was invariably allied to an unfailing sense of chivalry in their attitude to the game and to people. Both will have achieved more than they knew, in England and the West Indies and also in Australia, where the tour of Worrell's team is rated on a higher plane than that of any other visit by any team before or since.

There were many openings waiting for Frank if he had lived, including, of course, the career within the University of the West Indies on which he was embarked when at the age of 42 his life was cut short. Like Learie Constantine he was brought to an admiration for the British, and an ambition to better Anglo–West Indian relationships, by the kinship that grew up with the warm folk of Lancashire during his years there as a Manchester University undergraduate and a cricketer. Radcliffe and Worrell were as proud of one another as Nelson and Constantine.

We have, of course, modern English names which identify with special emphasis in the popular mind with all that is best in cricket. When a 30-foot banner, a work of some distinction in itself, was hung from the boundary pickets during the last of the 1974/5 Tests at Melbourne which read: 'MCG Fans Thank Colin – 6 tours' it said what all Australians felt: and the same sort of tribute might equally have been devised for Cowdrey in the West Indies, or in India, or in New Zealand. Applause at the entrance of a batsman unfortunately is no longer in England a polite general convention, growing in volume according to the stature of the individual. Quite distinguished cricketers come in now to a cool silence. But for many years Colin was always received with a warmth which was more than a tribute to the senior playing figure in the game, to the man with more than a century of Test caps, more than a century of centuries.

As I write, Colin may have played his last first-class innings, though if the need were dire I would not put it past him to come up with his 108th hundred within the next year or two. He will certainly go on playing, and he will certainly go on giving back to the game in service off the field something of what he has had from it.

The same may be said, I'm sure, of a man to whom Cowdrey gave his Blue, M. J. K. Smith, and with whom he has played innumerable Tests, sometimes one being captain, sometimes the other. There was a time, in his Oxford days, when I admired Mike more as a footballer than a cricketer – his brief but brilliant half-back partnership in 1955/6 with David Onllyn Brace, a case of a rare natural flair for a game perfected by the fusion of intelligent minds directed to a common object – but his cricket grew on one, his powers of leadership, so apparently casual, 'low-key', as they say, even more so. I never heard of anyone who did not enjoy playing under Mike. The years of his captaincy were those that just followed the scrapping of the amateur and professional definition : no one could have suited the situation better, his only misfortune being that the great England bowlers of the last decade and more were almost finished, and Test resources generally were on the spare side. He ran, in company with Billy Griffith, a model MCC tour to Australia – and who could want a better testimonial than that ?

So much for two England captains : when Ray Illingworth comes into the reckoning we are considering a man sprung from different soil, for whom, from his earliest days, cricket in a sense was a different game. Colin and Mike would be the first to say that they owe much to cricket. It has been at the centre of their lives over many years : their personalities have been tested and broadened by it. When the differences in status were abolished by decree they became professionals automatically; and with young families to bring up the change may have made it possible for them to stay longer in the game than they might otherwise have done. As leaders they conformed to the pattern of the day, tough, practical, tight in tactics, ever-conscious of the financial consequences to their sides of success and failure.

The name of Illingworth could be added to this last sentence, making three leaders whose grasp of the reins to the casual outward eye did not differ very much. Yet in Ray's cricket philosophy there were, and are, deep differences deriving from the fact that for him, playing in the heart-lands of the West Riding at Farsley, no less, cricket was *the* way forward, from manual employment and relatively stringent circumstances to a broader and more prosperous life. We southerners can only strive to imagine what the goal of a blue cap with a rose of whichever colour as its crest has meant down the cricket ages, for a century or more, to generations of young York-shiremen and Lancashiremen, brought up in the hard industrial North.

In Ray's case the struggle for a toe-hold in the Yorkshire XI coincided with a tense, explosive dressing-room with the threat of fresh turbulence seldom far below the surface. Jim Kilburn, the historian of modern Yorkshire cricket, summarized the situation, as usual, sparsely and succinctly :

The Yorkshire lack was not so much in talent as in unity. The team was neither grimly efficient nor gaily inconsistent. Play, by the sight and occasionally by the sound of it, was not being enjoyed and Yorkshire were made aware that they were far from the most admired or respected of opponents.

To such an atmosphere men reacted according to temperament. Len Hutton, says Kilburn, 'left first-class cricket with a feeling of relief rather than regret'. Willie Watson migrated with a smile to Leicestershire. Individuals reacted according to temperament. I recall Ken Taylor saying to me in Calcutta when he was playing for my side against what was almost the Indian Test team, in a game that was being contested with all possible enthusiasm by both sides : 'I never knew that cricket could be enjoyed like this.' His talent would probably have flowered more freely elsewhere.

Illingworth no doubt gave as good as he got with his fellow-players, and the disagreement that led to his quitting Yorkshire concerned a contract. Yet, though he left to take up the Leicestershire – and from that the England – captaincy at the age of nearly 37, in 1969, it is since then that, under his own captaincy, his best cricket has been played. That very year, the chance of Cowdrey's torn Achilles tendon led to his choice as Test captain, a post he held for a span of 31 Tests, until at the end of the 1972 summer after the crushing West Indian defeats the selectors turned to a younger man. By then he had proved himself as shrewd a tactician as had led England for a very long time; since then his influence on Leicestershire is attested by their results beyond any question or argument. (One searches for a less well-worn adjective to describe Ray's captaincy, but 'shrewd' is exactly right : he sums up the relevant factors to a nicety, the enemy's strengths and weaknesses in relation to his own side's, the conditions of pitch and weather. Beyond this is an intuition which has been built on long experience, by thinking and talking cricket ever since his teenage days with Pudsey St Lawrence.)

I have had my say about the events at Sydney in the game that brought back the Ashes in 1970/1, and the responsibility of the captain for the fracas which culminated with the stern rebuke uttered by the Cricket Council after the team returned home. No doubt all concerned are sorry at this distance for the things that were said and done in the heat of the moment, surrounding the central figure of Umpire Rowan. The only point that might be noted finally, in the light of what I have said about the respective backgrounds and cricket upbringing of Illingworth and Cowdrey, is the unfortunate absence of rapport as between Ray, the captain, Colin, who after much misgiving accepted the vice-captaincy in Australia for the fourth time, and David Clark, the manager, who had won golden opinions some years before as manager of Mike Smith's side in India.

There was no open dissension between these three, so I am assured. It was just that their minds did not meld. If the sense of unity at the top had been stronger the general outlook of some of the team would have been less abrasive : the Ashes would still have been won, and there would have been no bitterness or regrets. That, at least, is how I see it all, looking back : those of us who thought that differing personalities would unite in the common cause were proved wrong.

Still on the topic of England captains, one had to admire Mike Denness's dignity and cool self-possession whether in prosperity or adversity. Two facts will probably be remembered about his leadership : the failure of his side in Australia against Lillee and Thomson, and a degree of criticism from certain quarters that many people thought prejudiced and unwarranted. Here are two other facts that may help to put his contribution into better perspective : of the nineteen matches played by England under his captaincy in a little over two years six were won, five lost, and eight drawn. Of the five wins four were by an innings, and in each of these four he made a hundred. Not a few of England's more highly-acclaimed captains might envy this record.

Switching away from leadership for a while one turns naturally, in saluting the foremost cricketers of the last thirty years, to the bowlers, for, except for a short period in the '6os, they have acquitted themselves so much better than the batsmen. What an admirable pair, in their prime, were Trueman and Statham, the one generally the more explosive and more liable to bowl the unplayable one, the latter the perfect foil, tireless and with the heart of a lion, perhaps the most accurate of all fast bowlers. Trying himself out in a net after a minor injury in Salisbury, Rhodesia, I once saw Brian knock the stumps down six balls running. If this does not sound extraordinary you can safely lay a fast bowler any odds against doing so.

A greater contrast in personality could scarcely be imagined, as between Fred the extreme extrovert, his feelings, whether of pain or pleasure, plain for all to see, and Brian (nicknamed either 'George' or 'The Whippet') utterly unemotional, philosophical, just prepared to put everything into every ball for as long as his captain required. Fred, like many another artist in the bowling line, needed handling, and he was not always lucky, whether for England or Yorkshire, in the combination of authority above him. The place in which in particular I saw him bowl marvellously well and consistently, day in, day out, was the West Indies in 1959/60. Fast bowlers do not hope for glamorous figures on those adamantine pitches, but in ten matches he took 37 wickets, 21 of them in the five Tests. Walter Robins managed that tour, and the pair of them, each with a personality a little larger than life, established an excellent understanding – in which humour was a strong ingredient.

Frank Tyson's name is secure in history for the blistering speed that brought England victory in Australia in 1954/5. No subtleties for him! He had the back and shoulders, the legs, and, above all, the heart and determination for fast bowling, and for the short period of his peak I have never seen his speed exceeded. When he came back from Australia in the spring of 1955, fit and strong and just coming up to 25, it seemed the cricket world was at his feet.

I always remember the first ball he bowled in the first Test against South Africa that summer at Trent Bridge, and the face of its recipient, Jackie McGlew, as seen through the glasses, registering the extremes of astonishment and alarm. Frank took eight for 79 in this match, won by England by an innings; but, after that, one injury led to another, he played only two more Tests in England,

and all too swiftly the cutting edge became blunted. A slow, sandy pitch at Northampton was no help to him: his career probably would have run a different course had not Lancashire, the county of his birth, shown a strange lack of interest in him – even though Harry Makepeace, the head coach, after a net trial, had said he could make him an England bowler! Another addition, this, to the ranks of distinguished rejects: Mead by Surrey, Rhodes and Verity by Warwickshire, Jack Hobbs, of all men, by Essex . . .

Of John Snow, another Test cricketer of the top class, one cannot, alas! write with such undiluted enthusiasm; but when in the mood he served England as well as any.

So much for English speed – and indeed, looking back, before the advent of Trueman and Statham there had been none at all since the resumption in 1946. When MCC went to South Africa in 1948/9 Alec Bedser and Cliff Gladwin had the new ball, and the wicket-keeper stood up from the start of the tour to the finish. Bedser, though he had played for England since the first Test of 1946, reached his peak in 1950, by which time he had mastered the leg-cutter, and for the next five years did more than enough to establish his greatness as one of the best of all medium-pacers. If anyone objects to the phrase as belittling Alec's speed I freely admit there were days, if the pitch seemed right for it, when his big shoulders rocked and his big head shook as the arm came over, and Godfrey Evans jumped to lessen the jar as the ball smacked into his gloves. Invariably Evans stood up to Bedser, just as Maurice Tate always wanted his 'keeper up over the stumps. I rate Evans as the best of all the great 'keepers of the last half-century *in Test Matches*, and it ought always to be added that he was a conspicuously fair one. In this, and in his marvellous cheerfulness and optimism even when things looked at their darkest, he contributed much to the spirit that normally existed between the sides during his time.

Judging by his current comments over the air, and also by his glowing biography of Gary Sobers, Trevor Bailey's philosophy of cricket has broadened since his playing days. Some of his innings were the ultimate in boredom, bearing moreover little relation at times to the needs of the moment; but what a lot he gave on the credit side – much skill with the new ball, some great catching near the bat, and at least one high-class defensive innings when it really was called for, at Lord's with Willie Watson in '53. For a relatively small man his stamina, too, was remarkable, considering that he was usually the only all-rounder in the side.

Of post-war spinners now retired four stand out high above the rest: Jim Laker and Tony Lock, of Surrey, Bob Appleyard and Johnny Wardle, of Yorkshire. All credit to Lock for modifying his action without official prompting in 1959 – and far less credit to all concerned, myself included, for having winked at the contravention for so long. The fact however remains that of his 174 Test wickets all but 51 very expensive ones were taken in his unregenerate days. It therefore becomes a question, strange though it may seem, whether his most valuable contributions to cricket may not have been his highly successful captaincies of Leicestershire and Western Australia.

Laker's supreme skill as an off-spinner on English pitches is a legend that will last as long as the game is played. To complete his credentials he needed a truly successful Test series abroad, and this he was denied, by fate and circumstances, to say nothing of an arthritic spinning-finger. In the light of history it may be strange that Appleyard was preferred to him when MCC under Hutton toured Australia in 1954/5, but that is only because the latter's career was so sadly cut short by ill-health. Appleyard was a true artist, as also was the left-arm Wardle both in the orthodox style and as a wrist-spinner. In South Africa in 1956/7, chiefly with 'chinamen' and googlies, Wardle took 90 wickets – the best performance overseas by a slow bowler in my time.

Turning to the batsmen – and restricting myself to those whose cricket began after the war – I can merely voice the general opinion of friend and foe and rate Peter May head of the list. Ken Barrington's record – and figures must be duly respected when one is looking back over a career – are superior by quite a bit: Barrington 6806, average 58; May 4537, average 46. Ted Dexter's record is almost identical with May's. Tom Graveney and John Edrich, playing more Test Matches, have scored a few more runs, each with a slightly inferior average. And away out of sight of them all in weight of achievement is Colin Cowdrey with his 7865 runs (only exceeded by Sobers), average 43. (Geoffrey Boycott, of course, is among this elite in terms of runs and average; but I am attempting in this chapter a brief tribute to men who have served English cricket conspicuously well. I cannot therefore logically include someone who, for whatever sad, misguided reasons, has for four years declined to serve at all.)

Why, I wonder, among this impressive array, is May almost universally accorded the accolade? Well, we have Don Bradman's word for it that the most important thing in a batsman's make-up is concentration. Other qualities of the heart and mind come strongly into the reckoning, coolness of judgement, a proper degree of aggression, courage against fast bowling. We must add also a sufficiency of physical strength and stamina. But the Don's famous dictum obviously presupposes a sound technique, and in a man's method there are degrees of excellence.

Peter looked wonderfully solid against all types of bowling on all sorts of wicket. If one gives marks for the other virtues I have mentioned he scores well in all of them, and in particular concentration – which in his case amounted to an unremitting, iron determination. Remember that he and Tom Graveney were the first of the new generation who looked to have the ability to fill the shoes of the pre-war generation who at first filled the prime places, Hutton, Washbrook, Edrich and Compton. David Sheppard, now Bishop of Liverpool, had many of May's qualities, and would no doubt have been esteemed as highly as most I have mentioned but for the claims of the Church.

When Len Hutton, full of the game's honours and with a knighthood coming up, bowed out in 1955, Peter was suddenly elevated both to the captaincy and the role of batsman-in-chief. He was three summers down from Cambridge and in his twenty-sixth year, junior by a few months to Percy Chapman, hitherto the youngest of all captains of England. In the next six years he led England 41 times – more than any man has ever done. In terms of Tests played it was the most intensive of all periods, and it is therefore not surprising, family and business claims apart, that at the end of it he had had enough. In his tribute in *The World of Cricket* Richie Benaud refers to Peter's two hundreds in the Australian XI match at Sydney in 1958/9, the second of them scored between lunch and tea, as 'batting that can rarely have been bettered by an English player anywhere in the world'. He sums up:

May was a fine player as well as being an extremely pleasant one; a cricketer of sensitive nature who could be as hard as nails on the field without ever slipping from the peak of sportsmanship. I would put him at the top of the captaincy tree during my time, ahead even of the victorious Hutton in 1954/5.

A handsome tribute, from a chivalrous enemy. As to the comparison between Hutton and May as captains, the latter certainly took the great Yorkshireman whom he greatly admired as his model. Len was an enigma to most of his contemporaries, and, I think, consciously set out to be. He was inclined to oracular judgements, and enjoyed seeing people puzzling them out. So I doubt whether Peter truly understood him, though he and Colin Cowdrey came closer to it than most. Peter had one slice of luck when he took up the captaincy in that it coincided with Gubby Allen becoming chairman of selectors. Their time in office exactly coincided – 1955 to 1961 inclusive. From the first there grew up between them a particularly close understanding which involved not the chairman airing his views uninvited during a game but being readily accessible at intervals and close of play if the captain sought his advice. Peter very often did, of course, but the important distinction should be noted.

Allen's successor, Walter Robins, besides having been a magnificent all-rounder, had one of the sharpest minds in cricket. Indeed, in a general-knowledge paper covering every aspect of the game I would not put up anyone to beat him. But he was impatient and disdainful of the safety-first ruts that the game had got into in the early '60s, and some of the leading players, while agreeing maybe in their hearts with much that he said, found it too strong medicine. Most of us grow mellower, I suppose, with age, but poor Walter became if anything rather less so; in retrospect these early years of the '60s must have seen the first onset of the hardening of the brain arteries which after a long and particularly distressing illness proved fatal towards the end of the decade. Thus the rapport between chairman and captain came to a sharp halt, which was ill-luck on Cowdrey and Dexter, between whom the succession to May depended.

Dexter, to whom the honour went when Cowdrey fell sick at a critical point of the season, was a marvellous leader by example. Though less consistent than May he had many of his qualities as a batsman. At his best he stood comparison with Hammond, while those ancient enough to recall the Golden Age said no one had batted with such superb disdain since Maclaren. He gave one the feeling, as did Sobers but not so many more of the great ones, that he always *wanted* to be at the more difficult end.

Tactically he was less successful, apparently too ready to throw orthodox principles overboard in favour of sudden hunches. Strangely for such an outstanding natural games-player he was fascinated by theory. One had the idea he was probably thinking deeply about something, but that it might not be altogether relevant to the job in hand. He had good days indeed when things went his way, but one felt he might sometimes have profited from a wise head to turn to, as his predecessor had had in Allen.

It happened that Billy Griffith and I drove Peter May up to Headingley, aged 21, to play his first Test Match against South Africa. He never saw the first ball bowled to him from the Kirkstall end. It shaved the leg stump for four byes, whereafter he played beautifully for 138. Four years later Peter brought his young Surrey prodigy, Ken Barrington, up to St John's Wood to be driven up to his first Test, also against South Africa, this time at Trent Bridge. 'I hope you bring him the same luck,' he said. But Ken survived only three balls for a blob, played once more in that series, making top score in the first innings, and was not chosen again for four years.

Barrington was not a graceful sight at the crease, like many another successful England batsman, but he had a fine eye and a very rare degree of application, and though he generally played the anchor part he could hit as hard and well as anyone – as happened in 1965/6 at Melbourne when he made the fastest hundred of the series in $2\frac{1}{2}$ hours. As I have written before, his value to England, great as it was, would have been much enhanced if his potential as a leg-spinner had not been so neglected.

John Edrich's steadfastness as an England batsman is likewise attested in the books, and especially his record against Australia. In the century of England v Australia matches only three Englishmen, Hobbs with twelve, Hammond with nine and Sutcliffe with eight, have hit more than his seven hundreds. Maurice Leyland had seven, too, another left-hander who in phlegm and tenacity John resembled.

The last of my elect six post-war batsmen, Tom Graveney, cannot match the others in his record against Australia, though he certainly can against the West Indies, and in every other cricket sphere. There was an elegance in all he did that was more redolent of the classic age, and he can rest content in the knowledge that only seven men in history (of whom Hammond was the last) have bettered his 47,793 runs, and only nine (Compton the most recent) have scored more than his 122 hundreds.

A survey such as I have attempted inevitably leaves room for criticism, as to those omitted. Perhaps I can divert some of it by recalling briefly other fine post-war cricketers who have had their moments wearing the England colours – purple moments, for instance in the cases of Reg Simpson and Bob Barber, a more phlegmatic diligence from Geoff Pullar, Peter Richardson and Brian Luckhurst; equally we have owed much to the stamina and craft of David Brown, Fred Titmus and David Allen. By the time this sees the light of day let us hope fresh names are making the news against Australia – preferably a couple of batsmen of true Test quality, and, not least, another high-class spinner to make a pair with Underwood.

15
Fond Places

When my wife and I flew in to Barbados for our annual visit last February there was more than ordinary activity on the St James's coast at Holetown, since they were celebrating in carnival style the 350th anniversary of the original British landing in 1627. A monument marks the spot where some English farmers and their workers arrived on the island, which is shaped like a pear but named – by earlier Portuguese who did not settle – after the fig. There had been Arawak Indians before the Portuguese, but the latter found an empty but forested island – including the fig trees. The English, too, found the island uninhabited, but put down their roots, and grew first tobacco and very soon sugar. From Africa came the slaves to reap the sugar – the ancestors of the race that peoples and rules the island today.

The anniversary, and the fact of its being held, give as clear a clue as any to the character of Barbados; for British it became in 1627 and British it remained uninterruptedly until, following gradual stages, it was proclaimed an independent sovereign State within the Commonwealth in 1966. Unlike all the other islands in the Caribbean chain it was never fought over. The French often threatened but never came, the Dutch came once and were repulsed: and so it is that, apart from Westminster itself, only Bermuda, another speck in the ocean far away to the north, has a parliament of greater antiquity under the Crown.

Without allowing myself to be drawn to the extent of a single paragraph into the strengths and weaknesses of British administration in the colonial period, I would maintain that it was this background of security and justice stretching back almost into the Middle Ages – unbelievably harsh though this justice was, by modern standards, in the eighteenth and nineteenth centuries – that shaped the Barbadian character, and gave it its self-confidence and pride. For nine years we had a house on the island, and I cannot really start a chapter with such a title anywhere else.

The Barbadians, despite the ease of communications and a climate second to none in the Caribbean, remain integrated to an extraordinary degree. Though East Indians populate most of the West Indian islands and there are many Chinese, few of either have come to rest here. Among the traders you would be pressed to find a Jew. Many prosperous people have come from North America, and some from the British Isles and Europe, either to make holiday homes or to settle in retirement, but the proportion is insignificant. There are several thousand white Barbadians, of course, some of whom can trace their lineage back to the earliest days, and over the centuries inter-union has resulted in many coffee-shades. Few Barbadians, I dare say, are black-black. The point is that all are essentially Barbadian, slow though the now elderly generation of whites were, generally, to anticipate and assimilate themselves to the new independent order. The official ratio, by the way, is 95 per cent Afro-West Indian, 5 per cent European.

In November last year we were present at an occasion which particularly underlined the strong sense of identity common to Barbadians, a service of thanksgiving in Westminster Abbey to mark the 10th Anniversary of their Independence. How extraordinary, I thought, as the transepts and the choir and much of the great nave of the Abbey filled with Barbadians and friends of Barbados for this beautiful service, that it should have been set up in honour of a country about the size of the Isle of Wight, with a population akin to that of a London borough. The Duke of Kent, accompanied by the Duchess, represented the Queen, as they had done at the Independence ceremony. We had a sermon of the utmost power from Canon S. S. Goodridge, principal of the Barbadian theological college of Codrington, and just to remind us that one of the staple exports of Barbados is cricketers the lesson was read by C. B. Williams, known in his youth as 'Boogles' and now His Excellency the High Commissioner in London, who came to England with the famous 1950 West Indies side under John Goddard.

It is safe to say that nowhere in the wide world, England certainly included, do cricket and the Anglican Church exercise an influence so strong as in Barbados. When judges and ministers of the government come to Kensington Oval, as they consistently do, the game is the *lingua franca*, and its technicalities are discussed as among equals. Cricket is bred in the bone.

Whether the signal was ever sent at the outset of the First World War, 'Carry on, England, Barbados is behind you,' I am not sure, but the story fitted in with the Little England legend which until recently was the cliché generally tacked on, in a derogatory sense, to references in books of travel by writers who saw Barbados – not without some justification – as a bastion of white privilege in an otherwise cosmopolitan Caribbean. The place names are English – Hastings, Worthing, Beachy Head – and the island is divided into parishes called after the saints and apostles in whose honour the various Anglican churches were built. The countryside, not tropical in character like the other islands, even has something of the look of the Home Counties, especially after the cane has been reaped.

To those who can still afford to slip away for a while from their own cold winters, Barbados has much to offer: lovely bathing, sunshine, golf – indeed most forms of sport – and a steady trade wind to temper the heat. All this, and a dignified people who respond to visitors in their own coin: if you are aloof so will they be. Equally they react – like most of whatever race, I find – to the first gesture of friendliness. Then their humour soon comes to the surface.

Literacy in Barbados is rated at 97 per cent, and the provision of opportunity commensurate with individual ability is a perennial problem to which at least a degree of emigration would really seem the only answer. But those of lesser learning can be hard to understand, especially when they become animated, not only on account of accent but because English words have tended to develop Barbadian meanings. I am typing this particular chapter in Barbados with a gardener working outside. When we got talking I found he was concerned that he might be disturbing me. On being assured that this was not so he grew philosophical, saying it was up to each man to use the talents God had given him. There was he working away with his hands and I *spraining* my brain on the typewriter. He might almost have asked whether he was *humbugging* me, for in Bajan to 'humbug' means to get in the way or to interfere, either physically or mentally: a useful word. (Anyone interested should consult Frank A. Collymore's *Notes for a Glossary of Words and Phrases of Barbadian Dialect*.)

Beyond the garden on the landward side the buses ply up and down from Speightstown to Bridgetown. Some of them are modern and comfortable, others, known as 'pick-ups', are distinctly primitive. One fat old body unwedges herself after a crowded journey on a bare wooden seat, exclaiming : 'Aw, me botsie gone to sleep.' 'Ah know,' says her friend, 'I heard 'un snoring in Payne's Bay.'

After which, perhaps, we too should move on, I with apologies to those acquainted with other of the West Indian islands upon whose charms and virtues I might well have dilated given room. I could have found something agreeable to say, too, maybe about the people if not perhaps the terrain and climate of Georgetown, Guyana, and on this score content myself with one hitherto-unrecorded fact.

During the 1973/4 MCC tour of the West Indies I was mystified, until a clarifying letter followed, by a strongly-worded wire from the *Daily Telegraph* saying that on no account was I to set foot in Guyana. Apparently they had published an article or articles about Britain's sole former colony on the South American mainland to which its government had taken such strong exception that all and anyone connected with the paper had been declared *persona non grata*. So my colleagues and the team were deprived of any jolly speculation whether I should be locked up or merely turned back at the airport, and my work was undertaken by Tony Cozier. My instructions were to remain in Barbados and rejoin them later in Trinidad – which was no great hardship. It was not thought politic at the time to publish any explanation, so I suppose it was concluded that the *DT*'s ancient correspondent was growing lazy. Having completed a stint of 270 Tests, reported and/or broadcast (usually both) and with no ambitions to add to the number, let me add that this was one of only two Tests I was expected to cover and failed to. The other was the Fourth Test between South Africa and England at Johannesburg in 1956/7 when I was in hospital having a knee cartilage removed which I had ruptured while batting.

This can, of course, be no more than a more or less random reflection of places visited and enjoyed, ignoring, only two years after the publication of my book on the eight post-war MCC tours, the whole sub-continent of Australia, and also the Republic of South Africa, which cannot strictly be described anyway as fond, happy though one's memories are of friends both there and in Rhodesia.

It may seem passing strange to mention now among one's fond places another holiday island visited (up to the time of writing) only for a fortnight – but so far as my wife and I are concerned the phrase fits exactly in regard to Corfu. One warms to places, or, more rarely no doubt, one is allergic to them. Personally I have usually been attracted to islands, partly no doubt because they are generally associated with sea and sunshine. The West Indies apart, I think of Bermuda on that first-ever tour with Sir Julien Cahn, of our enthusiastic welcome there and the excitements of the cricket; of Jersey where the Arabs came to life; of Singapore even, though my memories of that farther bastion are of necessity bitter-sweet. Perhaps one is drawn subconsciously to islands since we British owe our freedom over the centuries to the fact of being islanders ourselves.

Similarly, as it happens, the Corfiots owed it to geography that though the mainland of Greece was subject to Turkish domination for centuries the infidel never gained a permanent foothold in Corfu. When Christendom was divided the religious jurisdiction of Corfu passed from the Pope in Rome to the Patriarch of Constantinople, and the island has remained firmly in the Eastern Orthodox tradition ever since. This was my first sojourn in a country where the Orthodox Church held sway, and it needed little time to see and feel how deeply grounded in their religion were the people of this fabulously picturesque, sunny and altogether benign island.

The climate – at least in mid-September when we were there – suited us as well as the 'feel' of the place: yes, and there is even cricket. In fact it was cricket which was responsible, indirectly at least, for our visit since two old friends, Ben Brocklehurst and Ian Orr-Ewing, both of whom first became acquainted with Corfu through taking sides out to play, had long lauded its charms, and it was the former who kindly organized our stay. These are the two moving spirits at the English end of the Anglo-Corfu Cricket Association which exists to foster the game there.

Corfu cricket first came to my notice almost 20 years ago when John Forte, then the British Vice-Consul, wrote to me at the *Daily Telegraph* asking if I could persuade cricketers at home to send superfluous equipment to Corfu to assist a revival of the game there. As a result of a letter in the paper under his name readers responded generously, the two Corfu clubs of Byron and Gymnastikos were re-stocked and, with Major Forte's participation and encouragement, cricket was firmly re-established on the Esplanade in the heart of the town. The latest development is that the Greek Government has promised to provide indoor practice facilities for the young in winter.

Greece being then still under the Turkish yoke, the British seized Corfu after the defeat of Napoleon in 1814 at Leipzig, and made it the capital of the group of islands which under British suzerainty became known as the 'Ionian Republic'. Wherever the army became stationed cricket naturally followed, and there is at least one print surviving of the game being played in Corfu under the shadow of the Old Fort early in the occupation. This ended, by the way, in 1864, after exactly 50 years, when, principally to strengthen the new Greek dynasty on the assumption to the throne of King George I, Britain amid mutual expressions of goodwill ceded the islands to Greece.

By the aid of John Forte's guide-book *Corfu, Venus of the Isles* and its companion, edited also by him, *Wheeler on Corfu*, signs of the British connexion are easy to pick up. The *Letters of Private Wheeler* were written when he was stationed in Corfu in the eighteen-twenties, but only saw the light of day, thanks to his great-grand-daughter, in 1948.

The Esplanade is the *grande place* of Corfu town, overlooked by the Royal Palace, now partly a museum, built by the first Lord High Commissioner, Sir Thomas Maitland, originally to house the members of the Order of St Michael and St George which he had persuaded the Prince Regent to institute as the ruling body of the Ionian Republic – under him as Governor or Grand Cross. 'King Tom' was a rough, hard-drinking Empire-builder, 'hot as pepper', whose death from apoplexy seems not to have been either an unexpected or an inappropriate end. However, he established the habitual marks of British rule, suppressing corruption, purging the judiciary, and exercising a just if despotic sway – so that even before his death the subject peoples put up in his memory the fine classical rotunda that dignifies the end of the Esplanade farther from the Palace.

Thereabouts, too, is a bronze statue to Maitland's successor, Sir Frederick Adam, who cemented relations by marrying a Corfiot bride, a dark, stern-eyed beauty with, however, according to Wheeler, 'a beard that would ornament a Huzzar'. Casting his eyes elsewhere, Adam found comfort in the arms of a lady over the hills and across the island in the remote bay of Paleokastritsa. It was a difficult journey, but the matter was neatly resolved when Adam decided that this was the ideal spot for a military convalescent home (or 'rehabilitation centre'), and therefore set the sweating soldiery to building a road. Our pioneering forebears were nothing if not resourceful. The Corfu–Paleokastritsa road is today the best on the island, and opens up the scenic beauties of the west coast to what is at times too thick a stream of tourists, multi-national from most of the countries of Europe but, on our evidence, with the British still predominant.

Of other nationalities the Germans were the most prominent – and the most obtrusive. As they paraded the narrow courts and lanes of the inner town of Corfu one wondered whether they were aware that the bomb scars still apparent in several places were caused by their countrymen in 1943 when their Italian allies surrendered, and changed sides. In the fighting between Germans and Italians a quarter of the town was destroyed, the Germans winning temporary occupation before they evacuated in front of the advancing British in the following year. I heard from several Corfiots how the Germans bundled captured Italian officers into sacks and threw them into the sea.

There is, by the way, one other tangible mark of Teutonic involvement in Corfu. The casino at Gastouri was the former Achillion Palace, built by the Empress Elisabeth of Austria and bought after her assassination by the Kaiser, Wilhelm II. His contribution to the palace ranks high surely as an example of sublime bathos : he caused a statue of the wounded Achilles to be credited with the inscription – TO THE GREATEST OF THE GREEKS FROM THE GREATEST OF THE GERMANS.

I must resist the temptation to wander further into these historical byways except to pay pious tribute to the patron saint of Corfu, St Spiridon. It was not he who brought Christianity across the Ionian Sea, but Saints Jason and Sosipatros to whom is dedicated the beautiful little Byzantine church at Garitsa. Comparatively speaking St Spiridon is a parvenu, his remains having been brought to the island as late as 1460; but his subsequent achievements could scarcely have been more spectacular. First, he is credited with having on Holy Saturday, at a time of famine, diverted a grain ship bound elsewhere, thus ensuring a happy Easter for one and all.

More than that, he raised a Turkish siege and drove off the infidel with the aid of a band of acolytes with blazing torches seen clearly in the night sky 'clothed in white Samite, mystic, wonderful'. Another Easter miracle was the first of two deliverances from plague, the second being associated with All Saintstide.

Each of these four visitations is annually celebrated by a procession round the town, the saint being stood upright in his silver casket and paraded with the utmost solemnity in the presence of the entire population. The faithful are allowed to kiss his ornamental scarlet boots, and in Private Wheeler's day the sick were laid out on the processional path that his shadow might pass over them. In the days of the British, 'God Save the King' from the military band signalled the start of the saint's journey from his church: and he received a 21-gun salute from the ships in the harbour dressed overall.

On first arrival I happened to remark that everyone seemed to be called 'Spiro', and was duly enlightened. The girls, it seems, are christened Sperita.

Whether or not it was St Spiridon who inspired a benevolently rich Greek named Tsaoussoglou to add to the manifold attractions of the island by laying out a golf course, the answer is eminently satisfactory. The fertile Ropa valley that lies behind the bay of Ermones on the west coast is refreshed by a network of streams which have been used with much skill to add to the hazards of the course. Scarcely one of the 18 holes is completely free of possible water trouble, and there are several carries to cause the golfer, whatever his ability, to have to choose between various degrees of discretion and valour.

The lay-out is imaginative, and the tees are flexibly placed to cater both for the long hitter and the veteran. The full championship length is 6221 metres, and the standard scratch score 72. But the most striking thing about the course is the quality of the turf both on green and fairway. Not even at Mount Irvine, Tobago, have I putted on a truer surface or on greens more uniform in texture and colour. They were sown with Penn Cross bent from Pennsylvania.

There is a noble club-house, where one can eat inexpensively and well, even at 60 drachmas to the pound, and there should be a swimming-pool and all the amenities of a country club by the time these words are in print. It would complete the picture, I would add, if Mr Tsaoussoglou saw fit to add a few adjoining cottages for the benefit of golf visitors. The young English professional, Mel Pyatt, who also acts as manager, told me that golf is somewhat slow to catch on with the Greeks. However, he was playing daily with Mr Karamanlis, who was on holiday, so maybe the Prime Minister will lead the fashion. At present nearly all the golfers are visitors.

Lastly, the cricket. It is played on a coconut mat laid on concrete, a lively surface as I had first discovered 40 years earlier in Bermuda. The rest of the field is very roughly-grassed – which adds to the hazards of the game and makes utterly imperative the first axiom, 'watch the ball'. The Corfiots – from what I saw of them – though their batting technique may have its limitations field marvellously well despite the difficulty.

There is a rare gusto about the proceedings, thanks to the eager involvement of the crowd which sits, hundreds strong, at café tables in the shade of an avenue of trees flanking a colonnaded street built by the French, during the Napoleonic phase, after the style of the Rue de Rivoli.

Watching thus comfortably, and sipping either the local *ouzo*, which is fiery and tastes of aniseed, or another British gift to Corfu, ginger-beer, it occurred to me that these were almost the only cricketers in the world most of whom have no English. Thus if you are bowled you are *apo xyla*. The pitch is *tapetto*, the crease is *simadi*, a full-pitch is *bombado*, and a bump-ball *psili tis gis*. Why as many of the phrases are Italian as Greek I cannot say – only that it adds an amusing dimension to the cricket when one cannot understand what is being said.

Ben Brocklehurst's side, despite the inclusion of the illustrious name of Bill Edrich, and also the Winchester and Cambridge bowler, John Roundall, was hard-pressed by its Greek opponents, and could only scratch up about 80. Roundall's speed and lift (at 6ft. 8in. he stands a shade higher than Tony Greig) caused problems, however, when Byron batted, and their No. 10 came in, amid feverish excitement, with five runs needed. When the Greeks were bowling it had seemed that the no-ball law governing the front crease could not yet have reached this European outpost of the game, and so far as I could see 'anything went'. But events were to prove otherwise. Five to win, and Roundall bowling. Miraculously he missed the leg-stump, via the inside edge of No. 10's bat, the ball hopping unpredictably over long-leg's hands for four. Scores level. It was too narrow a shave for the umpire. As Roundall's arm came over again 'No ball!' he cried, and that was that. Neither Bill nor I could remember before seeing a game lost and won on a no ball.

If I have given anyone the urge to take a holiday on Corfu they would discover a wide variety ranging from the humblest tavernas to the Corfu Palace and the Corfu Hilton, in the latter of which we eventually stayed in the acme of comfort since there had been some confusion about our booking elsewhere. There are a number of hotels on the sea, and a quiet one of much distinction lying back a bit and giving a superb view of the Albanian coast only a mile or two across the strait called the Castello, a residence in the Florentine style which was once the summer home of George II of Greece. (This reminds me that behind green gates and not at present visible to the public is the house where the Duke of Edinburgh was born. One imagines it deserves a more dignified name than 'Mon Repos'.) We swam in the clear water of Dassia Bay from the Castello's private beach.

You can rent a villa, or you can live simply, inexpensively, and with nothing to do but enjoy yourself at the *Cricketer* Taverna, nestling above a shining, secluded little bay near Paleokastritsa. Wherever you go are smiling people who seem to believe that in this island of churches and wayside shrines, olive groves and donkeys God's in his heaven and all is right with the world.

Since *SOCP* I have twice revisited India, thus repairing at least in a very minor degree the largest of the gaps in my cricket experience. The first occasion took in the first two Tests of the MCC tour of 1972/3, captained by Tony Lewis, with Donald Carr as manager. I was not able to see more than the Delhi and Calcutta Tests, and flew home with regret on all counts. For to the fascination of these two great cities and their inhabitants was added what for me was always the essential ingredient for the enjoyment of a tour, a happy and popular party. The Carr/Lewis partnership worked as smoothly as any I remember, and the team responded as English teams always will when the management strikes the right blend of discipline and tolerance.

Lewis was offered the captaincy, it will be recalled, when Ray Illingworth declined it – a decision on his part that seemed reasonable enough after four strenuous years as captain both of England and Leicestershire. Ray had just turned 40, and all the evidence suggested a highly taxing tour, including eight Tests, five against India and three against Pakistan. Geoffrey Boycott and John Snow, and one or two more who would have been doubtful selections anyway, also announced their unavailability. This caused much disappointment and some resentment in India, but, as is the way with human nature, it only fortified the MCC team spirit.

This, as it turned out, was almost, but not quite, the beginning of Boycott's proclaimed unwillingness to play for England, and there was one significant fact about the situation which the TCCB did not see fit to make public at the time : it was that Boycott was offered the vice-captaincy in addition to a place in the team, and after asking for time for consideration turned the job down. It was then accepted by Mike Denness. Lewis stood up to the demands of the tour physically, as well as with conspicuous success in every other way, but the following summer was always fighting a losing battle with his fitness. When therefore the TCCB decided they did not want Illingworth to take MCC that winter to the West Indies they called on Denness. However, if Boycott had gone as Lewis's vice-captain to India and Pakistan and had made a success of it he and not Denness would have been next in line of succession for the West Indies. Boycott would in all probability have fulfilled then and there his advertised ambition of becoming captain of England, and, who knows, might be so still. In any event the history of Test cricket these last four years would have been very different.

But it is time to join the team at Delhi where they are installed in all possible comfort at the Inter-Continental Hotel, and to enjoy a little golf prior to the First Test with an old friend, one of the most distinguished patriarchs of Indian sport, H. S. Malik. Golf in India has to compete with extremes of climate, but in December and January the courses, still green from the last monsoon and not yet scorched by the worst of the heat, play extremely well. Delhi Golf Club might almost have been the Berkshire, and it was an honour to be shown round by 'H.S.', who must have seemed to the rest of the MCC party a nimble and vigorous Sikh in his early sixties. He was in fact touching eighty.

H.S. learned his games in England before and after the first war, and has been a frequent visitor since, not least when he served as India's ambassador in Paris. He missed a Blue for cricket at Oxford, though he played quite a bit for Sussex, and won one for golf, having taught himself in the following way. H.S. was educated at Eastbourne College, and spent a summer holidays there in a house overlooking Royal Eastbourne. His interest in golf thus generated, he came by Harry Vardon's instructional text-book. Applying himself solidly to that until he had the basic techniques clearly in his head, he next ventured on to the course, and played round after round by himself.

The legend is that H.S. became scratch in a year, and though handicaps were then so scaled that the best were something like plus four there is no doubt that he soon became, as he has since remained, a very fine golfer and a distinguished ornament of the Oxford and Cambridge Golfing Society. I always recall the story of how, when still a young man, he was taken by a friend to West Herts where to his vast pleasure he found himself in the same match as Vardon. After he had watched H.S. for a hole or two the great man said to him, 'You know, I think your swing must be remarkably like mine.' It was the ultimate in compliments, and one can imagine H.S.'s gay turban brushing the clouds.

England won the Delhi Test after a proper dog-fight wherein, until the last morning – Christmas morning – the captain and Tony Greig came together in an undefeated stand of 101 for the fifth wicket that made the victory in the end look almost comfortable. It wasn't, by any means, happily though it all ended with Lewis in his first Test, after being for ages on 'a pair', justifying himself as a batsman with a handsome not out innings of 70. India, as may be remembered, under Ajit Wadekar had recently won Test series both in the West Indies and England, and were consequently hot favourites. The crowds that filled and overflowed the Ferozsha Kotla ground each day took the surprising result in a generous spirit that made the outcome all the more satisfying.

Now, one felt, with this MCC side in high fettle and one up, they might just come out on top at the end of a hard series – a thing that had not happened since Jardine had won against less sophisticated opposition almost forty years before. The crux would come in all probability right away at Calcutta over the New Year. It did, in front of 70,000 – or was it 75,000? – each day. No one could rightly say. Since my own side had played – and won – there against an Indian XI eight years earlier Eden Gardens had been made into a vast concrete bowl. Of the four Test pitches to come this was the one whereon English swing and spin might have the best chance of beating India, relying on spin alone. Unhappily Geoff Arnold, the best bowler at Delhi, went sick on the eve of the match, just as Derek Underwood was due to do in the following Test, played on a spinner's wicket at Madras. India won both these Tests by narrow margins, 28 runs at Calcutta and four wickets at Madras.

These were important misfortunes, but what finally turned the scales was England's batting strategy. Despite the lesson of the Delhi climax they ignored the basic axiom that even the best bowler will bowl only as well as he is allowed to do. In an atmosphere of fevered excitement I have only encountered elsewhere in the West Indies the fielders of both sides crowded the batsmen, and the frequency of appeals for bat-pad catches, and for LBW, made umpiring a nightmare. England may have had the worst of the luck with decisions, and there was consolation in that in Bedi and Chandrasekhar they were up against bowlers of world class. England had a little the better of both the last two drawn Tests without looking like shifting India's hold once they had taken the lead.

To the older Indian spectators the general ferment of this series must have made a strange contrast with the skilful but more relaxed cricket played in India between the wars, of which I had heard much from C. P. Johnstone, of Kent, who spent half a lifetime there. The princes, fired maybe by Ranji's example, played a big part in Indian cricket, both financially and, up to a point, on the field. Con Johnstone used to tell how when he and the Maharajah of Patiala were playing against Arthur Gilligan's MCC side His Highness when batting essayed a full-blooded stroke, missed, and then announced that in the effort one of his pearl earrings had flown off. There was general consternation at this, the game was stopped, and everyone scrabbled about until someone spotted it glinting in the recesses of his beard. This was old Patiala who used to send a minion out to do the fielding. His son, the Yuvraj, played once in a Test against Jardine, India being led by a magnificent cricketer, C. K. Nayudu.

It was deemed necessary, however, such were the castes and

languages involved, that on tour the captain should come from among the princes, and indeed the first three sides to England were led by, respectively, the Maharajahs of Porbander and Vizianagram and the senior Nawab of Pataudi, father of 'Tiger'. Porbander, a very modest performer, made only two runs on the tour – from a leg-glance at Cardiff, I seem to recall – but had a fleet of white Rolls-Royces for himself and retinue, and no doubt exercised some sort of lofty control. 'Vizzy' was an endearing little man and quite a reputable player who turned later to broadcasting, and carried on doing it into his sixties despite having been badly mauled by a tiger.

All titles now, of course, have been officially abolished. Thus the former Maharajah of Baroda, who managed the 1959 side to England and has since been President and a Trustee of the Indian Board of Control, is known in Delhi in his capacity of Member of Parliament as Fatesingh Gaekwad. But he is and no doubt always will be very much His Highness in his own State, as my wife and I learned when, on our way home from Australia two years ago, we were his guests at Baroda.

This was a fascinating glimpse of a relic of the old India, and one was also able to gather a brief insight into how a liberal and intelligent Indian born into a very different order adapts himself to the new. Laxmi Vilas Palace in its sheer pink bulk makes Blenheim Palace look almost bijou. It was the home of many of the old ruler's relations, and was the focal point of much activity – which included a talk given by me in the Durbar Hall to the Baroda Cricket Association. Under the Princes Agreement of 1949 the Palace apparently was not subject to wealth tax : should it become so the plan is to turn it into an arts centre and school.

We saw white tigers in the splendid zoo, and the daily crocodile-feeding by a man with one arm. Naturally we supposed the worst, only to learn later that the other had been lost in a train accident! In the museum were examples of European as well as Indian art, and portraits of the princes of long ago. We were shown round by India's captain of the '50s, Vijay Hazare, who is now Comptroller of the household. Vijay's master (generally known to his English friends as 'Jackie') shoulders the duties of a full life with an enviable Oriental calm. (He is among other things an author, having written on the palaces of India as well as a biography of his great-grand-father.) While his liabilities have increased the old responsibilities remain; but he was clearly happy, devoting himself to the service of his people.

India holds haunting memories for me and, it seems, for all who know it. The inherent problems are colossal, but will seem insuperable perhaps only to those who equate happiness with material prosperity. If it be not thought ridiculous to comment on so limited an acquaintance, let me record a general impression of philosophical acceptance the roots of which can only be religious. The staggering spiritual influence of Gandhi lives on in a people inured to hardship and disaster.

Partition, against which he spoke so passionately, was almost a *fait accompli* by the time of his murder but one asks oneself whether the tragedy of it might have been avoided if Jinnah, the architect of the Moslem State of Pakistan, against whom Lord Mountbatten, the last Viceroy, pleaded so forcefully if in vain, had succumbed a year or so earlier than he did to the cancer with which he was riddled, when the political future of the sub-continent was still being debated.

Though, as it was, much bloodshed could not be avoided in the end, the respect in which Englishmen seem to be held today in India suggests that they have a right to be proud rather than otherwise of the British achievement there over the centuries.

The penultimate hop on my journey of memory to fond places is a long one in every way, the Royal and Ancient Golf Club of St Andrews. I write as a humble member, junior in election and one of only 1800 in all, as compared with MCC's ten times as many. There are, obviously, similarities between the R & A and MCC in that both are private clubs which for the benefit of golf and cricket respectively have from time immemorial performed a public function of guidance and control. But today the differences are more significant than the likenesses, if only because of the contrast in numbers. MCC have a vast property to maintain, and must therefore assure themselves of an adequate income from entrance fees and subscriptions. The R & A have big and ever-growing administrative expenses, but their property begins and ends with the square grey granite club-house on the coast of Fife which is a fair counterpart surely in the minds of sportsmen to Lord's pavilion. The Old Course and the other links adjoining are common land administered by the St Andrews Links Trust, to which the R & A contributes the chairman and half the members.

On its own side of the clear demarcation line separating its functions from those of the national Golf Unions, the R & A through its various committees does a great honorary service to the game. It runs the Open and the Amateur Championships – the former a vast and ever-growing enterprise in itself; its selection committee chooses the Walker Cup and also some other representative British teams; it has committees that pronounce on amateur status and the implements of the game; and above all it is responsible for the Rules of Golf. Surely, you may say, such a catalogue of authority is an extraordinary anachronism in 1977? Up to a point it is, but membership of these committees is by no means confined to R & A members. Appropriate people are invited to serve on them from outside the club, and are given the status of temporary membership while doing so. For instance, the Rules of Golf committee is comprised of twelve R & A members and up to ten invited members from golf authorities at home and abroad. Naturally the closest liaison is maintained with the United States Golf Association. (Incidentally, the strength of the link with America is illustrated by the fact that of the 750 members who are ordinarily resident abroad as many as 275 may be American. No other country may provide more than 110.)

Two years ago we had an American captain, Joseph C. Dey Jr. by name, a figure well known in the world of British golf as the genius recently presiding over the destinies of the US PGA. He was indeed the second American to have been captain, following the immortal Francis C. Ouimet who as a young amateur made history by tying with the famous British professionals, Vardon and Ray, at Brookline in the American Open of 1913 and beating them comfortably in the play-off. What lover of the works of Darwin does not know the romantic tale by heart?

I did not see Joe Dey hit the fateful stroke at eight o'clock on the Thursday of the Autumn Medal whereby he drove himself into office, but I was present two years earlier when D. N. V. Smith, a fellow-member of Royal St George's and resident of Sandwich, had done likewise. It is a moment with a drama all its own as, with the caddies streaming down the course at distances flattering or otherwise to the prowess of the new captain, the tee surrounded

R   257

and faces peering from every adjacent window, Laurie Auchterlonie tees the ball, the victim allows himself a practice swing and then at the command of the starter 'plays away'. Donald Smith hit a perfect shot, and since most who are elevated to the captaincy are or have been good golfers a presentable stroke is the rule rather than the exception.

The then Prince of Wales was unlucky when, in 1922, he drove himself into office. An enthusiastic golfer but a nervous one, the strain on whom can well be imagined, he made brief contact with the heel of the club, the ball almost brushing his shoe before, according to repute, it came to rest just in front of the Valley of Sin short of the 18th green. Needless to say, Darwin rose to the occasion next morning in *The Times*, informing his readers that His Royal Highness had hit a low ball somewhat to the left.

It is a tremendous thrill, naturally, to play in a meeting of the R & A. Apart, however, from the first hole and the last – and there you have the Swilcan Burn with which to contend – the Old Course makes far too stiff and subtle an examination for the likes of me. Familiarity perhaps may breed less dread – a little less. Countless legends surround every hole, almost every bunker has a name, and many who read this book may be more familiar with it all than I am. As every golfer knows, the geography of the Old Course is simply all the way out (proceeding almost due north), a loop at the end, and all the way back. For those who stray off the line there are therefore the added hazards designed for the hole running parallel in the opposite direction.

It is this peculiarity that led to the immortalizing of the name of Benson. The admiral so called, a celebrated St Andrews character not long passed on, had just driven from the 12th tee when he spied an attractive girl in a bright red dress coming up the 7th. 'I wouldn't mind posting a letter in that letter-box,' he remarked as he allowed his gaze to linger – and promptly fell headlong into what will no doubt be for ever known as Benson's Bunker.

As with the Long Room at Lord's, the Big Room, made light by the bow window that extends its full breadth, giving on to the course, is much enhanced by the pictures, to which there has recently come a distinguished addition in the form of a full-length portrait of the Queen. The artist is Leonard Boden, whose eighth likeness of the Queen this was. It shows her, with the hint of a smile, in the green mantle of the Order of the Thistle, with the collar and silver star shaped as the St Andrew's Cross and with the Golden Image of St Andrew pendant from the collar. So says the official description.

Previously in the place of honour over the fireplace that faces one on entering the room was Orpen's portrait of the late Duke of Windsor as Prince of Wales in the golfing style of the '20s, with Fair Isle sweater and plus-fours. It was not universally admired, and the subject is credited with the comment that it was a very good picture of his shoes. The redisposition of the portraits caused by the Queen's arrival involved a degree of tact. Opposite the fireplace on the east wall is another of equal size on the west. It was not however deemed suitable that the monarch should be directly confronted by her uncle, who accordingly has been moved down the line, leaving H. G. Hutchinson where he was over his fireplace with old Tom Morris alongside him: two of the early greats together. Hutchinson won the first Amateur Championship held at St Andrews, the course being played (as it now is for a period in winter) clockwise, that is from the 1st tee to the 17th green.

Why the wrong way round, for goodness' sake? The legendary answer makes one curious to know more. Apparently on certain days or weeks it was ordained that the course be played in the contrary direction, including the period of this championship of 1886. The presiding authority in those days was the Lord Provost of St Andrews, and when he was appealed to for a relaxation of the rule out of respect to the occasion he stoutly refused. Were conflicting personalities involved? Hutchinson, who became one of the first writers of authority on the game, does not mention the matter; can some golfing Rosenwater add to the picture?

At the dinner which concludes the Autumn Meeting the second and last toast is to the New Members, and in 1973 Sir Iain Stewart, the captain, asked me to reply to it when, about a month before, the original choice, Alastair Cooke, was unable to appear. With the past captains in a serried row at the top table in their red coats, and a large company, this was an occasion the prospect of which was well calculated to spoil one's medal round. However, I found myself most kindly received. Obviously not much was expected of a mere cricketer!

So far as this chapter is concerned it is time to turn for home; but the way to Sandwich lies through Canterbury, and while my qualifications scarcely extend to even the most cursory tour of the Cathedral a focus for pilgrims of a different sort a mile or so to the seaward side is another matter. The St Lawrence ground is considered by all who have a fondness for Kent cricket with a pride which is part of its tradition. For one thing it is the headquarters of the Kent CCC, for another it is the scene of the oldest of all Weeks, setting the pattern for subsequent ones both in the county and beyond. The history of the first-class cricket 'weeks', sometimes called 'festivals', is a chequered one. Some have prospered a while and then, lacking sufficient support, have withered away. But on Kentish soil they have usually prospered, notably at Maidstone, at Tunbridge Wells, at Folkestone, and especially at Canterbury. Alas, that the Angel ground at Tonbridge, which was once to followers west of the Medway almost what Canterbury was to those to the east, is no more.

If it were not for its facilities and its associations St Lawrence would be among the best grounds in England. The turf is second to none (in the South at any rate : Trent Bridge and Worcester might claim comparison), and as to the square the only grumbles come from the bowlers. Like Lord's there is a cross-slope, which adds character to a ground if it be not too pronounced. Not least there is the famous tree, an ancient lime, the only one on a first-class arena actually within the field of play. It showed ominous signs of age a few years ago, but seems now to be enjoying either an Indian summer or a second childhood. Time will show.

But, of course, the field and what surrounds it are all of a piece, the pavilion, now much extended as compared with former days owing to the generosity of the late Stuart Chiesman (Colin Cowdrey's father-in-law) and accordingly named after him, and the two stands, one named after Frank Woolley, the other after Leslie Ames. In this form St Lawrence can take around 12,000, including members, in reasonable comfort, plus a thousand cars, and the capacity is taxed at most of the one-day matches, especially the Gillette and Benson & Hedges. Those intent on the best positions for their cars begin queueing at dawn for the opening of the gates at nine o'clock.

For the Week all is transformed (and the total capacity decreased) by the arrival of the tents, which from the Mayor of Canterbury's at square-leg to that of the President of the Kent CCC at long-on take up almost a quarter of the circumference. The various clubs and associations, identified by the flags they fly, book their accustomed places year after year, the general plan being to use the tents themselves for food and victuals, leaving a sufficient area in front of each for deck-chairs. Flower-boxes add further colour to the scene. Seeing the cricket thus, in the company of friends, is to do it *de luxe*, and if the sun is shining and the game itself lives up to the occasion it will be a day to cherish.

Many of the best amateur cricketers of the county, of all generations – and not a few venerable to a degree – will be found in the Band of Brothers tent, which is nowadays also open to members of I Zingari. The Buffs lodge next door to BB, and The Association of Men of Kent and Kentishmen a little farther down the line. The Rotary have their niche, and St Lawrence and Highland Court CC, and in some years the High Sheriff. Alongside the tree are the Old Stagers, who are indissolubly linked with the Week, having provided dramatic entertainment in the evening (now and for many years at the Marlowe Theatre) every year, wars apart, since its start in 1842.

It has been the essence of cricket from its earliest days that it attracted and brought together people of every age and sort and station, and though this characteristic is sadly less strong than of old it is to be seen illustrated to perfection in the Canterbury Week, where the broadest possible cross-section of Kentish folk come together year by year. The Buffs used always to supply a band, and only ceased to do so when some nameless visiting side objected to it as a hindrance to concentration, their objection being accorded far more attention than it deserved. Otherwise things are much as they have long been, and indeed of ancient institutions Canterbury Week surely changes less than almost any.

The young, it should be added, have their special place, pouring on to the field at the intervals in hundreds to play their impromptu matches, and only melting magically away as the umpires precede the players, threading their way through the throng. The one rule is, for obvious reasons of safety, that the boys play with soft balls only, a point which my old friend Rex Alston may have overlooked when he gave a description of the scene over the air which is still recalled with pleasure. I believe he omitted the adjective.

It is a temptation to linger at Canterbury, and it might be hard to drag away my Australian friend (whom I fear I've tended of late to forget) from those hospitable tents, but he will certainly enjoy Sandwich and not least an introduction to Royal St George's Golf Club. The reader who has accompanied me to these few fond places has been bumping into ancient history a good deal of the way, and he isn't due to stop now; quite the contrary, in fact, since Sandwich is both a thriving small town and a medieval relic of the first order – as is attested by the fact that it is the only town in Kent listed among the 51 throughout England by the Civic Trust and British Archaeological Society as specially worthy of conservation.

Our south-eastern tip of England has been the natural point of communication with the Continent for all but two thousand years – since in fact the time of the Romans who came in AD 40 and set up the camp from which they ultimately administered the whole of Britain a mile from Sandwich up the Stour River at Richborough. Sandwich was a Saxon stronghold of importance by 664, and in the Domesday Book was recorded as comprising 383 houses inhabiting 1800 people and belonging to the monks of Canterbury Cathedral. It became the premier English port, the Stour forming the perfect haven until in the sixteenth century the river silted up and the sea receded – to the detriment of the town's importance, though to the inestimable subsequent benefit of many generations of golfers.

From Sandwich Thomas a'Becket fled to France and came back to his martyrdom. Richard Coeur de Lion landed here on his return from the Crusades, and in token of gratitude for his deliverance from imprisonment walked barefoot from Sandwich to the Cathedral. When the Venetian trading fleets arrived the King and his court sailed down from London to make their purchases. Sandwich was the focal point, but in its prosperity became the target of attack by the French. In the worst raid – in 1457 – four thousand French landed down the coast at Deal, burnt and pillaged the outer town, and killed the mayor. So far as I can ascertain from William Boys's *History of Sandwich* (a classic published in 1792 and today worth around £150), they reached to the southward about as far as the end of the garden of Delf House where I live. The inner town was saved because its narrow streets, which make our traffic problem so acute today, could be successfully barricaded.

Out of respect for his memory the mayoral robe is black, and when the dignitaries of the Cinque Ports meet his dress stands out in sombre contrast with the scarlet and gold of the rest. Though the confederation of the one-time principal ports (Dover, Sandwich, Hastings, Romney and Hythe) continue now chiefly on sentiment and tradition, they came together for the vital purpose of defence and also mutual support against the demands of the Crown. It was the fishing fleets of the Cinque Ports that carried the English armies which perpetually and generally with success fought the French. Edward III, the Black Prince, Henry V, all embarked at Sandwich in ships which were the forerunners of the Navy. In return the Cinque Ports were granted many privileges.

One was reminded of these deep historic roots when Sir Robert Menzies was installed as Warden of the Cinque Ports with the old ceremony, took up residence at Walmer Castle, and for several years during his annual visits from Australia played an active part in the life of East Kent before illness overtook him. He is still Lord Warden and though confined to his home in Melbourne can at least reflect that his activities far exceeded those of his predecessor, Sir Winston Churchill, who loved the uniform but had more pressing matters to which to attend.

Delf House, by the way, and Delf Street in which we stand, are so named because the Delf stream runs alongside, partly visible, partly underneath the pavements and houses. The Delf, which was the town's only water supply until the end of the last century, had, according to the official guide to the town, a descending scale of use. The upper reaches on the Deal side were for drinking, then around our part it was used to water the animals (hence Horse Pond Sluice); next it served the tanneries and breweries, and finally 'when it passed outside the Town Wall to the Gallows field, it was used to drown witches and sundry felons'. It shows in fact outside Delf House, but to be honest it is not nowadays always fit to be seen.

Visitors are often mystified, as well they might be, by the tolling of the tenor bell of St Peter's, one of our three ancient churches, prompt each evening at eight. One explains it is the Curfew which has been rung from time immemorial, recent wars excepted. It used to be the signal for the turning-out on to the streets of the hogs and geese to dispose of the day's refuse. We are spared the goose-bell at five in the morning when all livestock had to be chased home under pain of impounding by the Common Sergeant – but we still have our sergeant, and an impressive sight he is in his regalia, in attendance on the mayor.

I was talking a page or two back about cross-sections of society, and I suppose that Sandwich might claim a wider one than most places of its size. We have miners who work at the nearby coalfields, employees of varying skills who earn their daily bread on the industrial estate over the toll-bridge on the Ramsgate Road : tradespeople and professional men and women in plenty : 'week-enders' owning cottages and normally seen only on Saturdays and Sundays : and lastly a sizeable company of the retired, some of whom put down roots first as 'week-enders' and graduated, so to speak, from there. Many of these, but by no means all, are golfers and members of St George's. Some are men of substantial achievement, a few have even contrived to become or remain rich. Happily, though, there is nothing remotely resembling an exclusive area of the town. Houses and cottages of several sizes and periods are to be found in every street. Sandwich Bay, where many desirable residences have recently been scattered among clusters of older modern houses, is different, but that is a couple of miles away, beyond St George's and on the way to Prince's, which lies, all 27 holes of true links golf, northward along the shore towards the hoverport at Pegwell Bay.

In the year of Queen Victoria's Golden Jubilee certain gentlemen from the Wimbledon Golf Club staying at Sandwich and reputedly on the look-out for this very thing came upon the spacious stretch of sandy wind-swept dune country lying immediately back from the sea and decided that it had all the qualities to make a great links course. The club they formed grew rapidly in stature, and within seven years had staged the first Open Championship held in England. There have been eight more since, to say nothing of ten Amateur Championships and two Walker Cups. Hagen and Vardon each had two victories, but the best-remembered win was that of Henry Cotton who in 1934 put an end to an American sequence of 11. As the golf world knows, the fact that there has been no Open at Royal St George's since 1949 is no reflection on the course but a straight problem of transport which the bypass would only solve if a spur could be built from Worth – and that is scarcely likely in the present economic climate. Still, we can continue to stage the Amateur and the Walker Cup, while for three years now the PGA Championship sponsored by Penfold, the biggest British professional event apart from the Open, has been played and televised. Arnold Palmer's historic conquest of the wind in the last round in 1975 when he came from behind to win was no doubt our most memorable modern occasion, but it was worthily followed next year when Neil Coles beat Gary Player and Eamonn Darcy in a play-off after they had tied on 280. That is level par. Writing before the 1977 Championship the fact is that, so far, the course has fully held its own with the top pros despite being by modern standards a few hundred yards short.

In physical terms St George's has certain limitations which with familiarity one tends not to notice. For instance, the club-house, which was originally a farmhouse, is so far from the 1st and the 18th that one can scarcely see a stroke played. There is no sight of brave deeds or ghoulish pleasure from putts missed and matches thrown away. You have no view of the sea. Yet no committee would ever get away with a reconstruction that involved a major alteration to those two admirable holes. Again, there is no alternative starting tee nearby. A car is needed to get to the 10th. This means that the pace of the course is invariably two-ball, and that four-balls, the most common form of week-end play on many courses, are completely beyond the pale. Our most popular form of contest is the foursome, and not only among the older members. Moreover it is normally finished in $2\frac{1}{2}$ hours or a few minutes over. For me there is no pleasure to exceed a well-contested foursomes with friends, especially playing with a young partner who can hit the ball a long way.

In one respect St George's is today, I believe, unique in that caddies are almost always available, and at what for these days is a moderate fee. They range in age from 12 to almost 80, and in 20 years I haven't come across a surly one, or one who showed dissatisfaction with a tip. All but the youngest know the game, most from having played it, for there is a Permit Holders' Club – a rough equivalent to the Artisan Clubs elsewhere – with a nominal subscription and rights to play at certain times. An annual foursomes match that might run to around 20 pairs a side between the Club and the Permit Holders with much conviviality afterwards is an expression of the goodwill and friendliness which one always associates with St George's.

Only the cynic or male chauvinist pig will suggest that the spirit of the place is in any way connected with the fact that there are no women members. Wives and daughters have the choice of Prince's adjoining and the Royal Cinque Ports, that other great course, nearby at Deal. Moreover women may play, and several do, so long as they and the members accompanying them keep discreetly clear of other matches : and as women do not officially exist, so to speak, no green fee is payable in respect of them.

Another way in which St George's differs from some other clubs is that one never hears of anyone playing for money. The normal stake is a ball or perhaps 'a ball, a ball, a ball' – that is to say, the method known as 'Nassau', with one invested on the first nine, one on the second and one on the match. The only man who with two or three friends may have played for something substantial was the late Ian Fleming. They were inclined to debate whether to play for one 'unit' or two – but as no one else knew what the unit was, whether large or small, they were none the wiser. No one perhaps was more devoted to St George's than Ian. He was captain-designate when he died, and was staying in Sandwich Bay when stricken with his last and fatal heart attack.

James Bond enthusiasts will remember the great match with Goldfinger at Royal St Mark's for a ten-thousand-dollar stake, and how Bond after suffering various sorts of knavery wins at the 18th having transposed his opponent's Dunlop 1 for a Dunlop 7 (at that time the markings were very similar) and so causing him to play the wrong ball.

An institution has grown since his day which might have appealed to the clubable side of Ian Fleming. As many members as choose to come foregather on Thursdays before lunch – according to the weather and the time of year it might be anything from 8 to 24 – all the names are popped into a hat and foursome partners are drawn for. All are fairly senior. Some are has-beens, some are never-wasers. One might be drawn with an old international golfer or former captain of the R & A (there are, I believe, five of these at present active at St George's) or some fairly contemptible hacker such as – well, yours truly. It's all very keen, we are known, in-evitably, as Dad's Army, and (as it happens) our Mainwaring is a Captain RN (retd).

16
Reflections

As I embark on this last chapter the great Centenary Test at Melbourne has just ended, in a blaze of glory, and euphoria hangs in its wake. Cricket's command performance came off with a vengeance. Alas, I could only read and listen in snatches to the first Anglo–Australian Test I have missed in all but 40 years. Indeed the truth suddenly hit one: the beginning of Test cricket was a century ago, and here have I been for exactly half that time scribbling and talking about the game. For it was in September 1927 that I marched across the road from Fleetway House in Farringdon Street and up Shoe Lane to the sports room of the *Evening Standard*. Straightaway I found myself watching the best cricketers and the best Rugby footballers, and mixing with them, and being paid for the pleasure. The life is not all honey. Like every other job it has its frustrations and disappointments – and, contrary to what many believe who have never tried it, writing for all but the very few is hard work. *Ergo*, to have written millions of words about games (something between 6m and 10m might be a fair estimate), much of it at speed, represents a fair degree of toil and sweat – especially when one recalls the intrinsic discomfort of the average Press-box. Yet when I think of other careers to which I might have aspired I am thankful for the chance that guided me into games-writing, and the luck that has steered my course therein.

Since anyone who has occupied a prominent platform for so long must have had an influence of some sort, whether for good or ill, I suppose it may be of interest to give an idea of what I have aimed to do. The chief correspondent of a newspaper that gives as much space to games as the *Daily Telegraph* can divide his work into two parts. There is the reporting on one hand and there is the rest of it on the other: commentary on matters of the moment, criticism of selections, previews of matches, news stories, and from time to time, of course, obituaries and book reviews.

For the reporting I worked to a conscious formula which was

developed in that period soon after the war when sporting interest was at its height and newsprint at its scarcest. One had to compress, and to try, however vainly, to believe the old Fleet Street axiom, no doubt first pronounced by some stony-faced sub, that you can say everything that needs saying in half a column. You can't – but it's a good discipline to make the attempt. When one analyses what the reader wants to know about a game, are his needs not satisfied if he is given the answer to the three questions: *what* happened, *why* did it happen, and *how* did it happen?

Obviously there are other techniques which appeal to many, and I never envied colleagues on other papers who, towards the end of a rather ordinary day's play, had to scratch their heads to make the most of some incident which would hand the sub-editor on a plate a heading from his opening paragraph. I began by giving a general picture of how things stood, mentioning those who had been chiefly concerned. The heroes, if any, were assured of a place up front. If the chap in the train had time only to discover the mere outline of *what* had occurred, I tried to give him the gist of it in a few paragraphs.

The next phase – *why?* – was analytical and necessarily more technical though one aimed to guard against putting off the reader (he was in the majority, after all) who would not claim to be an expert. One assessed the pitch, which is the most important key to every day's play, and usually mentioned the weather, perhaps also the ground and crowd. (The game is not played in a vacuum.) An appreciation of any outstanding performance came in here. Lastly, the descriptive section, which might run to half or more of the whole for a big occasion : *how?* At the end I read it all through, asking myself whether in haste I had left out anything important or ignored someone who deserved to be mentioned. After dinner I often read it through again, knowing that I could still make an amendment by telephone and catch the main edition.

As to the other sides of one's work, I always found previews the most difficult to make interesting, and have a theory that few people read them. Judging by letters received – which is not a bad guide, granted the journalistic belief that for every one who actually puts pen to paper a hundred or so probably had the mind to – I have found that readers enjoy obits. They also get incredibly worked up about the choice of Test teams.

As soon as space allowed I was given my head on Mondays with general commentaries on whatever aspect of the game seemed topical, and in these I roamed pretty widely, trying to bring in cricketers of all sorts. Much esoteric material from the wide world of English cricket and beyond got an airing here. No doubt I also rode my own hobby-horses: hence the comment of the critic who said that the familiar sound of an English Monday morning was of Swanton barking up the wrong tree.

Clearly my philosophy of cricket was repugnant to some, just as gibes about the alleged reactionary attitude of MCC and authority generally were unacceptable to me. Just over 20 years ago the *Daily Express* seemed to be waging a campaign of denigration against Lord's and all it stood for, and I decided, if Arthur Langford, the editor, and also Michael Berry (now Lord Hartwell), my own *DT* editor-in-chief, were agreeable, to have a go at them in the *Cricketer*.

Both being encouraging, I embarked with relish on the business of giving them some of their own medicine. A reader from Colwyn Bay had sent me an *Express* article entitled: 'It's time to brush those cobwebs off the snob Lords of Cricket', saying he found it 'somewhat disturbing'. The article consisted of a catalogue of mischief alleging, broadly speaking, that MCC was a citadel of privilege and reaction, utterly deaf to the needs of the public and in particular to the young. What had MCC ever done for 'poor boys', for instance? What chance had any of them to enter the sacred portals of the pavilion?

The facts were that what was then the MCC Youth Cricket Association had by this time affiliated associations in 33 counties, that scores of thousands of LCC schoolboys by a regular arrangement had been shown the pavilion treasures of Lord's, that 7000 schoolmasters of every sort had been put through classes run by the Association at Lilleshall, and that as a result of a scheme run in conjunction with a boys' paper no fewer than 204,535 boys had watched first-class cricket free that preceding summer after their day's schooling was over. Then there was the *MCC Coaching Book* with its country-wide sales of many thousands. Thanks to Harry Altham and Gubby Allen, the *Express* on this score were about seven years out of date. Other wholesale assertions were equally easy to demolish, and I did so with a polemical vigour that I look back on with pleasure.

My article ran to three pages under the titles: 'MCC and the *Daily Express*. Fact *v* Froth : A Little Spleen returned.'

There was said in those days to be a 'Suppress' list of those who for one reason or another were not to be mentioned in the *Express*, or at least not in any favourable light. I reckoned that my article richly qualified my name for inclusion, and had an amusing piece of evidence years afterwards to support my hunch. Sir Robert Menzies in his active days as Lord Warden of the Cinque Ports visited the annual Sandwich Art Exhibition, saw an action portrait of Frank Woolley, with the pavilion at Canterbury in the background, and bought it. Ann was the artist, and naturally was particularly pleased that the great man arranged for the picture to be sent to Melbourne and in due course presented it to the Melbourne Cricket Club. It hangs now in the pavilion there. This made a little gossip story which appeared in one or two places, the artist being described as Mrs E. W. Swanton, wife of – *et cetera*. But in William Hickey's *Express* version Ann was just 'a Sandwich housewife'! I need scarcely add perhaps that the *Express* coverage of sport since those days has become much more responsible, and my name has even been civilly mentioned. So perhaps bygones are bygones.

More recently (to be exact, in the *Cricketer* of October 1973), I thought the moment had come to say something with a sting in it about another persistent critic of cricket authority – and, for that matter, of most cricketers who happen to be born south of the Humber. The occasion was the unexpected appointment by the selectors of Mike Denness to captain MCC in the West Indies that winter.

Writing of the press reaction to Denness's appointment in the *Daily Telegraph* I said that it had been mostly good apart from some odious, sneering comment from a predictable quarter. I imagined that most people would at once identify Michael Parkinson, that caricature of a Yorkshireman who is guaranteed to glorify anything and anyone who comes from his own small corner of the world and to denigrate almost all else. Naturally he had hoped for Illingworth and failing him Boycott, and considered the selectors' decision 'so barmy one wonders if perhaps they are joking'.

Later in the piece we were informed 'it is a certain fact that a confirmation of the bad blood between the two sides in the West Indies will have very serious consequences. Mr Denness is going to have a lot on his plate and one wonders about his appetite.' For my part I never remember seeing Parkinson at any match or cricket function I have ever attended. If he had seen the England and West Indian teams happily together at the closing party at The Oval he would have realized that his mischievous words were complete balderdash.

However my point is not so much to refute the views of Parkinson as to answer the queries of many as to whom I was getting at, and to make clear it certainly was not any *bona fide* cricket-writer.

It is not, of course, new. The same author had this to say at the time of the choosing of the last MCC team to the West Indies when Brian Close forfeited his chance by gross time-wasting in a critical county match at Edgbaston:

'To criticise Close on this occasion is to misunderstand the man and deny him his background. Close has been with the Yorkshire side long enough to know that Championships are not won by nice people. He is a hard, uncompromising captain whose simple ethic is that there's no such thing as a good loser.' Unfortunately for him the impartial tribunal which judged Close's case disapproved so strongly of his 'simple ethic' as enunciated by Parkinson that they censured him severely, and the side was accordingly taken to the West Indies by Cowdrey. This naturally called forth reams of contempt and a forecast of inevitable defeat – which, of course, duly failed to materialize.

Denness equally contrived to falsify Parkinson's prediction in the *Sunday Times*, contesting the series in a sporting spirit and, despite the difficult circumstances of his selection and the formidable talent arrayed against him, achieving a draw. The mischief lay, of course, in the implication that in modern cricket an abrasive, utterly uncompromising attitude is necessary for success. At this, I thought, the great Yorkshiremen from Hirst and Verity to Leyland and

Rhodes must be turning in their graves.

On a more serious level it will probably be realized that the relationship between the critic and the objects of his scrutiny, especially the players, is very often a sensitive area. I would like to think that, generally speaking, over the years I have won the respect of the players and brought most of them at least to the point of thinking that, to repeat the dull old cliché, the old beggar probably 'has the best interests of the game at heart'. When things are going well on the field – I am thinking particularly now of sides on tour – the tensions as between Press and players may seem almost in abeyance. It is when a side disappoints itself and its public at home, and the reasons for its ill-success come to be analysed, that friction is likely. The critic is only doing, after all, what he is paid to do, but one can well understand the feelings of the player who queries the credentials of X, Y and Z who sit in judgement over him, observing the field of play from the safe side of the pickets. Have they ever been out here in the middle in a Test Match? How much do they know about the game? It is the everlasting cry of the performer *vis-à-vis* the critic in every sphere of activity.

I suppose that over so long a period I have watched more cricket than most, and more Test cricket than anyone, although in this respect John Woodcock's breath will soon be hot on my neck. I am proud of my minor part in writing *A History of Cricket*, and of having conceived the idea, and organized and edited *The World of Cricket*, that encyclopaedic tome of 1100-odd quarto pages which in the middle '60s sold out an edition of 9000 in little more than a year at six guineas and could scarcely be repeated today, I would estimate, even granted someone had the energy needed to revise another edition, at £20. I am pleased at having had the chance of taking several distinguished sides abroad. Indeed I am happy with much that I have aimed to do in and for cricket while regretting some things written and spoken and done impetuously and on the spur of the moment. I recall with nostalgic feelings all the varied cricket, much of it very good cricket, that I have been lucky enough to play, stretched over thirty summers or so, and all the fun during and afterwards that went with it. I can say, as I have quoted Harry Altham as saying, and possibly with even greater emphasis, that only I know how much more I have received from the game than I have given to it.

With all this I have, however, one real regret – that instead of skirting about on the periphery of the first-class game I had had the opportunity for a season or two of seeing whether I could make some sort of a mark in it. All one can add is that to have played with so many University, county and indeed Test players in club matches is a consolation, and one moreover beyond the normal scope of the similarly ambitious club cricketer of today when the game is so compartmentalized – surely much to its detriment.

I have been accused occasionally of being apparently more favourably disposed to England's opponents than to England, and admit the charge in one respect and one only: it may have been true when almost all the initiative, the attraction and maybe the risk has come from the other side. No one loves to see England win more than I do, granted they have shown a reasonable degree of enterprise in achieving victory. A measure of defensive pawkiness seems to be a national characteristic and, incidentally, it is nothing new. As far back as I can remember J. W. H. T. Douglas, the personification of the bulldog spirit, was preferred to P. G. H. Fender, his superior by a mile as a captain of dash and ingenuity. Walter Robins, who had much of Fender in him in his relish for a challenge and as an intelligent tactician, stood no chance of retaining the England captaincy when Walter Hammond turned amateur. The latter, for all his greatness as a cricketer, was utterly defensive in his outlook, and when he and some of his successors have overstepped the ordinary bounds of caution, or have been content to see their batsmen doing so, it has been too much for me. 'Ah, he's a grafter!' is always said as a compliment when English cricketers foregather. The brilliant opponent is apt to be dismissed as 'a bit of a flasher'. Neil Harvey was being written off as such from the day when as a lad of 19 he made his début against England with a hundred at Leeds until he retired with more Test runs to his credit than any Australian bar Bradman. Come to that, the Don himself before he played his first innings on English soil was considered too unsound to be a likely prospect on our wickets by those who had played against him in Australia with MCC. There is no need to pursue the theme further except perhaps to ask any who doubt the validity of this general criticism one double-edged question: when can you remember England landing themselves in trouble by being too audacious – and how many times have they

S

not surrendered the initiative, and perhaps the match with it, by getting stuck in the rut of caution?

As I say, the ultra-defensive attitude is no new thing, and I am far from wishing to suggest that in this, that and the other respect the game is less worth watching and playing than it used to be. As regards fielding there's little doubt that the standard has risen. The art of throwing his greatly improved. Nor do I think (as I mentioned a couple of chapters ago) that there is any justification in the cry that has echoed through the ages – there are no personalities in English cricket any more. The only regret here is that so far as batsmen are concerned most of the best are from overseas. (I wonder if we have found a real top-classer in Derek Randall, who came so swiftly to fame with his splendid 174 at Melbourne. I do not feel qualified to give an opinion; but the answer may well be known by the time these words are being read.)

I suppose from the general tenor of this book I may be considered *laudator temporis acti* – in answer to which I can only plead that I have always striven hard to see present and past in due perspective. If I haven't succeeded it is not for want of trying. There is, however, one crucial department in which, as I have hinted earlier, I abominate the modern trend as pursued by a few cricketers at the top, and point to the utterly different attitude of their predecessors. I mean, of course, the current fashion of foul language on the field, the attempted distraction of the batsman by talking to him, putting undue pressure on umpires by excessive appealing, and inciting the crowd (and, for that matter, the Press also) by showing dissent from decisions.

This is a comparatively new thing. At least Lindsay Hassett, who played through the first decade after the war, said solemnly when we were broadcasting in Australia together after the MCC 1970/1 tour that throughout his career he never heard a player swearing at another on the field. Leslie Ames, whose span covered thirty years and ended in the early '50s, will say the same thing. What one might call vicious talking started among certain English counties, and became much more pronounced in the last few years of my time as a cricket-writer. An undergraduate shocked me six or seven years ago by saying what misery it was to play against certain counties and how the attitude of others was quite different. I even recall the sides that came in for favourable mention –

Glamorgan, Essex, Warwickshire and Kent. This does not condemn all the others, it should be added, since his University fixture-list contained only about half of them. Fancy seasoned cricketers perching close round the bat trying to talk out a raw teenager struggling for his Blue! And, for that matter, fancy umpires permitting it! What Frank Chester had to say would have been worth hearing.

So far as Test cricket is concerned standards took a turn for the worse during the 1970/1 tour of Australia. Things came to a head in the last Test in Sydney wherein the captain, Ray Illingworth, and John Snow tangled with Umpire Rowan, and Illingworth led his team off the field.

On the team's return the Cricket Council felt themselves obliged to issue their forthright statement of censure and warning, and, though he might not say so in public, my belief is that Illingworth has been brought up in far too stern and realistic a cricket school not to regret very deeply what happened at Sydney on 13 February 1971. The worst of it was that it helped to set a trend in brash, undisciplined behaviour which found imitators – more in Australia than in England. That Test was only Lillee's second, and he as the incoming batsman following the injury to Jenner that started all the trouble had a first-hand view of the affair. Significantly enough it was also Ian Chappell's first Test as captain of Australia, and it was not long afterwards that this fine cricketer began a running battle with Australian cricket authority that only ended with his retirement. What Vic Richardson, that great and highly popular sportsman, would have made of the words and deeds of some of the Australian sides led by his grandson, Ian, is not hard to imagine.

The fact is that a few of the world's top cricketers today – only a few as yet – act as though they believe that the more 'controversial' they can make themselves the bigger their commercial value in all the money-making fields which, granted an active agent, are now open to them. Lesser figures tend to ape the most successful: hence the danger surely that threatens the traditional spirit in which cricket has been played, and which has been a chief ingredient in its attraction for all sorts and conditions of men. Of course there have been some angry incidents in the past. Cricket is a hot-blooded game. But, apart from Bodyline which left a deeper scar, they have been quickly forgotten and forgiven. The heroes of my youth, the household names between the wars, were admired, as have many of their successors since, for their sportsmanship as well as for their skill at the crease or with the ball. Cricket at its best is an art-form subtle and beautiful to the eye. For me, and I believe for most of its followers, the charm vanishes completely when ugliness in the form of ill-temper and sharp play is allowed to intrude.

Some of the moderns will sneer at this maybe as a counsel of perfection that takes no account of all the added stresses that have been brought into the game now that in the sponsorship age so much money is involved. Courtesy, they may say, goes out when you've simply got to win.

There are several answers to this argument about the evil influence of so much cash, but one need do no more than point to the golfers. They play golf for infinitely more money than comes the way of the cricketers and yet when is any golfer on the tournament circuit described or seen on television as behaving other than impeccably and with his feelings completely under control? And can there be a more agonizingly frustrating game than golf, or one that makes greater demands on the nerves? When they talk in public (as they are being asked to do all the time) the great golfers are modest in victory, generous in defeat. They behave in fact as civilized and thoroughly likeable people, and the follower admires and identifies with them. (As I write, the news comes from Scotland that, five months before the event, the Open at Turnberry is a sell-out.)

The golfers are bound by strict rules of conduct laid down by their own professional body, and – without airing the subject any further – I would suggest that the attitude of the Cricketers Association is equally important in our game, and that the more they and the TCCB see eye to eye on this matter, and the more closely they work together, the better.

But, without pushing this theme into the background, let us turn our thoughts finally to Melbourne and to a match which can be cited for ever as an incomparable illustration of the unpredictability that is at the heart of cricket's appeal. Australia scored 138 and 419 for nine declared; England 95 and 417 : a win therefore for Australia by 45 runs, the precise margin of their victory in the first of all Test Matches at Melbourne exactly a century before.

What computer could conceivably have come up with a game of such sensational contrasts? Once again truth turned out far, far stranger than fiction.

We could not tune in to the ball-by-ball commentaries in Barbados, sad to say, otherwise sleep in many a home would have been disturbed, for the game naturally caught the imagination of the Bajans, whose sympathies, I was gratified to find, were almost wholly with England. One was there in spirit, among the ancients wondering what they were thinking and saying about it all. One comment that got as far as Barbados will have been relished by many. It was from Harold Larwood. After paying due tribute to Lillee, as one great fast bowler might be expected to do to another, he added, 'But I don't like these antics. Even when we got Bradman out we didn't go round hugging. We just rested while the next bloke came along.'

Among Australians the most pithy comment regarding behaviour came, as might have been expected, from Jack Fingleton in a retrospective piece in the *Sunday Times*. Having warmly commended David Hookes, the highly promising young left-handed bat from South Australia, Jack wrote:

It was a pity Greig snapped at the lad when he was caught at short-leg. Hookes couldn't see the catch, and was entitled to wait for the umpire. He snapped back at Greig, so he is obviously well equipped for modern cricket. He showed his maturity when reporters went to him to know details of the snarling. 'Greig just said "Well batted," and I said "Thanks." '

This abusive back-chat is known euphemistically among the Australians, I gather, as 'sledging'. But Asif Iqbal, after the Pakistani visit to Australia a month or two earlier, had condemned in print the behaviour of his opponents on the field in blistering terms from which Australians, I understand, were still blushing. The captains could rectify matters no doubt if they had a mind to, and I hope that by the time these words are being read the captains of England and Australia will have become convinced not only of the dangers of this sort of thing but of the indignity of it all. This one aspect apart, everyone I have since met who was in India and Australia has been full of admiration for Greig as a courageous young leader both on and off the field. Considering the frailty of the English batting it was a remarkable achievement to have beaten India 3–1 on their own pitches, while as for the Melbourne match the recovery on the last two days could only have been achieved by a side of high morale with faith in itself and its captain.

Thanks to the admirable arrangements made by the Victorian authorities the Centenary Match was in the end a success surpassing all reasonable expectation. The two teams must surely have been infected by what, by all accounts, was a reunion of rare warmth and spirit, and have realized afresh that the game is more important than any individual, however illustrious. It cannot need emphasizing how the future depends on the way these foremost players and their contemporaries react to the financial transformation that cricket has recently undergone.

Now for the first time the County Championship is to be sponsored by Schweppes – an important development, since it puts the various English competitions in much truer perspective. On the face of it cricket has never been so prosperous, and it is much to the good that the first-class players can now be paid at a rate more or less relative to their ability. There is a healthy living in the game today, and for those at the top there will probably continue to be, if they can produce cricket of skill and challenge in an atmosphere of good sportsmanship.

I concluded the last edition of *A History of Cricket* by saying that the key to the health and prosperity of the game lay in the hearts and minds of the players. This maybe is not an original sentiment, and it may even be considered a banal one. Yet I end by repeating it, for no game holds up such a clear mirror to character as cricket, and this is the property which has been the secret of its appeal and fascination from Hambledon right through to the present.

Index

285